Contents

PART THREE • *Introduction to Social Structure in American Society*   **79**

PART FOUR • *Introduction to Social Settings*   **135**

Human Behavior and the Larger Social Environment

A New Synthesis

Miriam McNown Johnson

University of South Carolina

Rita Rhodes

University of South Carolina

PEARSON

Boston   New York   San Francisco
Mexico City   Montreal   Toronto   London   Madrid   Munich   Paris
Hong Kong   Singapore   Tokyo   Cape Town   Sydney

This book is dedicated to our fathers,
William Arthur McNown and Charles Arthur Rhodes.

Series Editor: *Patricia Quinlin*
Editorial Assistant: *Sara Holliday*
Marketing Manager: *Kris Ellis-Levy*
Editorial-Production Administrator:
Annette Joseph
Editorial-Production Service:
Holly Crawford

Photo Researcher: *Leah M. Eisenstadt*
Composition Buyer: *Linda Cox*
Artist: *Asterisk, Inc.*
Electronic Composition: *Peggy Cabot*
Manufacturing Buyer: *JoAnne Sweeney*
Cover Administrator: *Linda Knowles*
Cover Designer: *Roger Boecher*

For related titles and support materials, visit our online catalog at www.ablongman.com.

Library of Congress Cataloging-in-Publication Data

Johnson, Miriam McNown
      Human behavior and the larger social environment : a new synthesis / Miram McNown Johnson, Rita Rhodes
      p. cm.
      Includes bibliographic references and index.
      ISBN 0-205-37825-0
      1. Social ecology.   2. Social psychology.   3. Social institutions—United States.
4. Social structure—United States.   5. Social service—United States.   6. United States—Social conditions—21st century.   I. Rhodes, Rita M.   II. Title.

HM861.J64 2005
302—dc22

                                                                        2004049015

Printed in the United States of America

10 9 8 7 6 5 4   RRD-VA   09   08   07   06

Photo Credits: p. 15: AP Wide World Photos; p. 34: Tom Lindfors Photography; p. 57: David Young-Wolff/ PhotoEdit; p. 81: AP Wide World Photos; p. 93: Asian Week; p. 121: Lynn Johnson/Aurora & Quanta Productions Inc.; p. 137: Mark Richards/PhotoEdit; p. 157: Hackett, Richard/Omni-Photo Communications, Inc.; p. 175: EyeWire Collection/Getty Images - Photodisc; p. 188: Kateland Photo.

Preface

The purpose of this text is to help students understand the broader social context within which human behavior occurs. It is the authors' opinion that an appreciation of how large systems obstruct or promote the well-being and development of individuals and families is an essential foundation for social work practice.

In writing this text, one of our goals was to make the material useful to beginning social work students without overwhelming them. We made decisions based on our belief that it is not important for students to learn and memorize specific definitions or lists so much as it is imperative that they be able to reflect critically on new ideas and apply abstract concepts to different situations. With this in mind, we have applied the following strategies. First, we have used a limited number of perspectives and theories that students can learn thoroughly and well. Second, although we have explored many sources, we usually offer a single, simple definition of a term. Our definitions may not agree entirely with what other authors have written, but they work well for material presented in this book. Third, we have reduced some concepts, perspectives, or theories to their most essential elements in an effort to make them more understandable. In doing so, we have sacrificed some complexity that might be appropriately incorporated at more advanced levels of study. Finally, we have arranged concepts in ways that are arguably arbitrary; some social work authors and sociologists have organized them differently. After multiple drafts, we found this arrangement works best for us and for our students.

This book was written with consideration given to the Educational Policy and Accreditation Standards of the Council on Social Work Education (2001). In particular, the text addresses the foundation program objectives of understanding forms of oppression and discrimination and applying critical thinking skills. Within the content area of human behavior, this text is particularly strong in covering "the range of social systems in which people live" as well as "the way social systems promote or deter people in maintaining or achieving health and well-being" (p. 11). In addition, the text integrates content on values, diversity, and populations at risk and social and economic justice. The application of our "preferred perspectives" (diversity and strengths) promotes social work values throughout the text. Information is presented that contributes to students' knowledge of, affirmation of, and respect for persons of diverse backgrounds, including class, color, race, national origin, ethnicity, culture, religion, disability, gender, and sexual orientation. "Factors that contribute to and constitute being at risk" (p. 11) for a variety of populations are examined.

Organization of the Text

The text is composed of four sections and eleven chapters. The authors recommend that it be used in the first semester of a two-semester foundation HBSE curriculum, with the second semester devoted to understanding family and individual development from a variety of alternative as well as traditional perspectives.

Part I is an introduction to the basic theoretical perspectives that social scientists use. In addition, we include preferred social work perspectives. Chapter 1 explains the major perspectives that systematically reappear in the chapters that follow.

Part II presents eight social institutions, beginning in Chapter 2 with politics and the economy. The political economy profoundly influences all other social institutions as well as other contexts of human behavior. Chapter 3 addresses those social institutions that are, for the most part, government related: social welfare, education, and criminal justice. Chapter 4 covers three social institutions that are not government supported: health care, religion, and the mass media.

Part III discusses social structure in American society. Chapter 5 examines social stratification, giving particular attention to the issue of social class in American society. Chapter 6 considers the role of cultural diversity in influencing individuals and families, while Chapter 7 presents information on gender, sexual orientation, and disability.

Acknowledging that human behavior is dependent on context, Part IV gives attention to the social settings that individuals and families inhabit. Chapter 8 covers locational communities. Chapter 9 discusses organizations with special attention to human service settings. Chapter 10 presents residential institutions, which are a likely major employer of social workers in the twenty-first century. Chapter 11 addresses the behavior of individuals in formed groups and extends the discussion of settings to include social movements.

In summary, this text represents our effort to reinforce the unique social work outlook that human behavior is shaped by systems beyond the intrapsychic and familial domains. In these political times, it is essential that students recognize the power of large systems to harm the most vulnerable among us. We believe that such an understanding will well serve the next generation of social workers.

Acknowledgments

We would like to express our deep appreciation to the following people: Leon Ginsberg, Dean of the College of Social Work, for his support and encouragement; graduate assistants Adrienne Tripp, Ja'Shaun Brailey, Sarah Fimian, and Delander Sumpter for their diligence; research assistant Toni Jones for her resourcefulness; Tucker ("Tucky") Taylor and the other employees at Thomas Cooper Library for their endless patience; and Patricia Quinlin and Annemarie Kennedy at Allyn and Bacon and freelance editor Holly Crawford for their understanding and assistance. We are also grateful for the feedback provided by students on ideas used in the manuscript. We also extend our gratitude to the following people who reviewed our book for Allyn and Bacon: Bruce Dalton, East Tennessee State University; Marian Harris, University of Washington, Tacoma; Ameda A. Manetta, Winthrop University; Anne Medill, Northern Arizona University; Andrew T. Nilsson, Eastern Connecticut State University; Melanie D. Otis, University of Kentucky; and Deb Valentine, Colorado State University.

Miriam would like to thank Steve Johnson, Matthew Johnson, Elizabeth Johnson Boecher, Roger Boecher, and Mildred Morrison for their continuing faith in her. Rita would like to thank Katherine Mathisen and David Mathisen for continually instructing her about human behavior as only adolescents can. We would both like to thank the hosts of other relatives, friends, and colleagues who repeatedly encouraged us with the question, "So how's the book coming?"

We would also like to note our appreciation of Dixie, Mingus, Reeces, and Oreo, who kept us company through many long days of working at Rita's dining room table. The first three kept our minds sharp by insisting we take regular breaks to toss balls for them in the backyard. Oreo, who is not into fetching balls, contributed her random feline thoughts by walking across the keyboard when we left the laptop unattended.

I

Building on an Integrated Foundation

1

Introduction to Perspectives and Theories

WHERE WE BEGIN

Abigail Garvey was seeing her last client for the day. Abby guessed that Lucy Barlow, like many of her recent clients, would be asking for information about the resources that were available for newly unemployed workers in Oak Grove. Abby was already aware of how precarious Lucy's economic situation was, having made a referral for her to Consumer Credit Counseling for help in managing her family's credit cards a few months previously.

Lucy had been a long-time client of Abby's. Lucy had met with Abby seven years ago, when she graduated from high school, for career planning. Lucy was undecided on whether to enroll in classes at the local tech college or take a job at the local textile plant. Lucy decided to take the plant job because, as she pointed out, she could begin earning money immediately and marry her high school sweetheart, Zachary. Abby tried to point out alternatives but Lucy was determined to join Zach and her older siblings in the community's typical employment pattern. Abby remembered thinking at the time that she wished that Lucy, who was bright and seemed ambitious, had the ability to consider a wider range of options. Six months later, Lucy was married. A year later, she had her first child and ten months after that, twins. The wages at the plant were not bad, and with Lucy and Zach working different shifts, obtaining childcare was not a problem. Now the plant was *closing. It was the fourth factory to shut down in Oak Grove in the course of five years. The plant was moving to Mexico, where local workers would receive $8 per day to do what Lucy and Zach had done for $11 an hour.*

Abby was not much older than Lucy. She had foregone four years of salary and had postponed marriage and having children in order to obtain her BSW. Despite her training, the words "I told you so" came to mind when she considered Lucy's predicament. Abby had always thought that the most difficult part of counseling was watching her clients make poor choices. On the other hand, how could anyone have predicted that the textile plant would close? Blaming Lucy, or telling her what she should have done seven years ago, obviously wouldn't help now.

Like Abby, some social workers may believe that clients' problems originate in their own poor choices, but social workers are trained to use more than common sense, instincts, and good intentions in analyzing situations. They are taught to understand that human society and all of its parts interact in complex ways that are not easily reduced to simple, linear, cause-and-effect explanations. Lucy's decision to terminate her formal education at age 18 is not necessarily the cause for her family's impending economic crisis. Abby needs to consider that Lucy is an employee of an organization, a member of a community, and a participant in an economic system that also shaped her financial decisions.

There are discernible patterns in human behavior and in the social systems that humans create. Lucy's problems are not unique to her, her employer, or even her community. Social work school taught Abby that while she must respect Lucy's individual choices, there are sophisticated descriptions and explanations of circumstances that will help her select an appropriate intervention.

In addition, there are multiple ways of understanding the same events. Lucy will present her view of what is happening and why. Her boss and the executives at company headquarters might see things quite differently. Abby will review her own perspectives. Abby will conclude that all of these points of view have elements of truth, but that one or two of them are more useful in understanding Lucy's situation, in selecting a practice model, and then in formulating a course of action.

Shifting Perspectives in Social Work

A *perspective* is a particular point of view that reflects "taken-for-granted" assumptions or a system of beliefs. Perspectives provide a broad conceptual and value framework within which theory development or selection takes place (Chess & Norlin, 1991). Most people would agree that a perspective is not intended as a guide for practice. Perspectives have strong explanatory power and are thus useful for assessments, but do not prescribe specific forms of intervention. Instead they allow the thoughtful selection of one or more practice theories.

As a profession, social work has borrowed extensively from other disciplines, including the social sciences (e.g., sociology, psychology), the life sciences (e.g., biology, genetics), and the humanities. There is no perspective or body of theories that is totally unique to social work, although some perspectives and theories are more often used than others.

Historically, social workers and social work educators have shifted from one perspective to another. During the 1960s and 1970s, the social work profession moved from an emphasis on intrapsychic phenomena to an orientation that also paid attention to social environments and larger social systems (Leighninger, 1978). The systems perspective served as a theoretical bridge to address person *in* environment as a unitary focus rather than the false dichotomy of person *and* environment that had characterized earlier stages (Hearn, 1979).

The systems perspective also views behavior patterns as interactional and reciprocal rather than linear. In other words, rather than an explanation that says, in effect, a particular action on the part of A results in a predicable response from B, systems theorists would say that B is influenced by A, but A is at the same time also influenced by B. A and B could be individuals, families, or groups, or an individual in a family, or a group in an organization, and so forth. The limitations of a linear model seemed to be corrected by an emphasis on thinking systemically.

By the 1980s, the social system approach, which emphasized system stability, was beginning to be challenged. Although social workers continued to pay attention to person-in-environment concepts, some believed that a clearer understanding of how and why systems change was needed. The ecosystems perspective, which has strong roots in systems theory, replaced the system perspective with greater attention to process and what happens across encounters, reflecting the reciprocal relationships between organisms and their environments. Both perspectives are described in greater detail next.

Perspectives Used in This Text

Because this text is concerned primarily with the broader contexts of human behavior, it draws heavily on sociological perspectives. In their analyses of macro (large) systems, sociologists predominantly rely on two perspectives: the functionalist perspective and the conflict perspective. Two other perspectives, the social constructionist perspective and the rational/social exchange perspective, are often used in the analysis of smaller systems and individual interactions. We (the authors) believe, however, that the social constructionist perspective and the rational/social exchange perspective offer useful insights in examining some social institutions and social settings. We include the ecosystems perspective because it is especially relevant for social work practice in that it views human behavior as part of reciprocal relationships with and within a context of many levels of systems that are interconnected. Finally, we include both a diversity perspective and a strengths perspective because they are central to the profession's value system.

Two of the perspectives used in this text, the ecosystems perspective and the functionalist perspective, are partially derived from and closely related to the systems perspective. *Systems* are defined as organized wholes comprising component parts that interact in a distinct way and endure over time (Anderson, Carter, & Lowe, 1999, p. 294). The *systems perspective,* also often called *general systems theory,* (see von Bertalanffy, 1968) is an interdisciplinary construct developed to identify common principles of organization that can be applied universally to all phenomena. In other words, this perspective assumes there is a similar underlying order to everything in the world. Other basic assumptions of the systems perspective include the following:

- Each system has a structure; the parts have a relationship to each other.
- The whole is more than the sum of its parts.
- Everything is connected; a change in any one part affects the system as a whole.
- All systems are, at the same time, made up of smaller (sub)systems and are parts of larger systems.
- Each system has a boundary that separates it from other systems and gives it its identity.
- As systems evolve, they become more complex (e.g., the parts become differentiated and more specialized).

While physical scientists use a systems theory perspective to analyze everything from atoms to galaxies, social scientists use it to analyze social systems and their interactions. A *social system* is a social unit, such as a family, group, organization, or community, comprised of elements that are functionally related and interdependent. The parts of social systems do not need to be in close physical proximity to each other. They may have psychological rather than physical boundaries because they exist in social reality rather than in physical reality. The structure of a social system is determined by social roles and shared expectations; often members share common goals.

The assumptions of the systems and social systems perspectives can be illustrated with a school of social work. The school is more than a collection of individuals and spaces, more than faculty, staff, and students, offices and classrooms. It is part of a larger system, a college or university. It contains subsystems, such as student associations and faculty committees. Professors relate to students as instructors, advisors, and mentors; they relate to the administration as employees. In a large school, some staff may have specialized functions (e.g., accounting, clerical support, supervision of other staff or student assistants). The obvious boundaries of the school include building and classroom walls, but also might include psychosocial boundaries, such as ID cards, registration rolls, professional jargon, or a value system that is unique to the profession. It is easy to see how everything is connected and how one part affects the others. For example, if a professor in a foundation course fails to properly prepare students, instructors in subsequent courses will have to change their lessons to accommodate the students' deficiencies.

Terms used to describe change processes from a systems perspective include *equilibrium, steady state,* and *homeostasis.* When there is limited change and minimal interaction with the environment, the result is referred to as *equilibrium.* When there is greater change and considerable interaction with the environment, the result is referred to as *steady state.* For example, if a field instructor becomes incapacitated at midsemester and is unable to continue to supervise interns, a new instructor may be recruited to replace him with minimal disruption in the system (equilibrium). If a replacement cannot be found, the students may have to be reassigned to other agencies that will make the necessary accommodations to offer the students an appropriate learning experience (steady state). The term *homeostasis* is often used in reference to the adaptive capacities of organic systems. Thus, for example, the body maintains its internal balance by taking in water and nutrients and expelling waste. It maintains its temperature by sweating or shivering. These examples of equilibrium, steady state, and homeostasis illustrate a return to balance. In other cases, change may cause a temporary imbalance in the system, but ultimately result in a different but more successful balance. For example, in a social system, such as an organization or a community, the current system balance may be based on outdated practices or the exploitation of some people in the system. Optimal functioning may depend on a disruption of the present balance so that new, more successful patterns may emerge.

The Ecosystems Perspective

One of the common criticisms of the systems perspective stems from the abstract way it conceptualizes phenomena. Because systems concepts literally apply to all phenomena, they don't tell us much about any particular element or interaction. "Ecology, the biological science that studies organism-environment relations, offered concepts of these relations that were less abstract than those offered by systems theories and closer to common human experience" (Germain & Gitterman, 1995, p. 816). The *ecosystems perspective* (also called *the ecological perspective*), was introduced to social work by Carel Germain in 1973. It conceptualized the environment as "more than a static setting" for people's lives (Germain & Gitterman, 1995, p. 816). Concepts from ecology were used to supplement the systems perspective. This was consistent with the person-in-environment worldview of social workers (which Germain and Gitterman write as *person:environment* to signify how closely the two are intertwined).

> The ecological perspective makes clear the need to view people and environments as a unitary system within a particular cultural and historic context. Both person and environment can be fully understood only in terms of their relationship, in which each continually influences the other within a particular context. Hence, all concepts derived from the ecological metaphor refer not to environment alone, or person alone; rather, each concept expresses a particular person:environment relationship, whether it is positive, negative, or neutral. (Germain & Gitterman, 1995, p. 816)

Another construct of the ecosystems perspective is *adaptation,* or the various processes people use to achieve a better level of fit between themselves and the settings in which they find themselves. Social systems, as well as individuals, are involved in a process of continuous adaptation within and with their larger environments. In our school of social work example, adaptation would occur if the university lost funding for work-study positions and the school developed paid internships in various social service agencies to fill the gap for financially needy students.

Goodness-of-fit is the extent to which there is a match between an individual's or a group's needs, rights, goals, and capacities and the qualities of their physical and social environments (Germain & Gitterman, 1995, p. 817; Greene, 1999, p. 299). In our prior example, goodness-of-fit would be achieved if the school recognized that its student body was comprised primarily of full-time workers and changed its course schedule to offer mostly evening and weekend classes.

Other important ecosystems constructs include niche and habitat. Germain and Gitterman (1995, p. 818) define *niche* as the "status occupied by an individual or family in the social structure . . . [often related to] color, ethnicity, gender, age, poverty, sexual orientation, or physical or mental states." *Habitat* is defined as places or settings where individuals can be found (p. 818). Whereas it is impossible to analyze the natural social and physical environments of humans as distinctly separate from each other, in this text we find it useful to concentrate on niches in Part III and discuss places where people live and work—locational communities, organizations, and residential institutions—in Part IV.

The Functionalist Perspective

The *functionalist perspective* (often called *structural functionalism*) also is closely related to the systems perspective. It is used by sociologists, who are less interested in individual adjustment or smaller social systems than in how society works. They use functionalism to understand larger social systems and the functioning of society as a whole. "According to this perspective, a society is composed of interrelated parts, each of which serves a function and (ideally) contributes to the overall stability of the society" (Kendall, 2001, p. 22). Drawing on systems perspective and social systems theory, one assumption is that large societal systems reflect a general orderliness and that they maintain a balance or stable state. If one part changes, all the other parts are affected and the system may no longer function smoothly.

Systems, ecosystems, and functionalist perspectives assume that systems are constantly changing, but that these change processes are incremental (slow and in small steps) and are self-correcting when the system gets out of balance. Functionalists believe that all social phenomena serve the purpose of maintaining the social system. Functionalists see a useful function in everything in society, including elements, characteristics, or processes that most people would view as negative, such as poverty or racial inequality (Davis & Moore, 1945). Because maintaining the status quo supports the interests of those who already hold power and wealth, functionalism is often criticized by those who believe the existing system is unfair.

Theorists who espouse a systems-related perspective (ecosystems or structural functionalism) emphasize small, incremental, and self-righting changes. There is little expectation that the environment will be markedly changed. This point of view differs substantially from the position of conflict theorists (discussed next) who routinely call for fundamental structural change.

The Conflict Perspective

The *conflict perspective* is another perspective commonly used by sociologists. It is most often linked with Karl Marx, who wrote about inter-class struggle. Unlike the functionalist perspective, conflict theorists argue that social systems are not united or harmonious, but are divided by class, gender, race, or other characteristics that reflect differences in social power as much as anything else. According to this perspective, "groups in society are engaged in a continuous power struggle for scarce resources" (Kendall, 2001, p. 23). In the conflict perspective, problems are defined as social and structural rather than individual, meaning that they can be solved only by social change, not by individual adaptation.

> It's not the fact that there are rich and poor that generates egalitarian struggle, but the fact that the rich grind the faces of the poor. It's always what one group with power does to another group—whether in the name of health, safety, or security—it makes no difference. The aim, ultimately, of the fight for equality, is always the elimination of subordination . . . no more toadying, scraping and bowing, fearful trembling. (Walzer, 1983, p. 13)

Early social workers recognized structural inequality and oppression, but as a profession they have not until recently drawn on the conflict perspective as a way to conceptualize human behavior in the social environment. The development of empowerment theories (Lee, 2001; Solomon, 1976, 1987), which have their roots in the conflict perspective, has led to a renewed interest in utilizing this perspective as a way to explain social injustice and privilege. *Empowerment* is a proactive response to assist people who experience systematic forms of harassment and oppression through raising consciousness, and enhancing self-efficacy.

Critics of the conflict perspective note that, particularly without adoption of an empowerment approach, social workers using this perspective may overemphasize polarization and antagonism, viewing clients simply as victims and their opponents as oppressors (Robbins, Chatterjee, & Canda, 1998, p. 85). On the other hand, in contrast to other helping professions, social work has a specific commitment to empowerment at both the personal and societal levels.

The Rational/Social Exchange Perspective

The *rational/social exchange perspective* is based on the assumptions that human beings have the capacity to reason, make choices based on consideration of available alternatives and anticipated consequences, and act in their own best interest. Human behavior is believed to be purposeful and goal directed. At the individual level, rational decision-making theories (e.g., rational choice theory, social exchange theory, fair-exchange theory, reciprocity) suggest that people make decisions based on a cost-benefit analysis.

The rational/social exchange perspective has also been applied to larger social systems (groups, organizations, communities, societies) based on the "doctrine of *utilitarianism*—a belief that the purpose of all action should be to bring about the greatest happiness to the greatest number of people" (Kendall, 2001, p. 178). Nevertheless, beyond the individual level, rational decision making by a collective body encounters many barriers, including lack of agreement on political, social, economic, and cultural values and goals; inability to compare competing costs and benefits; and the fragmented nature of policy making in large bureaucracies (Dye, 1998, pp. 25–27). Often benefits can be identified only for specific groups, and many of those are conflicting. Another barrier is that individual actors may look out for their own interests rather than that of the collective body or constituency. The reality is that, at the level of larger systems and social institutions (organizations, communities, government), policies that generate the maximum social gain—the most benefits for the most people—are difficult to develop. In fact, Dye argues that rational decision making "rarely takes place at all in government" (p. 25).

The Social Constructionist Perspective

The *social constructionist perspective* emphasizes the role of the human mind and the shared subjective understanding of localized experiences in defining the social world. ("Localized experience" refers to the notion that all people live in a specific cultural and historical setting that shapes their perceptions.) The constructionist perspective is based on the assumption that there is no objective reality; rather, reality is defined by perceptions and is, in fact, a social construction (Schutz, 1967). From a constructionist perspective, sociological phenomena, such as society and social institutions, considered by most people to be elements of objective realty, are no more than creations of human thought processes. Although constructionists do not deny the reality of such social phenomena, they suggest that it is important to study the subjective interpretations of them made by individuals and groups. In sum, this perspective suggests that reality is socially constructed through social interaction and people act in accordance with their constructed reality.

> *Standpoints* are truths or knowledge created through awareness of reality gleaned from particular social locations. The concept of standpoint assumes that all people see the world from the place where they are situated socioculturally. What is considered to be real depends on one's standpoint and is grounded in experiences related to one's position within the sociocultural topography. (Van Den Bergh, 1995, p. xxvii)

Thus, the social constructionist perspective is useful in reminding social work practitioners that members of minority groups or other marginalized people may experience a social reality that is quite different from the one experienced by members of the Euro-American middle class.

One criticism of social constructionism is that, if everything is subjective and therefore relative, there is no basis for judging situations or determining preferred outcomes (Robbins, Chatterjee, & Canda, 1998, p. 317). Critics of the social constructionist perspective also worry that if social problems are understood as merely the perceptions and claims of particular groups, then there is no basis for taking action (Best, 1989).

Preferred Perspectives

The Diversity Perspective.   In the past, the idea that America was a "melting pot" held prominence. Today most social workers do not accept this as a productive point of view, but rather embrace the notion that celebrating different racial and ethnic cultures is healthy for individuals, families, groups, organizations, and communities. Acknowledging and valuing human diversity is central to the profession's value base and essential for culturally competent practice. Still, it is important to distinguish between strengths-affirming segmentation of identities and divisions that rest on inequality and serve not to validate differences but to facilitate discrimination (Cohen, 2003, p. 408). Social workers must celebrate diversity while at the same time negotiating resolutions to conflicts in a way that promotes justice and fairness for everyone.

The Strengths Perspective.   Another point of view that reflects social work values is the *strengths perspective* (Saleebey, 2002). "While recognizing the fallibilities of people, the strengths perspective brings some balance to the understanding of the human condition" (Saleebey, 2002, p. 265). The strengths perspective views all individuals and groups, regardless of their histories, as having value and capabilities, with resources, skills, motivations and dreams that must be considered when working with them such that they gain more control over their lives. This perspective offers a basis from which helpers become agents of the client system, which is regarded as having special expertise. Critics of the strengths perspective say that it ignores problems or simply reframes them in a more positive light.

How Theory Informs Practice

A *theory* is narrower than a perspective. It is a proposition that explains or predicts something. In other words, it is an educated guess, based on both previous knowledge and observations. Most scientists treat theories as hypotheses to be tested, not as factual statements. In other words, a theory is *provisional;* that is, it is used only until a better explanation comes along. A theory may *describe* (how things happen as they do) or *explain* (why things happen as they do). *Prediction* is based on recognizing a recurring pattern so that future events can be anticipated. Prediction may occur without a full understanding or explanation of cause and effect. Usually predictive power alone is not sufficient to develop effective interventions.

On the other hand, explanatory theories provide a basis for the development or adoption of models of intervention. *Models* provide guidance on how to practice in a range of situations. They focus on what to do by describing patterns of activities and highlighting certain principles that give practice consistency (Payne, 1997, p. 35).

In this text, we concentrate on perspectives and a limited number of related theories that help to explain human behavior. A good understanding of these provides the foundation for selecting appropriate models for intervention. Students will spend more time exploring theories of change and models of practice in other social work courses.

In general, we would like to think that models flow neatly from theories and that theories are grounded in coherent perspectives. The reality, however, is that the relationship between these three elements is messy. For example, sometimes an innovative practice intervention precedes the development of a theory that explains why it works, and there are some theories that offer no applications that can be translated into intervention. Payne (1997) suggests that when all three elements—perspective, theory, and model—are fully developed and in place, the practice of effective social work is more likely to occur.

Key Points

- A social worker's perspective affects how he or she assesses a client's situation.

- Sociological perspectives are useful in examining larger systems.

- Diversity and strengths perspectives are derived from the social work profession's values.

- Social work practice is more effective when perspectives, theories, and models are fully developed and applied.

Questions to Think about and Discuss

1. How is it helpful for a social work practitioner to look at a situational context from more than one perspective?

2. Do you think more emphasis on diversity or more emphasis on common values and needs is helpful in today's world?

Internet Search Terms

Conceptual frameworks	Functionalist perspective	Social/cultural perspectives
Constructionism	Multiple perspectives approach	Sociological perspectives analysis
Ecosystems	Resiliency	Symbolic interactionism
Empowerment	Social-conflict perspective	Systems theories
Exchange theory	Social constructionism	

Part II

Introduction to Social Institutions

Social institutions are among the more abstract notions we present in this book. *Social institutions* are defined as patterns of human interaction that meet the basic social needs of a society. These needs include reproduction and socialization of the young; establishing a hierarchy of power; producing and distributing goods and services; dealing with questions about meaning, such as the purpose of life, the reason for suffering, and what happens after death; transmitting knowledge and skills across generations; treating the sick and injured; providing for dependent members of society; maintaining social order; and disseminating information. Sociologists recognize several basic social institutions that exist in all societies in addition to the family; among these are government/polity, economy, religion, education, and health care. Some recognize or acknowledge additional social institutions. In this book, we will discuss three additional social institutions: social welfare, criminal justice, and the mass media. These eight social institutions have been selected because they are particularly relevant to social work.

Even though the idea of a social institution might be difficult to grasp, everyone has had experience with the cumulative effects of each of the social institutions discussed in this section. They have as much influence on social work clients as any smaller social system because they provide the context within which families, organizations, and communities operate. The collectivity of social institutions is what constitutes a society.

We restrict ourselves to three or four major perspectives in our discussion of social institutions. These four perspectives are those used by most social scientists/sociologists to explain social institutions: the *functionalist perspective,* the *conflict perspective,* the *rational/ social exchange perspective,* and the *constructionist perspective.* These perspectives were defined and described in Chapter 1.

It makes sense that a rational perspective would apply (at least in principle) to the economy and to government-supported social institutions. The reader should not be surprised, however, to learn that the rational perspective is not easily applied to the health care system, mass media, or religion. Although specific organizations within these systems have centralized administrative and decision-making bodies—and there may be alliances and coalitions that act in concert to meet social needs or to promote particular agendas—there are no central coordinating or planning bodies that are charged with (or have the authority for) setting priorities or making policies regarding those systems as a whole.

We believe that social institutions have the capacity to oppress. They also have the capacity to promote well-being, although for many social work clients, that is not what they experience. Thus we will explore the effects of each social institution as a context for individuals and families, looking in particular at how they obstruct or promote well-being.

In this section, we begin in Chapter 2 with what we believe are the most significant social institutions, that is, economics and politics. In Chapter 3, government-related social institutions—social welfare, education, and criminal justice—are examined. In Chapter 4, non-government-related social institutions—health care, religion, and mass media—are addressed. These last six social institutions are examined each in its own right, and also in relation to the political economy.

2

The Political Economy

We have devoted an entire chapter to the two most important social institutions in America, that is, the economic system and the political system. We will introduce the two separately, but at the end of the chapter we will discuss how closely they interact. This interaction is so complete that we will label it the *political economy* and thereafter treat it as a single institution.

The Economic System

The *economic system* organizes and regulates a society's production, distribution, and consumption of goods and services. The American economic system is based on *capitalism*. In an American context, capitalism is usually understood as being synonymous with the business world. The three basic characteristics of capitalism typically cited by economists are private ownership, unfettered market competition, and pursuit of profit. These present a clear contrast to the characteristics of *socialism,* which are public ownership, central planning, and collective goals. These pure ideological models seldom exist in reality; instead, many countries have mixed economic models. Even the United States does not have a "pure" form of capitalism, as the government is actively involved in several aspects of economic control.

Issues and Trends

Corporate Capitalism. A *corporation* is an artificial being, existing only in the law (Peterson, 1991). As one outspoken Native American environmentalist notes,

> Corporations exist beyond time and space. . . . They do not die a natural death; they outlive their own creators. And they have no commitment to locale, employees, or neighbors. This makes the modern corporation entirely different from the baker or grocer of previous years. . . . Having no morality, no commitment to place, and no physical nature . . . a corporation can relocate all of its operations to another place at the first sign of inconvenience: demanding employees, too high taxes, restrictive environmental laws. The traditional ideal of community engagement is antithetical to corporate behavior. (Mander, 1991, pp. 133–134)

The "profit imperative" and the "growth imperative" are fundamental corporate drives.

A corporation has a charter that establishes it as a separate legal body that has its own rights, privileges, and liabilities distinct from those of its members. Originally chartered by the monarchy and created as extensions of the government to "promote the general welfare," over time corporations "changed from temporary creations beholden to the state to permanent businesses with a vested interest in serving private capital" (Palmer, 2003, p. 53). In 1886 the Supreme Court ruled that corporations have many rights similar to individuals, and corporations have since assumed that they can exercise rights to free speech, privacy, equal protection, and against self-incrimination (Hartman, 2002). While small businesses and individual entrepreneurs are often glorified by politicians, the reality is that contemporary American capitalism is about large corporations.

Corporate capitalism dominates the economic system. There are millions of corporations, but only a small number—fewer than several hundred companies—control the vast majority of economic activity (Peterson, 1991).

Sociologists often differentiate between *work establishments,* the actual place where someone works, and *firms,* the parent company or organization (Stockard, 2000). An example of a work establishment would be a local Kentucky Fried Chicken restaurant. An example of a firm would be its parent company, Pepsico. A majority of workers, especially those in the service sector, go to work in establishments with fewer than one hundred employees. A third of all workers, however, are employed by very large firms. Corporations such as automobile manufacturers (e.g., General Motors) and gigantic retailers may employ hundreds of thousands of workers. Wal-Mart is the largest employer in 21 states and the largest private employer in Mexico.

Conglomerates are giant corporations that result from mergers and takeovers of smaller corporations. Beginning in the later 1960s, conglomerates began to appear as a result of the mergers of firms with diverse products and services. For example, the enormous profits of the petroleum industry in the 1970s allowed Gulf Oil to buy the Ringling Brothers and Barnum and Bailey Circus (Hodson & Sullivan, 1990).

Noticing that the government had shown little interest in restricting mergers and monopolies, corporations changed strategies during the 1980s, divested themselves of unrelated firms, and began to acquire firms in the same or similar industries. By the late 1990s, this trend involved mergers of more than 5,000 firms a year and transactions of more than $1 trillion, over five times the level of a decade earlier (Stockard, 2000, p. 378). Many of the acquisitions involved "hostile takeovers," that is, the purchase of a company against the wishes of its owners.

There are probably no entities other than national governments that are big enough to stand up to the power of giant conglomerates. Corporations that devote themselves to generating profits and owe allegiance only to their stockholders have little interest in the welfare of employees, consumers, or the environment.

Corporate power is felt not only within this country, but internationally as well. Multinational corporations profess loyalty to no single nation. In fact, many are larger and more powerful than nation-states (Morgan, 1986). They may manufacture component parts in one (or several) countries, assemble the parts in another, have their corporate headquarters in yet another, and sell their products throughout the world.

Changing Patterns of Employment.   Today, the economy of the United States has shifted from industrial manufacturing to an economy that is predominantly service oriented and information based. The new economy provides few openings for unskilled laborers in well-paying manufacturing jobs. Employment in the *service sector* is split between positions requiring technical skills (such as computer programmers) and poorly paid jobs requiring minimal skills. For example, in the fast food industry, cashiers no longer have to enter prices and make change; they simply hit keys with pictures on them and the customer's change is automatically calculated and discharged. Even the interaction with customers is scripted ("Do you want to supersize that?"). Employment in this part of the service sector does not pay enough to support a family and is unlikely to provide benefits, such as health care insurance and retirement plans.

In search of greater profits, companies moved manufacturing jobs first to the anti-union South and then overseas to reduce labor costs. Employees have little bargaining power in such situations, either individually or collectively. By 1999, only 9.4 percent of private sector workers were union members (Frank, 2000).

Downsizing refers to large-scale worker lay-offs. (Downsizing may also be called "reduction in force" or RIF.) *Outsourcing* means contracting to have tasks normally done within the company performed under a contract with another company. Commonly outsourced jobs include custodial work or payroll functions. *Offshoring* is the term used when the jobs are still controlled by the company itself but moved overseas. Most of the lost jobs are in manufacturing or in telephone call centers (Uchitelle, 2003). An example of this trend is the transfer of customer service and tech support jobs to India where English-speaking, college-educated, entry-level recruits earn $3,650 a year—good wages in India, but only a fifth of what an American would be paid for similar work (Carmichael, 2003; Waldman, 2003). Even such traditionally American products as Levi's blue jeans are now being manufactured overseas (Mayhew, 2003). Recently, more highly skilled jobs are being offshored, including aeronautical engineers, software designers, and stock analysts (Uchitelle, 2003). Whereas factory lay-offs used to be temporary and employers called workers back once a recovery began, outsourcing and offshoring practices reflect structural, permanent changes in the broader economy.

Since 1979, when manufacturing employment peaked in this country, one in four factory jobs has disappeared (Vieth, 2003). Although other kinds of jobs have been created, the new jobs tend to pay significantly less (McCracken, 2004). Beyond the effects on individuals and their families, unemployment also has larger consequences, including community break-down and a rise in social conflict: Unemployed persons tend to withdraw from social and civic activities and direct their anger at a variety of targets, including immigrants, minorities, welfare recipients, and the very rich (Thio, 1998, p. 405).

Beginning in the 1980s, American companies learned that by using "temps" they could hold down wages, reduce the costs of employee benefits, and lay off surplus staff at any time. Although many people (such as students, homemakers, and older adults) work part-time by choice, a significant number do so only because they cannot find full-time employment. *Contingent work* is becoming a characteristic of the American workforce (Larson, 1996). The contingent workforce is made up of part-time and temporary employees. A majority of jobs in the private sector are filled by contingent workers (Reskin & Padavic, 1994). Temporary workers are the fastest-growing segment of the contingent workforce (Kendall, 2001). Manpower, a temp agency, is now America's largest private employer (Korten, 1995). Many contingent workers can be classified as *underemployed,* that is, they are overqualified for the position they fill. For these workers, job security and employment benefits are an illusion.

Consumerism. Some sociologists have argued that the real focus of the American economy has shifted from one of production to one of consumption—or even "hyper-consumption" (Ritzer, 1999). This trend has been fostered by the development, since World War II (in order of their appearance) of franchises, shopping malls, "superstores," discounters, home shopping networks, "cybermalls," and "mega malls." The average American is consuming more than twice as much as he or she did 40 years ago. Since 1950, Americans have used up as many of the earth's resources as were used in all the rest of human history. Environmentalists are alarmed that Americans are both extracting resources at rates the planet cannot sustain and producing waste at levels that the planet cannot absorb (Korten, 1995).

The shift in consumption patterns probably began in the 1920s when producers starting marketing directly to consumers, rather than to retailers. From the start, advertising was more about creating consumers than selling individual products (Croteau & Hoynes, 2003). Although the marketing industry claims that they simply provide information so that buyers can make informed choices, many would say that through massive advertising campaigns corporations actually create "needs" (or more accurately, "wants") as much as they provide goods and services in response to consumer demands. A further discussion of how the mass media encourage consumerism is presented in Chapter 4.

In addition to advertising, another development that has fostered a consumer society is buying on credit. Credit card companies lure people into consumption by offering easy credit and then entice them into still further consumption by offers of "payment holidays" and increased credit limits (Ritzer, 1999). Schor (1998) describes these organizations as "credit pushers," acknowledging the addictive effects of buying on credit. This point of view is shared by Manning (2000), who also expresses concern about how credit card companies target college students. The results are predictable. According to data collected by the Endowment for Financial Education, there were more personal bankruptcies filed in 2002 (about 1.5 million) than there were graduates from colleges and universities (about 1.2 million) (Rosen, 2003).

Understanding the Economic System

Functionalist Perspective.   Functionalists suggest that corporate capitalism improves the quality of living for many of the world's citizens. The free trade that is necessary for multinational corporations promotes greater competition and greater productivity. This leads to lower prices and a higher standard of living. While functionalists acknowledge that developed countries lose unskilled jobs to poor countries, this is explained as a temporary "glitch" as corporations in the more developed countries create jobs demanding skills in technology. Poor countries also benefit as new jobs improve living standards.

Functionalists also believe that the opportunity for everyone to be a stockholder, as well as a consumer, is a major positive feature of the American economic system. In effect, everyone, including workers, can also be "capitalists" and share in the profits and the prosperity of a growing company and a strong economy.

Conflict Perspective.   The laws of supply and demand and the push for profits are not necessarily consistent with the well-being of workers or consumers. Conflict theorists (including Karl Marx) suggest that those who own the means of production will always exploit the laboring classes. These theorists stress that in order to keep labor costs low and profits high, capitalists view workers as expendable commodities who can be exploited to meet the needs of the company.

For conflict theorists, downsizing is an obvious example of owners valuing profits over the well-being of their employees. Downsizing from this perspective is not just about efficiency. It is directly linked to the profits of the stock market. A common strategy to increase stock prices has been to lay off employees (Frank, 2000). The newly unemployed workers are assured that this process is, in fact, good for the economy and hence good for everyone (Korten, 1995).

Another indicator of the exploitation of workers is the enormous disparity between the salaries of workers and those who employ them. CEO salaries grew as downsizing became a management strategy. One economist (Frank, 2000) reported that in 1980, CEOs of large U.S. corporations earned 42 times as much as the average worker. By 2000, the ratio was more than 500 times as much. While both production and productivity per labor hour increased continuously during the last half of the twentieth century, labor's share of the income fell drastically (Berberoglu, 1994). If the minimum wage had kept pace with productivity since 1968, it would now be $13.80 per hour rather than $5.15 (Whittington, 2001).

Rational/Social Exchange Perspective.   If the explanation of any social institution can be said to be firmly rooted in a social theory, it is capitalism and social exchange. Adam Smith, one of the earliest of the economic theorists, suggested that it is self-interest that makes capitalism—and industrial society—function. In business, managers, workers, and customers make decisions based on their own interests. There is no room for sentimentality or idealism. The "market," acting without interference, will find the correct balance so that consumers get the best value for their money and workers are paid what they are worth. Companies that offer shoddily made products or sloppy service are put out of business as consumers seek better deals elsewhere. Workers who do not contribute a value comparable to their wage are laid off. Efficiency—payback on investments—is the key.

Proponents of capitalism assume that the principle of self-interest operates not just among individuals but also between larger systems. For example, a community or even a state, competing with other localities, might offer tax breaks to entice a corporation to build a new plant within its boundaries, thus creating jobs for its citizens.

Constructionist Perspective.   Even something that sounds as rational and objective as economics can be partly explained in terms of how members of a society interpret the meaning of work, wealth, and economic exchange.

One well-known theorist, Max Weber, suggested that the development of capitalism as an economic system was based on the belief system of early Protestants. The Protestant followers of John Calvin believed that worldly success was a sign of their being in God's favor. According to Weber, Calvinists' religious convictions led them to reinvest their wealth, thus laying the foundations of capitalism.

Later generations of Calvinists retained their personal discipline and their belief system became a work ethic, wherein hard labor and thriftiness were closely associated with morality. The *Puritan work ethic* is firmly established in the American psyche. It suggests that people should work even under conditions that are unfair or harmful. The injunction that welfare recipients accept jobs that will not cover their child-care costs is an example of the power of the belief that working is not simply a means of self-support, but also a moral imperative.

Another point of view that has facilitated the growth of American capitalism is the meaning of credit and how it is used (Calder, 1999; Hine, 2002; Ritzer, 2001). At the beginning of the twentieth century, borrowing was frowned upon. Nevertheless, by the 1950s, there was a definite change in attitudes toward money, and households took on debt in the pursuit of consumer goods (Gottdeiner, 1997). Credit card debt doubled in the United States between 1990 and 1996, while savings declined (Ritzer, 1999). The quality of acquisitiveness used to be discouraged, if not condemned; now Americans are told that consumption is equivalent to patriotism.

Thus, in terms of the socially constructed meanings of work and wealth, we see both continuity and change. Work is still viewed as having inherent value. Wealth, while no longer seen as a sign of salvation, is highly regarded as an indicator of personal worth.

The Impact of the Economic System on Individuals and Families

How the Economic System Obstructs Well-Being.   Even the greatest advocates of capitalism acknowledge that it is an unfair system, rewarding some very well and leaving others behind. For those at the bottom of the economic hierarchy, the inequity is especially notable. According to the 2000 census, in the midst of the best economic conditions in decades, 9.2 percent of families residing in the "richest country in the world" were still living in "abject poverty" (Economic Policy Institute, 2002a). In the next few paragraphs, we will discuss inequities in relation to income, wealth, food, housing, and employment.

An accumulating body of data, reported by the Economic Policy Institute (2002b), documents the growth in inequality between economic classes in America. The pattern in the 1980s was for the top wage earners to pull away from the middle and the middle to pull away from the bottom. In the 1990s, the bottom and middle wage earners grew closer together, while the top pulled even further away from the rest.

A usual way to measure inequality is to divide American society into quintiles (fifths) and then make comparisons. In 2000, for example, the poorest fifth received 4.3 percent of national income while the top fifth received 47.4 percent. See Table 2.1.

In 2000, the average annual income of the poorest fifth of American families was $12,990, a 1 percent increase since 1990; annual income of the richest fifth of American families averaged $137,480, a 15 percent increase since 1990 (data from the Economic Policy Institute and the Center on Budget and Policy Priorities, reported in *Time,* January 31, 2000, p. 25). This disparity in income is accounted for, in part, by the low wages paid to those at the bottom of the income scale and has the effect of making the rich, richer and the poor, poorer.

The current minimum wage for U.S. workers is $5.15 per hour; it has not been increased by Congress since 1997. A worker employed 40 hours a week and earning the minimum wage cannot adequately support a family of four. According to the poverty guidelines of the government, a full-time worker would have to earn at least $8.70 per hour to support a family of four at the poverty level.

Class difference is not just about wages and salaries. An accurate measure of *wealth* includes all assets (savings, stocks, bonds, life insurance policies, real estate holdings, paintings, jewelry, antiques, and so forth). The wealthiest Americans can live on the dividends from their investments without having to touch the principal or work for a salary. In 1995, half a million U.S. households (one-half of 1 percent of the population) owned 39.3 percent of all assets (Household Economic Studies, 1995). This makes the United States first among prosperous nations in the level of inequality of income (Smeeding, 2004).

In 2000, 4.1 million American children lived in poverty despite the presence of a full-time worker in the household. This represents an increase from 1998 when 3.8 million children lived in poverty with a full-time worker. The Department of Agriculture reports that 33.3 million individuals or 12.1 percent of the U.S. population experienced food insecurity during 2000. See Table 2.2 and Figure 2.1.

In addition to insufficient food, lack of affordable housing is a critical issue for the working poor. Writing for the Habitat for Humanity newsletter, the director of Harvard University's Joint Center for Housing Studies summarized America's housing crisis (Retsinas, 2002). Referring to federal guidelines that suggest that housing should not consume more than 30 percent of a family's income, he noted that one in eight American families spends more than 50 percent. He concluded that for those full-time workers who make only

TABLE 2.1   *Percent of National Income Received by Each Fifth of the U.S. Population*

	1950	*1975*	*2000*
Highest fifth	42.7	40.7	47.4
Fourth fifth	23.4	24.2	22.8
Third fifth	17.4	17.7	15.5
Second fifth	12.0	11.9	9.8
Lowest fifth	4.5	5.6	4.3

Source: U.S. Bureau of the Census, 2002. *Population survey: 2002.*

TABLE 2.2　*2002 Federal Poverty Guidelines*

Size of Family Unit	Poverty Guideline	Required Gross Monthly Income	Required Approximate Hourly Income
1	$8,860	$738	$4.26
2	$11,940	$995	$5.74
3	$15,020	$1,252	$7.22
4	$18,100	$1,508	$8.70
5	$21,180	$1,765	$10.18
6	$24,260	$2,022	$11.66
7	$27,340	$2,278	$13.14
8	$30,420	$2,535	$14.63

Source: Federal Register. (2002, February 14). *Poverty guidelines for the 48 contiguous states and the District of Columbia.*

the minimum wage, there is no county in the United States where they could afford to rent a two-bedroom apartment. Given these data, it is not surprising to learn that the homeless population in America is growing. In 2001, homelessness among families increased by 22 percent. Many of the adults in these families were employed (Warkentin, 2002).

Social scientists divide the labor market into two categories. The *primary labor market* provides jobs that carry with them many benefits, including career advancement opportunities. Examples of occupations in the primary labor market are management positions and the professions. Jobs in the *secondary labor market* require few skills, provide minimal benefits, often involve dirty or dangerous conditions, and may offer only part-time or seasonal employment;

FIGURE 2.1　*Food Insecurity and Hunger in the United States*

❏ 33.3 million *individuals* or 12.1% of the U.S. population experienced food insecurity during 2000.

❏ 11.1 million *households* or 10.5% of U.S. households experienced food insecurity in 2000.

❏ Rates of food insecurity among the following groups were significantly higher than the national average of 10.5%:

✔ Households below the federal poverty level: 36.8%

✔ Households with children, headed by a single female: 31%

✔ African American households: 20.5%

✔ Hispanic households: 21.4%

Note: Food insecurity is defined as not having access at all times to enough food for an active healthy life, necessitating recourse to emergency food sources or other extraordinary coping behaviors to meet basic food needs (U.S. Bureau of the Census. *Statistical abstracts of the United States: 2000*).

Source: U.S. Department of Agriculture. (2000). *Prevalence of food security, food insecurity, and hunger for households and persons.*

examples include store clerks, fast-food cooks, and farm workers. People of color and women make up the majority of workers in the secondary labor market.

An example of the secondary labor market is the meat-and-poultry packing plants that draw Latinos—some of them undocumented Mexicans—to the Southeast (Butler, 1998). There they do much of the unpleasant work of transforming hogs into hams and sausages, and chickens into breasts and drumsticks—work that most Americans wouldn't do for twice the pay.

Capitalism depends on having a large reservoir of unemployed "reserve" workers who are willing to work for minimum wage whenever such work is available. The "acceptable"— that is, desired—level of unemployment advocated by the federal government has changed from a goal of zero (full employment) after the Great Depression to two to three percent during 1960s and then to five to six percent as of the mid-1980s (Heilbroner, 1993).

The picture of the extent to which the economic system exploits vulnerable populations in particular is partially captured by the overrepresentation of certain populations in statistics on poverty. Over 24 percent of African Americans and over 21 percent of Hispanics lived below the poverty line in 2002, as compared to 9.6 percent of all American families (U.S. Bureau of the Census, 2003).

How the Economic System Supports Well-Being.   While it is easy to identify oppressive elements in the modern American capitalist economy, it is important to note ways in which the economy also enhances the well-being of many citizens. The high standard of living in this country, especially in terms of consumer goods (e.g., wall-to-wall carpeting, household appliances, electronics, automobiles), is undeniable. Even the rapid growth of the service sector and its accompanying low wages and job insecurity presents an opportunity for many of the least skilled workers in American society, including high school dropouts, non-English-speaking immigrants, and people with disabilities. For example, one of the authors shops at a grocery store where a popular, good-natured "bag boy" is mentally retarded.

The Political System

The *political system* is the social institution that establishes a hierarchy of power and leadership. It is where decisions are made and carried out, either directly or indirectly. The *government* is the formal organization that has the legal authority to maintain social order by resolving conflicts among members of the society and by protecting its citizens from threats that come from outside its borders.

The United States is a representative democracy. This means that political decisions are made by bodies of representatives elected by the people (e.g., city or county councils, state legislatures, and, of course, Congress) rather than directly by the people themselves. Usually decisions are made based not only on what constituents want, but also on a complex process of negotiation and trade-offs, as well as the direct and indirect influence of "special interest" groups.

In Chapter 6, we discuss "mainstream" American values. One of these, *individualism*, has had a profound effect on our political system. Americans prefer to have a relatively weak central government (Lipset, 1996). Because of Americans' strong belief in individual rights, they are generally opposed to government "bureaucratic interference" in anything from health care to the Internet. Most citizens of the United States dislike the idea of "big government." Nevertheless, there is widespread support for government spending to clean up the environment, combat crime, improve transportation, and strengthen the educational system. Thus Americans can be characterized as *ideological conservatives* and *operational liberals* (Thio, 2000, p. 361). They criticize their government as too powerful, too intrusive, and too wasteful while at the same time demanding more services.

Issues and Trends

Political Influence. Election campaigns are increasingly commercialized and expensive. See Figure 2.2. The rising cost of political campaigns at all levels means that politicians and political parties are constantly concerned with raising funds. As a result, individuals with money (or more often, groups and organizations with money) exercise a great deal of influence over the political process. Without good financing, potential candidates do not become actual candidates (Dye & Zeigler, 1993). Some of the resources provided by campaign funding include consultants, pollsters, speechwriters, and media experts. Dye and Zeigler suggest that good consultants have become more important than political parties in successful election campaigns.

A *special interest group* is an alliance of people concerned about some political issue. Influencing legislation is called *lobbying*. The term often has a negative connotation but lobbying is used, mostly legitimately, by special interests groups of all types. These include the National Association of Social Workers, the American Public Welfare Association, and the

FIGURE 2.2 *Campaign Spending in Recent Presidential and Congressional Races*

In 1996:

❑ Total spending on all federal campaigns including presidential was $2 billion.

❑ The average winning Senate candidate spent $3.8 million compared to average campaign expenditures of $595,000 in 1976.

❑ The average winning House candidate spent $680,000 compared to average campaign expenditures of $73,000 in 1976.

❑ *Soft money* (outside the legal limits on contributions to federal campaigns) contributions to the Democratic and Republican parties totaled $263 million compared to $86 million contributed to the 1992 Presidential campaigns.

❑ The top five soft money contributors were Philip Morris ($3 million), Seagram & Sons ($1.9 million), RJR Nabisco ($1.4 million), Walt Disney Co. ($1.4 million), and Atlantic Richfield ($1.25 million).

In 2000:

❑ Presidential candidate George Bush spent $191 million. Candidate Al Gore spent $110 million.

❑ The Republican party raised $715.5 million during the 1999–2000 election period and the Democratic party raised $520.4 million.

❑ The pharmaceutical/health products industry contributed $15.3 million dollars in soft money to the two major political parties: 69% to Republicans, 31% to Democrats.

Sources: Federal Election Commission, 1996–2001; Center for Responsive Politics, 2002.

Child Welfare League of America as well as better-known groups, such as the National Rifle Association, the American Association of Retired Persons, and tobacco companies (Ginsberg, 1994). In addition to contributing to campaigns, special interests groups and their lobbyists may affect legislation by testifying before lawmakers' committees, mobilizing support or opposition to a bill by asking members to call or write letters, and even drafting proposed legislation.

Many special interest groups are not allowed to make political contributions directly. They use *political action committees* (PACs) to promote their political agendas. PACs are organizations that solicit and distribute political contributions as their primary purpose (Ginsberg, 1994). PACS have been organized by labor unions, trade associations, environmental groups, and religious groups. The number of PACs grew from 608 in 1974 and 3,798 in 1999 (DiNitto, 2000). Contributors give to PACs rather than to a political party when they want to support a specific political cause (Dye & Zeigler, 1993).

The Power of Incumbency.   In addition to the benefits associated with simple name recognition, *incumbents* (politicians already holding office) tend to have huge advantages in fundraising, and in communicating with voters through free mail privileges, regular access to the mass media, and speech-giving opportunities. David Broder, a political columnist who writes for the *Washington Post* recently identified another incumbent advantage. Following the 2000 census, in state after state legislators set aside their differences to redraw district lines to protect the incumbents of both parties; the result was that fewer than one-tenth of the seats in the House were susceptible to change (Broder, 2002).

The American public has become increasingly cynical about politicians while at the same time overwhelmingly voting to return incumbents to office. For example, in the 2000 Congressional races, 98 percent of incumbents (392 out of 399) in the U.S. House of Representatives were reelected.

PACs give most of their money to incumbents (Dye & Zeigler, 1993). The political watchdog group Common Cause (2000) reported that House incumbents had a 4 to 1 financial advantage over challengers and for Senate incumbents the ratio was 6 to 1. Scott Harshbarger, president of Common Cause, noted "this system is a gravy train for members of Congress—and a meal ticket for special interests, many of whom want something in return." The implication is that political outsiders have little power, and the status quo is supported.

Voter Apathy.   Given the situation described above, one is not surprised to find high rates of voter apathy in America. The voting rate has fallen in almost every presidential election for four decades (Patterson, 2002). Barely over half (51.3 percent) of eligible voters voted in the last presidential elections and two-thirds do not vote in Congressional races (*Statistical Abstract 1999:* Table 490). Voter enthusiasm is clearly correlated to perceptions of having a stake in the political system and the outcome of the election. Those who believe they have nothing to gain feel alienated and are unlikely to vote. See Figure 2.3.

Verba, Schlozman, and Brady (1995) note that American politics is prone to "participatory distortion." Citizens with more income, education, and age are overrepresented in almost every political activity, from contacting lawmakers to contributing funds; actually, voting is the least distorted political activity. People who hold intense opinions on issues such as gun control and abortion are also more likely to vote. All of these factors tend to favor Republican candidates (Patterson, 2002).

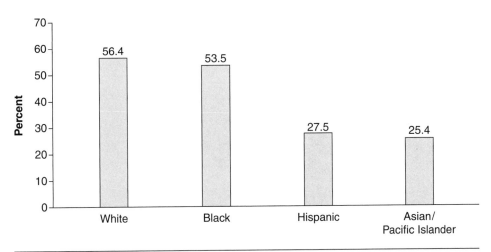

FIGURE 2.3   *Reported Voting in 2000 Presidential Election by Race (Voting Age Population)*

Source: U.S. Bureau of the Census, *Current Population Survey: 2001.*

Patterson (2002) argues that many voting policies in this country continue to reflect patterns of discrimination. For example, limited polling hours discourage lower-income citizens with inflexible work schedules. Outdated voting devices and inaccurate registration rolls found mostly in poor and minority neighborhoods suggest that barriers are not randomly distributed. Some states have made voting easier for their residents by allowing same-day registration and permitting absentee balloting by any voter, not just those who can show they are unable to participate on Election Day.

Office Holders.   Elective offices are filled predominantly by white men. Women and people of color are significantly underrepresented in proportion to their numbers in the general population in elective office at all levels. See Figures 2.4 and 2.5.

Understanding the American Political System

Functionalist Perspective.   Modern governments perform the necessary societal functions that private enterprise will not or cannot because there is no profit to be made. Examples include providing safety and protection (e.g., police services, national defense), building and maintaining infrastructure (e.g., roads, sewage treatment plants) and running public institutions (e.g., schools, courts, prisons).

Functionalists espouse the *pluralist model* of politics. They argue that there are many competing interest groups making the political process necessarily one of negotiation and compromise. Although few groups are powerful enough to force their agenda on others, many are able to thwart the goals of their opposition. Thus, power is widely dispersed and change is slow.

Conflict Perspective.   Some conflict theorists, notably C. Wright Mills (1956), have argued that most important political decisions are made not by elected officials but by a *power elite,*

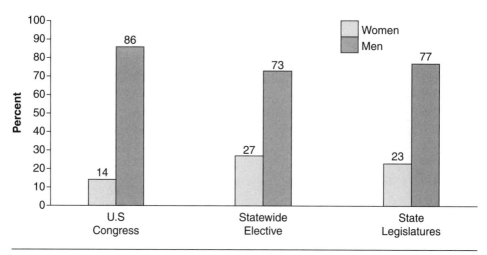

FIGURE 2.4   *Men and Women in Elective Office in 2002*

Source: Center for American Women and Politics. (2002). *Women in elective office.*

or ruling class, made up of extremely wealthy individuals who enjoy easy access to the centers of U.S. politics. Elites come from the upper classes—the wealthy and educated—and are usually white (Peterson, 1991). Nearly half of new members elected to Congress in the 2002 were millionaires (Salant, 2002).

Conflict theorists note that the power elite are not participants in some grand conspiracy, but simply are people of similar backgrounds who share mutual interests and agendas, often involving "the welfare of big business." Nevertheless, those who espouse the

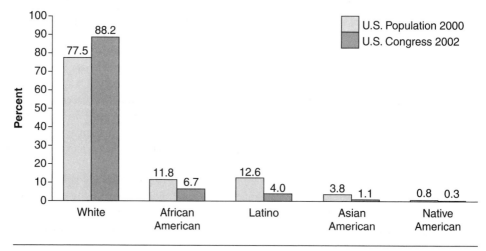

FIGURE 2.5   *Proportion of Minorities in Congress Compared to U.S. Population*

Source: Center for American Women and Politics. (2002). *Women in elective office.*

power elite model say that the concentration of wealth and power in a few hands is so great that the people at the top face little opposition. At the same time, the voices of many of the people in the middle and most of those at the bottom have little chance of being heard (Piven & Cloward, 1997).

Rational/Social Exchange Perspective.   Modern Western democracies were conceived in the "Age of Enlightenment," an eighteenth century movement that celebrated the essential rationality of humankind. Philosophers of the time proposed that the "rule of law" should replace the rule of monarchy. Inherent in this concept was the idea that citizens are capable of making logical choices in governing themselves through processes of deliberation and negotiation.

This nation's founders did not trust the general populace to make decisions directly. For example, they established the Electoral College to select the president. Most Americans believe that, especially if they have access to accurate and unbiased information, they can and should make many political choices for themselves. Sometimes politicians allow this process of *direct democracy* through the use of *referendums* on the election ballot. Typically, this happens at the state or local level.

Constructionist Perspective.   The constructed meaning of the United States of America has power to influence and shape political directions. Many Americans believe that their country has been especially chosen and blessed by God to lead the world (McLoughlin, 1978). One hundred and fifty years ago this idea was expressed in the concept of "manifest destiny"—the idea that God had provided the North American continent to be developed into a utopian society built on the principles of capitalism, Protestantism, and democracy. (This ignored the fact that indigenous Americans had a legitimate claim to the same territory, of course). Today this idea of American superiority is expressed or implied as belief in the country's inherent goodness or right in opposing "enemies" who are invariably described as "evil" and "godless."

With the exception of Native Americans, every inhabitant of the United States, or their ancestors, came from somewhere else. Thus "being an American" in the mind of the general public reflects voluntary allegiance to the United States. Despite support of the idea of freedom of speech, those who challenge mainstream values or criticize national policy run the risk of being labeled unpatriotic, if not "un-American" (Alter, 2003). The citizens of other countries derive their sense of themselves from a common history and ancestry; they do not become "un-French" or "un-Korean" by expressing unpopular points of view (Lipset, 1996).

The Impact of the Political System on Individuals and Families

How the Political System Obstructs Well-Being.   The presidential election of 2000 focused attention on basic inequities in the election process. A recent study (Income and Racial Disparities, 2001) of 40 U.S. congressional districts documented that the votes from low-income, nonwhite districts were more than three times as likely to be discarded as those from wealthy, predominantly white districts.

As discussed in the section on conflict perspective, the issues of poor people are not commonly addressed by our political system. The poor are isolated and marked off as deviant by "a predominantly middle-class political culture" (Piven & Cloward, 1997, p. 282). Because they have been left out of the mainstream political process, they have few options to make their voices heard. In the past, these have included public demonstrations, sit-ins, boycotts, and rent-strikes. "[D]isruptive and irregular tactics are the only resource, short of violence, available to low-income groups seeking to influence public policy" (Piven & Cloward, 1997, p. 284).

How the Political System Promotes Well-Being.   The U.S. Constitution and judicial system stand as examples to the rest of the world in their protection of the civil rights and civil liberties of minorities, women, people with disabilities, and older adults. Americans enjoy individual freedoms unknown in many countries.

As will be discussed in the next chapter, the American social welfare system, in particular the social insurances, have for the most part done a good job of preventing the impoverishment of retired persons, and workers who are laid off or injured on the job. In general, government regulations have kept manufactured products and the built environment safe, and the economy strong and growing. Even after the events of September 11, 2001, Americans have a reasonable sense of security and optimism about their future.

Economics and Politics Together: The Political Economy

Political economy is the term used to refer to the pervasive interaction of political and economic institutions. In the United States, politics and the economy are so intertwined that often it is difficult to see them or treat them as separate institutions. Many of this country's laws are based on the ideals of capitalism, and much of the "free market" economy is politically supported in one way or another.

The Power of Organizations

Piven and Cloward (1997) suggest that despite political oratory to the contrary, as individuals most Americans have little direct influence on the political process. Instead, political dialogue is carried on between organizations—between government agencies or legislative committees and professional associations, unions, PACs, and business groups—not individuals. Individuals don't have the time, resources, or the interest to regularly monitor and participate in the political process. The complexities of issues and the intricacies of policy making are simply too much for the average citizen to follow (Mackenzie, 1996). On the other hand, the focus of organizations—to protect the rights, income, occupational roles, property, or other economic interests of their members—makes ongoing interaction with political processes both necessary and potentially profitable.

We have already mentioned how giant corporations dominate the American economy and discussed Mills's theory of the power elite. Corporations are the major contributors to both political parties. In response, much of the activity of politicians is aimed at promoting the economic interests of large corporations. Among those contributing between $100,000 and $1,000,000 to the Democratic and Republican national conventions in 2000 were AT&T,

Bank of America, Blue Cross/Blue Shield, Boeing, Chevron, Daimler-Chrysler, Enron, Ernst & Young, General Motors, Hewlett-Packard, Lockheed Martin, Microsoft, Motorola, PepsiCo, Phillip Morris, Prudential, SunAmerica, Transamerica, Union Pacific, Unisys, United Airlines, UPS, and US Airways. See Figure 2.6.

> The . . . claim by corporations that they have the same right as any individual to influence the government in their own interest pits the individual citizen against the vast financial and communications resources of the corporation and mocks the constitutional intent that all citizens have an equal voice in the political debates surrounding important issues. (Korten, 1995, p. 59)

The amazing expansion of the influence of corporations over the federal, state, and local governments in the last 20 years has led to acknowledgment and criticism of *corporate welfare,* the direct subsidies and tax expenditures granted to businesses. *Time* magazine (Bartlett & Steele, 1998) reported that the state of Louisiana cancelled millions in property taxes to help various companies with "start up" costs; those receiving the tax breaks included Dow Chemical, Exxon, Georgia Pacific, International Paper, Procter & Gamble, Shell Oil, and Union Carbide. The government annually gives tens of millions of dollars to corporations such as Miller Beer, Campbell's [soups], and McDonald's to promote their products overseas (Rosenbaum, 1997). Another recent example of corporate welfare is the federal government's response to the September 11 terrorist hijackings. As reported by the *Houston Chronicle* (Masterson & Graves, 2001), ten days after the disaster Congress approved $15 billion in emergency assistance to the airlines and their stockholders ($10 billion in loans and $5 billion in grants). An industry analyst estimated that the airlines would report a total loss of only $3 billion after taxes at the end of the year. There were no provisions in the bill that any part of the funds should go to the 100,000 laid-off airline workers.

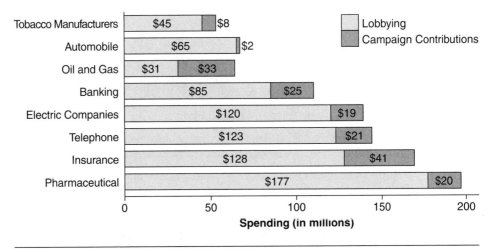

FIGURE 2.6   *Political Spending by Industry, 1999–2000 (in millions)*

Source: Center for Responsive Politics (2002).

Inequities in Government Benefits

Links between the government and the economy affect every citizen. Most Americans benefit financially from government programs, but the middle and upper classes benefit more (Abramovitz, 2001; DiNitto, 2000). The rich receive government assistance through various income tax deductions and government contracts and subsidies to their businesses; individuals in the middle class receive government assistance primarily in the form of home mortgage loans and associated tax deductions, and grants and loans for education. The poor and near poor receive government assistance in the form of welfare grants, food stamps, Medicaid, and earned income tax credits.

Regressive taxes are those that tax the poor at a higher rate than the rich (DiNitto, 2000). For example, some low-income workers may not pay any income taxes at all, but they do contribute to FICA taxes/Social Security withholding, which is charged against all of their earnings, for benefits they may not live long enough to collect. People with higher incomes do not pay FICA taxes on all of their earnings because there is a built-in maximum. Sales taxes are particularly regressive for low-income people. In states where groceries and medicines are taxed, the poor pay sales taxes on 100 percent of their income because they must spend it all to survive.

Without an awareness of the pervasive influence of the political economy, social workers may be tempted to believe that problems exist solely on the individual or family level. The poor in particular are vulnerable. They lack the resources to use the political system to address their needs. Even skilled social work practitioners cannot counsel their clients out of the difficulties created by the inadequacies and injustice of the larger society.

Looking Ahead

Not only are individuals, families, and communities affected by the political economy, but so are the other social institutions. We will explore these relationships in Chapters 3 and 4.

Key Points _____

- The United States does not have a "pure" form of capitalism; the government is actively involved in several aspects of the economy.

- Large corporations control the U.S. economy.

- Recent economic trends include the loss of industrial jobs, downsizing, outsourcing, and offshoring. Contingent work is becoming a characteristic of the American workforce.

- The United States is first among prosperous nations in inequality of income between the rich and the poor.

- A worker being paid the minimum wage cannot support a family.

- Americans criticize the government as too powerful, too intrusive, and too wasteful while at the same time demanding more services.

- Women and people of color are underrepresented in elective office. Incumbents have a tremendous advantage over challengers.

- Corporations have greatly expanded their political influence in the past 20 years, in part due to their financial contributions.

- Most Americans benefit financially from government programs, but the middle and upper classes benefit more.

Questions to Think about and Discuss _____

1. Should there be a different level of minimum wage for teenagers who are working for college savings or recreational spending money and for adults who are working to support themselves and their families?

2. Are your beliefs about spending, borrowing, saving, and investing different from those of your parents or grandparents? What factors have shaped your attitudes toward money?

3. Given the influence of money in politics, what role do you envision for yourself as a professional in working for social justice?

4. Can democracy survive when power and wealth are concentrated in the hands of an elite few?

Recommended Readings _____

Domhoff, W. (1998). *Who rules America? Power and politics in the year 2000*. Mountain View, CA: Mayfield.

Frank, T. (2000). *One market under God: Extreme capitalism, market populism, and the end of economic democracy*. New York: Doubleday.

Hesse-Biber, S., & Carter, G. L. (2000). *Working women in America: Split dreams*. New York: Oxford University Press.

Lapp, F. M. (1989). *Rediscovering America's values*. New York: Ballantine Books.

Manning, R. D. (2000). *Credit card nation: The consequences of America's addiction to credit*. New York: Basic Books.

Parenti, M. (1995). *Democracy for the few* (6th ed.). New York: St. Martin's Press.

Simon, D. R. (2002). *Elite deviance* (7th ed.). Boston: Allyn & Bacon.

Terkel, S. (1985). *Working: People talk about what they do all day and how they feel about what they do*. New York: Ballantine.

Internet Search Terms _____

Capitalism	Interest groups	Political idealogies
Consumer behavior	Labor-market segmentation	Political participation
Consumerism	Marketing	Pluralistic versus power elite
Economy	Market economy	perspectives
Global political economy	Political action committees	Power structure
Globalization	Political economy	Work ethic
Income distribution/inequality	Political elites	

3

Government-Related Social Institutions

In this chapter we present three social institutions that are, for the most part, government supported. These social institutions—social welfare, education, and criminal justice—are particularly important in the lives of many social work clients. We discuss the relationship of each of these social institutions to the political economy and their impact on individuals and families. Because most social work students take entire courses on social welfare, we will limit our discussion on that topic, focusing mostly on income maintenance programs.

Social Welfare

Social welfare is the social institution "that deals with the problem of dependency" (Popple & Leighninger, 2001, pp. 25–26). Dependency occurs when people are not able to perform expected social roles. Sometimes this occurs due to personal problems, and at other times it is the result of the failure of one or more social institutions. For example, one person may be unable to support himself financially because of mental illness and another may be unable to support herself because of a large number of layoffs in the local economy.

Public social welfare programs can be divided into categories, such as income maintenance, in-kind benefits (e.g., housing, nutrition), and social services (e.g., child and adult protective services, employment services, community mental health services). There are two basic types of income maintenance benefits. The *social insurances* are programs that were established to collect taxes in order to provide benefits to workers and their dependents in the event of the loss of their incomes. Examples of social insurance benefits are Social Security retirement, unemployment, and Social Security Disability benefits. Unlike social insurances, *public assistance* programs are based entirely on need. Their purpose is to provide subsistence-level income. In many people's minds, social insurance programs are linked to current or past employment; both recipients and taxpayers believe benefits have been dutifully earned. Public assistance recipients, on the other hand, are viewed as requesting a share of resources to which they have not contributed. Social insurance programs are financed at a level roughly four times higher than public assistance (Karger & Stoesz, 2002, p. 252), reflecting public attitudes about the two categories of programs.

Unlike the public sector (governmental programs), the *voluntary* or *private sector* is more likely to provide services rather than direct financial assistance, although "aid-in-kind" (e.g., food pantries, homeless shelters) is not uncommon. United Way and other private contributions support the many private, nonprofit agencies that define social welfare at the local level.

Issues and Trends in Social Welfare

Several trends in social welfare in the United States are worthy of comment. These include the inadequacy of public assistance payments, the fragmentation of the welfare state, the growth of the private, for-profit welfare sector, and welfare reform.

Inadequacy.   Conservative lawmakers fear that a generous level of public assistance benefits will make recipients unwilling to seek employment. Accordingly, public assistance benefits fall below the poverty level in every state in the United States (Karger & Stoesz, 2002, p. 275).

Americans pay relatively low taxes and allocate a smaller share of the nation's wealth for social welfare than most European countries. The United States fails to provide universal access to certain foundation programs that many Europeans take for granted: medical care for all citizens, children's/family allowances, and day-care programs.

Fragmentation.   The American welfare state is vertically fragmented across various levels of government. This results in striking discrepancies in eligibility requirements and benefits from one location to another and encourages "buckpassing" from one level of government to another. For example, in the last several decades, Washington has shifted many welfare responsibilities to the states in a process called *devolution*. Often, however, the money to support the programs does not follow. Welfare recipients living in poor states, such as Alabama, Mississippi, Texas, South Carolina, or West Virginia, usually receive less than beneficiaries in relatively wealthy, more liberal states, such as New York, Massachusetts, Minnesota, or Wisconsin.

The Growth of Private, For-Profit Agencies. Beginning in the latter half of the last century, private, for-profit agencies began to take over some of the functions that had previously been handled by public and nonprofit human service organizations. The combination of availability of government insurance funds and pressure to "contract out" for services led to the growth of human service corporations in the areas of child care; hospitals, nursing homes, and rehabilitation centers; behavioral and psychological treatment centers; and home health care. Some critics believe that there is an inherent conflict between the goals of providing high-quality human services and making a profit for stockholders.

Welfare Reform. The term *welfare reform* is synonymous with cuts in financial assistance for poor families. Politicians have emphasized the need for time limits on eligibility in response to public resentment. Pressure for "welfare to work" programs (moving recipients off the welfare rolls and into paid employment) reflects both a general disregard for single mothers and a growing societal acceptance of mothers working outside the home. The problem is that for many poor families, welfare is used as a kind of unemployment assistance or underemployment assistance (Karger & Stoesz, 2002, p. 297). This is because the work that is available is part-time or seasonal, offering only minimum wage and no benefits. In other words, most welfare recipients have worked, and are willing to work, but the jobs they find do not meet their basic needs. For others, there are additional problems that make finding secure, full-time, long-term employment difficult; these problems include physical and mental problems, special needs of children or other dependent family members, and lack of transportation.

Although welfare reform has, in fact, been "successful" in reducing the size of the welfare rolls, the impact on former recipients is still being studied. For those who have used up all of their eligibility and have no job and no other source of support, prospects are grim.

Understanding Social Welfare

Functionalist Perspective. Structural functionalist theorists say that the real function of income maintenance programs and social welfare services is not to "help people" but to make society more stable. Welfare systems evolved in industrialized countries to deal with the inevitable fluctuations and limitations of a modern market economy. They provide longer-term financial support to those who cannot work (e.g., older adults, people with disabilities) and temporary support to potential workers (children and the unemployed) so that there will be a reserve of workers available when they are needed.

Conflict Perspective. Conflict theorists believe it is a fear of the poor and disadvantaged, rather than sympathy for them, that underlies social welfare programs. These theorists would agree (in part) with the functionalists in saying that social welfare is not about helping the poor but rather about ensuring that their circumstances are not so desperate that they are pushed to disrupt the social order.

Several authors (e.g., Abramovitz, 1988; Piven & Cloward, 1993; Quadagno, 1994) writing from the conflict perspective have suggested that the hidden agenda of social welfare is to divide society by class, gender, and race. Abramovitz, for example, argues that social welfare replaces women's dependence on their husbands with a dependence on a patriarchal state. Quadagno believes that the American welfare system is used to preserve racial segregation. Others suggest that welfare programs create a conflict between age groups, as young workers earning minimum wage are taxed to support the Social Security benefits of wealthy retirees.

Rational/Social Exchange Perspective.   One might expect that as a relatively modern social institution, social welfare would reflect the result of a rational decision-making process on the part of policy makers. Although a cost-benefit approach is a part of rational decision making, DiNitto (2000) argues that rationalism should consider not just economic values, but social ones as well. Social welfare policies are distinctly irrational if one subscribes to values such as fairness and human dignity.

On an individual level, although welfare critics seem to believe that some recipients make a conscious choice to have another baby in order to receive a larger TANF grant, figures demonstrate that miniscule increases in benefits hardly compensate for having an additional mouth to feed, and no rational person would purposefully make that kind of decision. Few recipients make lifestyle choices based on what the welfare office has to offer. (See Table 3.1). On the other hand, a person who is permanently laid off at her place of employment might weigh the costs and benefits of taking the first available job versus accepting unemployment checks while she looks for a better position. In this case, unemployment benefits provide an opportunity for the individual to exercise her capacity for logical decision making.

Constructionist Perspective.   In analyzing social welfare, social constructionists might observe that certain categories of recipients are considered deserving and others are considered undeserving. Americans are generous and quick to offer assistance to victims of natural disas-

TABLE 3.1   *Temporary Assistance to Needy Families (TANF) Benefit Levels for Selected States*

Benefit Levels for a Family of Three (1 Adult, 2 Children) with No Income, June 2001			
High Level States	**Monthly Grant**	**Low Level States**	**Monthly Grant**
Wisconsin	$673	Alabama	$164
California	$645	Mississippi	$170
Vermont	$629	Texas	$201
New York	$577	South Carolina	$203
Rhode Island	$554	Arkansas	$204

Source: U.S. Department of Health and Human Services, Administration for Children and Families, Office of Family Assistance, TANF Annual Report to Congress.

ters, terrorist attacks, and other unexpected calamities. (This includes aid for residents of low-lying areas who neglected to purchase flood insurance or for people who choose to live in coastal vacation areas that are vulnerable to hurricanes.) They also give generously for individuals with unusual medical needs. Americans balk, however, at extending this generosity to people who are needy as a result of structural causes of poverty, such as residents of an inner-city area whose factory jobs have been exported to the suburbs or overseas, or a child in a family headed by a single mother who cannot secure a day-care arrangement that would allow her to get paid employment outside the home. Although these latter are poor through no fault of their own, they are not considered "deserving" of public support.

In the same manner, some social welfare programs have a stigma attached and others are perceived to be part of the entitlements of citizenship. In political circles, "welfare" is narrowly defined as public assistance. Many conservatives believe that any amount of funding is too much for the "undeserving" poor. This point of view is not applied to middle-class recipients of student loans, tax write-offs on mortgages and child care subsidies, or for retired workers who have "earned" their social security benefits, regardless of what may be huge differences between what was contributed and what is received. It also is not applied to government benefits handed out to large corporations (see *corporate welfare* under the section The Power of Organizations in Chapter 2). Negative attitudes toward public assistance are the result of a socially constructed worldview that blames the poor for their condition while ignoring the privileged status of the upper classes.

"Charity" is also a social and political construct. Using the tax code to their advantage, the philanthropy of the rich elite is often directed toward organizations that benefit them directly (such as opera companies or private schools). "Elite American philanthropy serves the interests of the rich to a greater extent than it does the poor, disadvantaged, or disabled" (Odendahl, 1990, p. 245). Middle-class families can use similar schemes in designating their United Way contributions to go to suburban agencies that provide recreational opportunities for themselves, rather than for inner-city agencies providing food or shelter to the destitute. Donors feel good about contributing to causes that help "deserving" others like themselves rather than charity that might go to the "undeserving" poor.

Relationship of the Social Welfare System to the Political Economy

All of the social institutions discussed in this chapter and the next are strongly influenced by the political economy, but this is particularly true for social welfare. Social welfare was born in industrialized, capitalist societies when it became apparent that the resources of families and religious institutions were not sufficient to deal with the problems associated with economic dislocation and inequity. Social welfare continues to be the vehicle for addressing problems generated by the political economy by providing an alleged safety net for those who are left out.

A primary concern at all levels of government is how to pay for programs and benefits. The core issue is the political question of how to respond to people who are excluded from full participation in a free market society. Because these people lack support in elite or political circles, the answer usually involves something short term and minimal. For example, welfare reform is perceived as an accounting problem rather than a people problem—the focus is on "fixing the bottom line" by reducing welfare rolls and thereby keeping voters happy.

The Impact of the Social Welfare System on Individuals and Families

How Social Welfare Obstructs Well-Being.   The United States is the wealthiest country in the world. See Figure 3.1. There is no justification for leaving some citizens (particularly children) without adequate food, shelter, or health care when a small but significant number of citizens live in extravagant luxury.

In many welfare offices across the country, lines are long, employees are impatient, the physical environment is shabby and uncomfortable, and the paperwork is challenging. Pressure for accountability encourages human service organizations to measure success primarily in terms of the number of people "processed" rather than the quality of service provided. Despite the humiliation that applicants sometimes are subjected to, the resources that are offered often do not meet even minimal needs, as defined by the government itself; that is, welfare benefits do not lift a family above the "poverty line." Some people in crisis will not ask for or accept assistance because of the difficulties involved in the application process, not to mention the associated stigma. More than half of the states use food stamp application forms that are 10 to 36 pages long (Karger & Stoesz, 2002, p. 474).

How Social Welfare Promotes Well-Being.   Although it is often accompanied by stigma, public welfare does not require recipients to be "grateful" or to meet standards unrelated to eligibility. In other words, it is distinguished from private charities that may impose expectations about applicants' lifestyles, religious beliefs, or family structure.

In general, social welfare functions best for people who have an employment history. For example, if an employee has an injury or illness that is job-related, he or she can expect to

FIGURE 3.1   *U.S. Ranking in Economic and Child Welfare Measures (among Top 25 Industrialized Countries)*

- ❏ First in military technology
- ❏ First in Gross Domestic Product
- ❏ First in number of millionaires and billionaires
- ❏ First in health technology
- ❏ First in defense spending

- ❏ 11th in proportion of children living in poverty
- ❏ 16th in living standards among the poorest one-fifth of children
- ❏ 16th in efforts to lift children out of poverty
- ❏ 17th in rates of children born with low birthweight
- ❏ 18th in income gap between rich and poor children
- ❏ 22nd in infant mortality

Sources: Children's Defense Fund (2001). *The state of America's children yearbook 2001;* United Nations International Children's Emergency Fund (1998). *Population and life expectancy. State of the world's children.*

receive medical benefits and cash payments through state-mandated workers' compensation insurance (DiNitto, 2000). The program helps those with short-term disability, those with longer-term partial disability, and those with permanent, long-term disability. Dependents of workers killed on the job also are entitled to benefits.

Education

The second American social institution discussed in this chapter is education. The function of education is to pass along a society's formal knowledge and skills in a systematic way, with emphasis on learning that will improve students' futures as workers and as citizens. Typically this involves *schooling*, or formal instruction by credentialed teachers, within special organizations (schools) designed for the purpose.

Issues and Trends in Education

Special Programs and Schools. Of particular interest to social workers are those schools and programs that were developed to address gaps in the system and the unmet needs of vulnerable populations. These include Head Start, charter schools, magnet schools, and voucher plans.

In the middle 1960s, the federal government began funding *Head Start,* a remedial program for disadvantaged preschoolers designed to give them the skills they needed to be ready for kindergarten and first grade. Whereas initial evaluations seemed to indicate that benefits were short-lived, long-term studies demonstrate better reading scores, a higher rate of high school completion, more college admissions, and higher rates of employment (Barnett, 1995; Svestka, 1996).

Charter schools are supported by public funds but operate more like private schools because they do not answer to a local school board. In 1998, about 700 charter schools were operating in the United States (Macionis, 2001). *Magnet schools* are public schools that offer special facilities and curricula, focusing on areas such as science or the arts. They were developed in urban areas to hold onto middle-class students who might have otherwise chosen to attend a private school. There are about 1,000 magnet schools in the country (Ravitch & Viteritti, 1996).

About 6 million of the 53 million children enrolled in kindergarten through 12th grade in the United States attend private schools (Wright, 2002). One-third of these private schools are affiliated with the Catholic Church and almost half (48 percent) are affiliated with other religious groups. Under *voucher plans* (also called *school choice*), parents can send their children to a private school and the government pays part or all of their tuition. The idea is to make public schools improve in order to compete for students (Clemetson, 2000). Opponents worry that private schools are not accountable to public scrutiny, and that these plans violate the principle of separation of church and state by providing tax based funding to religious schools. They argue that these plans take much needed monies away from already underfunded public schools, and they encourage racial and ethnic segregation. More than half of all private schools have minority enrollments under 9 percent (Wright, 2002). Another criticism is that private schools are not legally required to accept children with disabilities.

An increasing number of families in the United States have chosen to *home school* their children. In the early years of the movement, parents reported religious motives for keeping their children at home; currently, however, home schooling parents express concerns about the quality of the public schools, citing inferior teachers, overcrowded classrooms, and lack of safety (Hawkins, 1996; Kantrowitz & Wingert, 1998). In 1998, 1.5 million American children were home-schooled (Kantrowitz & Wingert, 1998). Over 90 percent of home schooling families are white (Hawkins, 1996; Kantrowitz & Wingert, 1998). Most home-schooled children are also involved in various outside activities with age-peers, including field trips sponsored by home-schooling organizations, sports, Scouting, 4-H, and church activities.

Safety.   Another contemporary concern in education is physical safety. Given the recent history of rare but highly publicized school shootings in this country, neither children nor parents believe that schools are safe places. Many schools have resorted to using uniformed guards and metal detectors. Even before the 1999 Columbine High School shooting tragedy, some school administrators were worried enough that they scheduled "drive-by shooting drills" in addition to fire drills (Toch, 1993).

Two other controversial issues related to education that are of interest to social workers are inequity in funding and dropout rates. These are discussed later in this chapter in "Impact of the Education System on Individuals and Families" section.

Losses in State Funding for Public Colleges, Increasing Tuition.   As public colleges and universities lose state funding, they have come to rely more and more heavily on income from increased tuition and fees, research grants, lottery funds, and philanthropists, combined with cuts in costs by reduced services, cut backs on scholarships and assistantships, increased class sizes, more part-time faculty, and the use of technology to reach a larger market through distance education and web-based courses (Brinson, 2003; Burbules, 2000). The costs of attending an institution of higher education has increased faster than the rate of inflation and family income; it increased 228 percent between the 1979/80 and 1996/97 academic years (National Center for Public Policy and Higher Education, n.d.). Not surprisingly, fewer children from low-income families can afford to go to college now, and it appears that federal tax credit programs are more likely to help middle- or high-income students than those in the lowest income group (Guerard, 2002; Quinn, 2003).

Challenges to the Use of Affirmative Action in College Admissions.   Affirmative Action allows colleges to consider a student's race in making admission decisions. Proponents argue that diversity in a student body is an essential ingredient in a well-rounded education (Bollinger, 2003). They also note that whites have long enjoyed "legacy privilege"—a practice that gives special consideration to the relatives and friends of the rich, powerful, and well connected. Kinsley (2003) points out, for example, that Harvard accepts 40 percent of applicants who are children of alumni but only 11 percent of applicants generally—a practice that not only confers unfair advantages but also makes the student body less diverse, not more so. Opponents of Affirmative Action say that not only is it a form of "reverse discrimination," but also that it benefits primarily middle- and upper-class blacks while reinforcing the idea that minorities are perpetual victims (Williams, 2003). An alternative that is being tried in many states is called "affirmative access." Under these plans, public universities admit the top graduates from state high schools, so that students from predominantly minority schools have an equal chance of being accepted (Fineman & Lipper, 2003). Critics say that such programs may result in more less-qualified students being admitted.

Understanding the Education System

Functionalist Perspective.   In addition to the obvious function of transmitting knowledge and teaching skills, structural functionalists suggest that the education system sorts children and youth and then trains them to fill positions at different levels in society. These theorists believe that schools fill a gate-keeping function by identifying the most qualified persons, selecting them for advanced education, and channeling them toward leadership positions.

The education system also socializes the young, instilling values of respect, obedience, punctuality, and perseverance. Particularly in the case of mandatory and free public schooling, it serves the purpose of acculturation for the young children of recent immigrants. This is especially important in a country with as much diversity as the United States.

Social institutions have both manifest and latent functions (Kendall, 2001). *Manifest functions* are those that are intended and obvious. *Latent functions* are unintended side effects, and those functions that are often hidden, or at least not acknowledged by participants. Some of these may be positive and some may be negative. Besides the obvious manifest functions of education, this social institution also has latent functions. These include providing free child care and supervision for a significant part of the day—which is particularly helpful for parents who are employed outside the home. Another latent function is keeping adolescents out of the labor market where they might compete for jobs with unskilled adults.

Conflict Perspective.   Social conflict theorists argue that the school system in the United States perpetuates class inequality. This is achieved by *tracking,* or ability grouping, based on standardized tests that magnify small differences (Tobias, 1989). Poor and minority students are assigned to remedial and vocational skills classes where they receive a diluted academic program, making it unlikely that they will ever catch up to their white, middle-class peers (Kozol, 1991; Oakes, 1985; Tobias, 1989).

The financial costs of higher education prevent many people with below average incomes from enrolling. Low-income students may be forced to attend a local community college where they will earn certificates and associate degrees that will lead to jobs with limited opportunities for advancement (Gilbert, 1998). When only the affluent can afford to attend prestigious colleges or restrictive programs, social and economic privilege is reinterpreted as personal merit. Our society reserves the most desirable occupational opportunities for those who have four-year or graduate degrees, even if educational attainment is unrelated to the demands and responsibilities of a particular job. In this way, *credentialism* (evaluating a person on the basis of his or her educational background) is used as a strategy to restrict certain careers to a small (and privileged) segment of the population (Collins, 1979).

Gillborn (1992) uses the term *hidden curriculum* to describe how schools teach obedience to authority and conformity to cultural norms in addition to the academic curriculum. Learning the student role prepares children for the routines of the work world. Conflict theorists note that middle- and upper-class youth are more likely to be encouraged to think critically and creatively, thus preparing them for leadership roles while the behaviors of lower-class children are shaped to accommodate the demands of the assembly line and the clerical pool.

Rational/Social Exchange Perspective.   Although some property owners complain that they have to pay high taxes even when they have no children in the public school system, most taxpayers understand the need for educated citizens and workers. (One of the authors has a t-shirt with this slogan on the front: IF YOU THINK EDUCATION IS EXPENSIVE, TRY IGNORANCE.) As a technologically advanced society, the United States relies on a literate workforce and must provide at least a basic education to all members of society to prepare them for their roles as citizens.

Contructionist Perspective.   Social constructionists remind us of the importance of percep-tions. Jonathan Kozol, who conducted a study that highlighted the alarming differences in funding levels between affluent suburban schools and inner-city schools, noted the effects of perceptions that "the poorest districts are beyond help" and that resources would thus be "wasted on poor children" (1991, p. 99). He concluded that these "children hear and under-stand [that] they are poor investments—and behave accordingly. . . . Expectations are a pow-erful force."

  The application of the social constructionist perspective to the education system has focused for the most part on *labeling theory* and *self-fulfilling prophecy* (Merton, 1949). Basi-cally, this suggests two parallel processes. The first affects the students individually. Once labeled "slow" or "a behavior problem," students will come to accept the label and act accord-ingly. Even when nonperjorative labels are used (e.g., "sharks" or "goldfish"), children know to which level they have been assigned (Tobias, 1989). The second process affects the teach-ers. Once they believe that a child is "bright" or "struggling," they will respond to the child according to their expectations of how that child will perform—challenging the bright ones and "dumbing down" lessons for the less able children, thus unintentionally creating the re-sults that were predicted.

  In a classic study, Ray Rist (1970) observed that after only eight days of class, a kinder-garten teacher divided her students into three groups. The "slow learners" were put at a table in the back of the room, and the "fast learners" sat at a table next to the teacher's desk. As the year progressed, the fast learners came to think of themselves as smart, and the teacher treated them as such. The children in the back received little attention. Rist himself concluded that the divisions were based on social class, as there had not been any testing done early in the se-mester. The same class divisions were retained in the first and second grades, thus consigning many students to a long-term negative educational experience based on one teacher's unin-formed assessment less than two weeks into their school careers.

Relationship of the Education System to the Political Economy

The education system in the United States reflects the political economy in several ways. Schools foster patriotism by teaching lessons in history, civics, and other social studies. Fur-ther, the values of individualism and competition assumed to be crucial to a capitalist economy are promoted in the schools.

  Schools provide captive audiences for advertisers. By accepting corporate donations or sponsorships, brand loyalty is introduced and consumerism is reinforced. Market-driven educational materials are integrated into the school day. For example, Exxon has produced a documentary on the beauty of the Alaskan coastline, McDonald's has created a nutrition chart, and kindergartners are taught to read through a program that uses corporate logos (Kilbourne, 1999, p. 46). While *Channel One* is offered free to school systems as a teaching tool for current events, the reality is that it serves as an unfettered conduit for corporations seeking to reach the youth market (Croteau & Hoynes, 2003). Resisting commercialization in the classroom is not without its consequences. In 1998, Mike Cameron, a senior from Evans, Georgia, was suspended from school for wearing a Pepsi logo shirt on a school-designated "Coke day" (Kilbourne, 1999).

Most surveys of political opinion demonstrate that public education is a primary concern for many American citizens. There is growing recognition that in order to be competitive in a global economy, U.S. workers need to be technologically competent. In response to public pressure for better performing schools, Congress passed *Goals 2000,* which was designed to set minimal national standards for school children. In spite of support for this agenda, the federal government is unable or unwilling to provide the supplemental funding that allows school districts to achieve these standards.

Some leading academics (Bok, 2003; Gould, 2003) are concerned about the increasing commercialization of institutes of higher education. With rising enrollments exceeding revenues, many schools are becoming more entrepreneurial (Raines & Leathers, 2003). Changes in their missions reflect an increasing emphasis on research, particularly in areas expected to produce commercially profitable intellectual property, and less on teaching the future citizens of their state. "Hustling for dollars" has become a major focus of public universities, with practices ranging from promotion of corporate-academic partnerships, to selling naming rights to buildings or even restricting sales of soft drinks to a single brand (Brinson, 2003). Universities are put in the position of marketing themselves in competition against each other, not just for students, but for cash (Brewer, Gates, & Goldman, 2002). For example, in order to make profits from their sports programs, universities reschedule major conference games to meet the broadcast demands of television sports executives, even though fans are inconvenienced, student athletes have to miss classes, and midterm exams are disrupted (Morris, 2003).

The Impact of the Education System on Individuals and Families

How the Education System Obstructs Well-Being.   Because public schools are largely supported by local property taxes, schools in wealthier communities or neighborhoods have more resources, and schools in poorer communities or neighborhoods have fewer resources. The result is great discrepancies in the quality of education provided to children living in different communities. As of 2003, in dozens of states across the country, citizens and educators had filed lawsuits to challenge existing patterns of funding of schools, seeking to reach a standard of adequacy, if not equity (Drake, 2003).

As discussed under the Conflict Perspective, tracking is usually based on the results of standardized tests. Such tests measure not only intelligence and aptitude but also culturally acquired knowledge. Thus, they may be biased against minority and poor students. "It's one of the most persistent issues in education: African American children, statistically, are more likely to be designated as special education students than white students. Conversely, a much higher percentage of white students are classified as gifted" (Fine, 2002).

Although a school system can be a model of diversity, segregated housing patterns are reflected in high rates of racial, ethnic, and class segregation in most schools. The vast majority of students in many urban public school districts are African American and/or Latino, while the vast majority of students in private urban schools and upscale suburban public schools are white. The term *de facto segregation* can be used to describe the pattern of racial segregation in schools that results from segregated housing.

According to one study (Delpit, 1995), rather than embracing diversity in the classroom, many white teachers, out of misdirected goodwill, make a conscious effort to be "color blind." The teachers' failure to acknowledge and celebrate the different heritages and cultures of their minority students makes the students feel invisible. Insensitivity to cultural differences in learning and communication styles hinders minority children, leading to low self-esteem and negative school experiences. For example, Heath (1982) observed that African American children seemed unresponsive to teachers' questions. She discovered that the students thought that questions such as "What is this?" or "What do you call that?" were silly because obviously the teacher already knew the answer. The children came from communities where people asked open-ended questions about whole events: "What did you see today?" or "What did you like best about your field trip?" In their homes, caregivers accepted many different answers, and the answers almost always involved telling a story, describing a situation, or making a comparison.

Children from cultural backgrounds with collectivist rather than individualist traditions may go out of their way to help each other; some teachers perceive this as cheating or not "doing their own work" (Gallimore, Boggs, & Jordan, 1974). Because of their strong cultural value of humility, Asian American children may hesitate to ask questions of the teacher or to take credit for, or show pride in, their work. Teachers need to take this into account when evaluating the classroom interaction of these students.

Children and families with limited English face extra challenges in dealing with school systems. Obstacles include the absence of bilingual teachers, the inability to communicate with school personnel, and the inability to understand school correspondence sent to the child's home (Dale, Andreatta, & Freeman, 2001). Some migrant worker parents report being intimidated by the educational system even when language assistance was available. The overall result of such factors is that Latino children have a higher dropout rate than other racial and ethnic groups (Feagin & Feagin, 1999).

Dropout rates are also related to socioeconomic status. The dropout rate for students in the lowest income quintile [fifth] of the population is seven times greater than the dropout rate for students in the highest quintile (U.S. National Center for Education Statistics, 1999). In other words, students who drop out are more likely to come from families where parents also are likely to have had little schooling. This pattern perpetuates intergenerational cycles of disadvantage.

Gender discrimination is also a concern in the school environment. Researchers Myra and David Sadker (1994) discuss the sexism found in America's schools in their book *Failing at Fairness: How America's Schools Cheat Girls*. Gender bias is particularly apparent in math and science courses. By the time they reach middle school, girls lose confidence in their ability to do math as well as their male peers, even though this change of attitude is unrelated to measures of actual performance.

How the Education System Promotes Well-Being.   This country has led the world in the proportion of young people completing different levels of mass education, first for elementary and high schools, later for colleges and graduate schools (Lipset, 1996, p. 21). In 1940 only 24.5 percent of the U.S. population had completed high school; in 2000 that figure had increased to 84.1 percent (Wright, 2002). In 1940, fewer than one in twenty Americans had completed four or more years of college; in 2000, it was one in four (Wright, 2002). The proportion of 20 to 24 year olds in higher education in America is almost double that of the most affluent European countries and Japan (Lipset, p. 21).

Within the past generation, federal laws have enhanced the opportunities for children with disabilities and for female athletes in school settings. The Equal Education for All Handicapped Children Act (PL 94-142) was passed in 1975. Renamed the Individuals with Disabilities Education Act (IDEA) in 1990, it mandates that students with disabilities receive a free and appropriate education. Many schools have attempted to *mainstream* children with disabilities so that they can attend classes with their nondisabled peers, as well as have access to special education teachers and classrooms, speech therapists, occupational therapists, and physical therapists (Weinhouse & Weinhouse, 1994). Historically most women had little opportunity for involvement in high school and college sports. Title IX of the Educational Amendments of 1972 prohibited sex discrimination in educational institutions receiving federal funds. This law has led to more funding for women's athletics.

Schools also go beyond instruction to meet some of the more basic daily needs of poor children. They provide screening for visual and hearing problems, some provide dental and mental health services, and most have school nurses. Over 15 million children receive free or reduced price school lunches (Children's Defense Fund, 2001).

Criminal Justice

The social institution of criminal justice is America's formal system of social control. It includes a loose confederation of more than 50,000 agencies at the local, state, and federal levels that often operate independently of each other (Bohm & Haley, 1997). The *criminal justice system* represents the parts of government that have the political mandate to protect members of society, but abuses of power can also unfairly strip citizens of their freedoms. The system includes a variety of law enforcement organizations (e.g., local police; county sheriff; federal marshals; Alcohol, Tobacco, and Firearms [ATF] agents; Immigration and Naturalization Service [INS] agents; the courts; and institutions for the incarceration of offenders—detention centers, reform schools, jails, and prisons).

There are many outspoken critics of the American criminal justice system. Currie (1998, p. 8), for example, states,

If we look squarely at the present state of crime and punishment in America . . . it is difficult to avoid the recognition that something is terribly wrong; that a society that incarcerates such a vast and rapidly growing part of its population—but still suffers the worst violent crime in the industrial world—is a society in trouble, one that, in a profound sense, has lost its bearings.

Issues and Trends in the Criminal Justice System

Crime Rates and Violence.   There are three major sources of crime statistics in this country (the FBI's Uniform Crime Reports, the National Incident-Based Reporting System [NIBRS], and the National Crime Victimization Survey), and each uses a different method of collecting and reporting data. In general, crime rates are down in this country since the early 1990s. Crime rates are affected by a number of factors, including how crimes are reported and tracked, or whether they are reported at all. For example, between 1975 and 1990 the number of reported rapes increased from 56,090 to 102,560 (Wright, 2002). A significant part of this increase may have been due to increased levels of awareness and reporting. Rates declined by13 percent between 1990 and 1999. Changing population demographics, especially the proportion of people between the ages of 18 and 24, may account for as much as 40 percent of the changes in crime rates (Bohm & Haley, 1997).

According to Bureau of Justice statistics summarized by Wright (2002, p. 311), victims of most crimes are poor, urban, young people of color. Except for rape and domestic violence, most victims are male. Youths are almost 20 times as likely to be the victims of violent crime as people over the age of 65. Poor people (i.e., those with household incomes of less than $7,500) are the most likely to be victimized by crime, especially violent crime.

The violent crime rate in the United States is about five times higher than Europe's and even worse when compared to rates in Asian countries (Macionis, 2001). An apparent recent decline in rates of violent crime in this country represents only a leveling off from unprecedented rises in the preceding several years (Currie, 1998, p. 22).

The United States leads the industrialized world in firearms violence. Although not everyone agrees (see Lott, 2000 for example), most reformers suggest that a major contributing factor is the extensive private ownership of handguns in this country (Violence Policy Center, 2000). Although handguns are often marketed as protection for law-abiding citizens against dangerous strangers, FBI data show that only 1.3 percent of handgun homicides in 1997 involved the justifiable killing of an unknown assailant (Violence Policy Center, 2000).

Of particular concern to social workers is the problem of *hate crimes,* criminal acts that are motivated by bias against someone's race, ethnicity, religion, sexual orientation, or disability (Henslin, 2001). Offenders convicted of hate crimes receive more severe sentences than those who commit the same act but without hatred as the motive. African Americans, Jews, and gay men are disproportionately the victims of hate crimes. After the events of September 11, 2001, increasing numbers of individuals of Middle Eastern heritage were unfairly targeted because of growing distrust of Muslims and Arabs.

The Incarceration Boom.   In a shift from earlier approaches that emphasized rehabilitation and deterrence, a new philosophy of criminal justice focusing on incarceration of large numbers of criminal offenders, including drug users and pushers, appeared at the end of the twentieth century (Feeley & Simon, 1992). This shift explains the recent explosion in the number of inmates. The adult prison incarceration rate was stable from the 1930s until the mid-1970s; between 1980 and 1994, the prison incarceration rate rose by more than 150 percent (Bohm &

Haley, 1997, p. 325). This occurred during a period when crime rates were stable or declining, and when the proportion of young adults in the population (those most likely to commit crimes) was also steady or declining. In 1996, construction began on 27 new federal prisons and 96 state facilities (Dyer, 2000).

The Violent Crime Control and Law Enforcement Act passed by Congress in 1994 introduced *three strikes penalties* for repeat offenders. Many states had "habitual offender laws" on the books before the three-strikes terminology became popular. These laws, including the three-strikes versions, require enhanced prison terms for repeat felony offenders (Secrest, 1999). The strongest criticism of three-strikes laws is that they are not targeting serious offenders. For example, 17,000 offenders were sentenced under the three-strikes law in California since 1994, but 75 percent of the third offenses were nonviolent (e.g., property and drug offenses) (Secrest, 1999). According to the Office of National Drug Control Policy (1998), three-quarters of the growth in the federal prison population during that time period can be accounted for by the incarceration of drug offenders, and the number of inmates in state prisons for drug-law violations increased by more than 400 percent over the same period.

Privatization.   Another trend in the criminal justice system is the construction and operation of prisons by private companies. The private sector has a long tradition of contracting to provide services to inmates, such as provision of meals, medical or psychiatric care, and education; the private sector also has operated detention facilities for juveniles for many years (Bohm & Haley, 1997). Now, in response to the incarceration boom, many states have asked private organizations to build and operate new prisons. It appears that not only can private firms open new facilities more quickly than can government agencies, but also they can save up to 20 percent in construction costs and 5 to 15 percent in operating costs, at least for minimum security facilities (National Center for Policy Analysis, 1995). Private companies are more cost efficient because they can pay less and provide fewer benefits for employees (Cripe, 1997), as well as limit promotions, reduce staffing levels, and require less training (Shichor, 1999).

Criminal justice and policy analysts disagree about whether privatization has been a success (Shichor, 1999; Torres, 1999). Those who argue against it worry that companies in the "prison business" are interested in keeping their facilities full, and use their lobbyists to encourage legislation that will result in even higher levels of incarceration (Shichor, 1999).

The Death Penalty.   The U.S. Supreme Court reinstated the death penalty in 1976, making the United States the only Western industrialized nation that still allows capital punishment. (Twelve states and the District of Columbia do not have capital punishment statutes). As of April, 2003, there were 3,525 prisoners on death row in America. Of these, 54 percent were people of color; 48 of these 3,525 prisoners were women and 82 were juveniles (Death Penalty Information Center, 2003).

In addition to the basic question of whether it is morally acceptable for a government to kill its citizens for any reason, critics of the death penalty argue that it is inherently unfair because poor, uneducated, and minority men are much more likely to suffer this penalty than are more affluent, well-educated, white offenders. There is a strong association between white racial prejudice and support for the death penalty (Aguirre & Baker, 1994). Dozens of scientific studies have demonstrated that the death penalty continues to be administered in a fashion that discriminates against African Americans and killers of whites (Bohm & Haley, 1997). One reason for this is that many poor defendants who end up on death row are assigned inexperienced, unskilled, or unprepared attorneys. In 1987, the U.S. Supreme Court ruled that state death penalty statutes are constitutional even when statistics indicate that they have been applied in racially biased ways (Bohm & Haley, 1997). Between 1977 and 1999, 598 individuals were put to death by the criminal justice system. Of these, 374 (62.5 percent) were white, 213 (35.6 percent) were African American, and 11 (1.8 percent) were "other" (Wright, 2002).

The death penalty is also administered unevenly across various regions of the country. Six southern states (Alabama, Florida, Georgia, Louisiana, Mississippi, and Texas) account for 70 percent of all executions since the death penalty was reinstated. The state of Texas has executed 199 prisoners since 1977, a third of all those executed in the entire country during the time period.

Reversing their 1989 ruling, in June 2002 the U.S. Supreme Court held that the Eighth Amendment ban on cruel and unusual punishment does indeed prohibit the execution of a capital offender who is mentally retarded. During the intervening time between rulings, 16 states had enacted laws prohibiting the execution of mentally retarded persons. Many other states are currently developing procedures to implement the court's decision.

Understanding the Criminal Justice System

Functionalist Perspective.   Functionalism is based on the assumption that members of society subscribe to the same values and presumes that the laws of society reflect that consensus. Punishing deviance reinforces agreement about societal norms.

Consistent with a functionalist perspective, one option is to *rehabilitate* (i.e., "correct") offenders. This approach emphasizes constructive improvement through external control (i.e., probation or parole, or incarceration) but also by offering skills training, counseling, and treatment for drug and/or alcohol abuse. The goal is for the offender to conform to societal expectations and become a functioning member of society.

The second option is to remove deviants by deporting, incarcerating, or executing them. Currie (1998, p. 30) reports that incarceration is modestly effective with "high-rate" offenses, such as robbery and burglary. It is much less so for violent crimes, such as homicide, because for some offenses, especially murder, the first serious crime may be the only one the offender commits. Both approaches—rehabilitation and removal—have the ultimate goal of keeping society in balance.

Conflict Perspective.   Conflict theorists would say that, like the social welfare system, the criminal justice system erroneously defines problems as occurring at the individual, rather than at the societal level, and therefore efforts to address social conditions are rejected (Macionis, 2001). "To look only at individual criminality is to close one's eyes to social injustice and to close one's ears to the question of whether our social institutions have exploited or violated the individual" (Reiman, 1998, p. 157).

Conflict theory looks to differences in socioeconomic class to understand and explain both deviant behavior and societal responses to it. Individuals from all class levels break the law, but they commit different kinds of crimes. People from lower socioeconomic class backgrounds are more likely to commit property crimes. Conflict theorists believe that chronic unemployment caused by the capitalist system leads poor people to commit property crimes in order to survive (Thio, 2000).

People from middle- or upper-class backgrounds are more likely to commit *white-collar crimes*—income tax evasion, bribery of public officials, embezzlement, fraud, and so forth. These crimes do not involve violence, but in their efforts to enrich themselves, white-collar criminals may cause significant harm to consumers, investors, or employees (Macionis, 2001). Recent examples would be the scandals at the Enron, Worldcom, and Tyco corporations that were uncovered early in 2002. The important difference is that the laws against white-collar crimes are relatively lenient and seldom enforced. Often it is corporations rather than individuals who are charged with law breaking. Even if individuals are charged, it is likely that they will be tried in a civil hearing rather than in criminal court. The odds are only a little greater than fifty-fifty that offenders charged and convicted of white-collar crimes will go to jail (U.S. Bureau of Justice Statistics, 1999).

Rational/Social Exchange Perspective.   Gordon (1973, p. 174) notes that "nearly all crimes in capitalist societies represent perfectly *rational* [italics in original] responses to the structure of institutions upon which capitalist societies are based." This is because most crimes are motivated by a desire for money or goods and thus are an understandable way of coping with inequity (Reiman, 1998). *Deterrence theory* suggests that people who are rational will refrain from committing crimes if they believe that the "costs" of the punishment will outweigh the "benefits" of the crime. Given current rates of recidivism, some criminologists doubt the value of incarceration as a deterrent.

Constructionist Perspective.   The definition of "deviance" varies according to cultural norms. No act is criminal or delinquent in and of itself, only the response of the criminal justice system, determined by political processes, makes it so. For example, prostitution is legal in Nevada but not in any other state. In some states, there are still laws on the books making homosexual behavior illegal; legislatures in other states have decided that privacy rights cover sexual activity between consenting adults in their own homes. Gambling is still illegal in many places, but most states now promote government-sponsored lotteries as a preferred alternative to raising property or income taxes.

Relationship of the Criminal Justice System to the Political Economy

All Americans are constantly bombarded by commercial messages that promote materialism. Currie (1985) suggests that mainstream cultural emphasis on individual economic success, along with the great disparity in economic statuses, contributes to crime rates in the United States. In their theory of *illegitimate opportunity structures,* Cloward and Ohlin (1960) argued that residents of inner-city slums have the same aspirations for "success" as do middle- and upper-class people. "At the very least, overwhelming numbers of the poor give allegiance to the values and principles of the dominant American culture" (Ryan, 1976, p. 134). The problem is that because they lack access to good education, training, and legitimate employment opportunities, they are attracted to alternate opportunities for making money: robbery, burglary, drug dealing, prostitution, pimping, gambling, and other "hustles."

As already noted, the construction and operation of prisons has become a big business. Between 1984 and 1996, there was a twenty-fold increase in the number of prisoners placed in correctional facilities run by for-profit corporations (Donziger, 1996). This "has created a large and politically potent constituency of those whose jobs and status depend on yet further expansion [of the inmate population]" (Currie, 1998, p. 7). In fact, Dyer (2000, p. 2) suggests that the most plausible explanation for the unprecedented growth in the U.S. prison population is the money that ends up in the bank accounts of the shareholders of some of America's best known corporations; underwriting prison construction by selling tax-exempt bonds is now estimated to be a $2.3 billion annual industry itself.

Dyer (2000) reports that prison labor is another area that benefits the American economy. In 1998 there were more than 2,500 prison and jail industries in operation in the United States. Prisoners are usually paid between twenty cents and $1.20 per hour to make everything from false teeth to parts for Boeing aircraft. Among the other companies that use prison labor are Microsoft, IBM, Compaq, AT&T, Victoria's Secret, Eddie Bauer, Chevron, and TWA.

The Impact of the Criminal Justice System on Individuals and Families

How the Criminal Justice System Obstructs Well-Being.   The United States has the highest incarceration rate of any nation in the world (Wright, 2002). Nationally, 478 people per 100,000 residents are incarcerated; the highest rate is in the District of Columbia, 971 per 100,000. Most industrial democracies have rates that cluster around 55 to 120 individuals per 100,000 (Currie, 1998).

The Criminal Justice System and Minorities.   Given the opportunities for discretionary decision making at various stages of the criminal justice process, there is ample opportunity for discrimination. People of color (except Asian Americans) are more likely to be under police surveillance, arrested, convicted, and incarcerated for offenses than are whites. Other factors being equal, minorities receive harsher sentences and serve long prison sentences (Petersilia, 1983). A study by Bridges and Steen (1998) documents that probation officers consistently portray African American youths differently from white youths in their written court reports, more frequently attributing blacks' delinquency to negative attitudes and personality traits. Although they are just 12.7 percent of the population, African Americans comprise 31.9 percent of arrests for property crimes and 40.2 percent of arrests for violent crimes (U.S. Federal Bureau of Investigation, 1999). The number of blacks behind bars jumped 69 percent between 1990 and 2000; nearly one in ten African American males between the ages of 25 and 29 are in prison (Wright, 2002).

Historically, police officers have been white although equal opportunity and affirmative action programs are changing that. More than 90 percent of judges are white; they are mostly male, and their background is typically middle, if not upper, class (Kendall, 2001).

Using Alabama as an example, Jesse Jackson (2003) notes that the prison population increased by 600 percent in the past 30 years, while the population grew by only 30 percent.

Over two-thirds of the prisoners are black. Only 16 of Alabama's 220 judges are black. None of its appellate judges are black. None of the district attorneys are black, and only 8 of 67 county sheriffs are black. "The back of the cell has replaced the back of the bus," Jackson argues.

The targeting of minorities is a long-established pattern of drug enforcement in this country (Thio, 1998). In the mid-1980s, Congress passed antidrug abuse acts that mandated harsh sentencing. These guidelines differentiated between crack (which is used by poor and minority people) and powdered cocaine (which is used predominantly by middle-class and wealthy people). A mandatory minimum sentence of five years occurs with the possession of 500 grams of powdered cocaine but only 5 grams of crack (Bush-Baskette, 1998). "[B]lacks constitute 13 percent of the country's drug users; 37 percent of those arrested on drug charges; 55 percent of those convicted; and 74 percent of all drug offenders sentenced to prison" (Harris, 1999, p. 5).

Racial profiling is the term used to describe disproportionate law enforcement activities that target people of color. Recent Supreme Court decisions have allowed the police to use traffic violations as a pretext to search for evidence (Harris, 1999). An African American driver on the New Jersey turnpike is three times as likely as a white driver to be stopped (Dyer, 2000). In June of 2003, the federal government admitted that racial profiling is an issue with its directive to federal law enforcement officers that forbids targeting religious, ethnic, or racial minorities (CBSNEWS.com, 2003). However, the directive makes a distinction between routine law enforcement and threats to national security or border security. Although it is broadly forbidden, the policy permits consideration of ethnicity or race if there exists "trustworthy information" that certain groups of people are engaged in specific criminal or terrorist activities. Some states are enacting their own bans on racial profiling.

Sometimes members of society see crimes as less socially significant if the victim is viewed as less worthy. This practice is called *victim discounting* (Schaefer, 2000, p. 260–261). Although almost half of all homicide victims in the United States between 1977 and 1992 were African Americans, 85 percent of prisoners executed were convicted of killing whites. Prosecutors are less likely to argue for a death sentence and judges are less likely to impose one when the murder victim is black (Zorn, 1995).

The Criminal Justice System and the Poor. The FBI does not collect or report data on the socioeconomic class of arrested and convicted persons. Although violent crime is a serious problem among the poor, especially in inner-city neighborhoods, the majority of people who live there have no criminal records (Harries, 1990).

The probability of getting arrested, convicted, and sent to prison is strongly associated with social class. Geis (1999) asks "Is it fair that a person who steals a television set should do prison time while a person who bilks the government out of millions walks away with a fine or a community service sentence?" (p. 154).

The Criminal Justice System and Women. Men are incarcerated at a rate nine times greater than women (Wright, 2002). However, the rate of arrests for women has been increasing faster than the rate for men (28 percent compared to 2 percent, between 1989 and 1999) (U.S. Federal Bureau of Investigation, 1999). In the two decades between 1980 and 1999, the number of women in prisons increased sixfold (Chesney-Lind, 2002).

Because there are so many more male than female inmates, prisons are not well prepared to meet the needs of women offenders. There are fewer educational and training opportunities in women's prisons than in men's prisons (Reid, 1987).

Prison medical facilities lack diagnostic and treatment tools essential for women's health care (such as mammograms) (Chesney-Lind, 1986). In addition, women's past lives have put them at particular risk for certain health problems. According to the Centers for Disease Control and Prevention [CDC] (2003), women often enter prison with sexually transmitted diseases and somewhere between 22 percent and 58 percent have Hepatitis C. Many women also suffer from depression and PTSD associated with histories of abuse.

Female inmates are more likely than male inmates to have children and to have been living with those children immediately prior to incarceration. Forty-six percent of female prisoners are single parents compared to 15 percent of male prisoners (Mumola, 2000). Women are likely to have their parental rights terminated as they are often the sole guardians of their children (Chesney-Lind, 2002). At the time of their arrest, 6 to 10 percent of women are pregnant (CDC, 2003). In 1998, more than 1,400 women had a baby while incarcerated (CDC, 2003). National survey information indicates that in the United States residential programs for inmate mothers and their infants or children exist only in the federal system and in about 11 states; in the other states, newborns are removed from their mothers immediately after the hospital stay (General Accounting Office, 1999).

The Criminal Justice System and Children.   Most states establish a maximum age under 18 years, the age of legal majority, for juvenile court jurisdiction. In some states, minors who are charged with certain offenses may or must be prosecuted as adults. Since 1992, 45 states have taken steps to facilitate the transfer of juveniles to adult courts (Wright, 2002). At least three states permit the execution of 14 year olds.

Diversion of Resources.   Federal spending on jobs and job training for low-income people was cut by half during the 1980s; at the same time, federal spending on "correctional activities" rose by more than 500 percent (Currie, 1998, p. 31). The United States devoted $34.1 billion to expenditures for adult correctional facilities in 2000. Even a portion of the dollars spent on the criminal justice system could have made a big difference in the education, housing, and treatment of the poor, especially poor children who otherwise may become the criminals of the future.

How the Criminal Justice System Promotes Well-Being.   In a society that is unable or unwilling to invest in prevention or rehabilitation, incarceration provides short-term security and protection by keeping offenders locked up. Many people believe that as a growing "industry," the building of new prisons offers economic opportunities in rural communities that have no other alternatives for generating new jobs. Prisons are appealing because "they don't pollute, they don't go out of business, [and] they don't get downsized" (Lamb, cited in Dyer, 2000, p. 16).

The authors found it difficult to identify benefits of the criminal justice system. Perhaps the better strategy to ensure security in this country would be the promotion of fair and equal treatment of all individuals, regardless of their race, class, gender, or age. The rights of the accused are not protected by our current criminal justice system, and the system does a poor job of keeping the members of society safe from harm. Van Wormer (2001, p. 227) suggests that "today we face not a crime crisis . . . but a criminal justice crisis. The solution to the problem has become the problem: the war on crime has become a war on people, Black people, poor people, drug addicts, and the mentally ill."

Looking Ahead

In the next chapter, we will examine social institutions that are not as closely associated with government. These social institutions are also an important part of the context of the lives of social workers and those they serve.

Key Points

- Even though the United States is the wealthiest country in the world, its social welfare system has failed to provide all of its citizens with adequate food, shelter, and health care.

- Problems of inequity in funding and lingering discrimination plague our school systems.

- The United States has the highest rate of incarceration in the world, but this approach to criminal justice has failed to ensure security for its citizens.

- Statistical analyses repeatedly demonstrate that poor people and minorities are unfairly treated by the criminal justice system.

Questions to Think about and Discuss

1. Some policy makers believe TANF recipients should be strongly encouraged to marry in order to reduce the welfare rolls. Do you agree?

2. Should women who are receiving TANF benefits be allowed to attend college?

3. Some people believe that education is the "ticket" out of poverty; others believe that education perpetuates social inequity. What do you think?

4. Do you believe that tax revenues should be used to pay tuition for children to attend private schools?

5. What do you believe is the best way for colleges and universities to ensure a student body that is diverse in terms of race, ethnicity, and class, while treating all applicants fairly?

6. Some social work students have already held paid or volunteer jobs providing quality services to clients and are now in school to get the "credentials" to make them eligible for a new title or higher salary. What proportion of your educational experience do you perceive to be getting past the "gatekeepers" versus acquiring necessary knowledge and skills?

7. What can social workers do to reduce hate crimes?

8. Would you be willing to have your taxes used to pay for equal-quality legal counsel for poor defendants?

Recommended Readings _____

Kozol, J. (1991). *Savage inequalities: Children in America's schools*. New York: Crown.

Seccombe, K. (1999). *"So you think I drive a Cadillac?": Welfare recipients' perspectives on the system and its reform*. Boston: Allyn & Bacon.

Timilty, J., & Thomas, J. (1997). *Prison journal: An irreverent look at life on the inside*. Boston: Northeastern University Press.

Wachtler, S. (1997). *After the madness: A judge's own prison memoir*. New York: Random House.

Internet Search Terms _____

Capital punishment
Correctional problems
Crime prevention
Criminal justice and violence
De facto segregation
Death penalty
Deregulation
Deterrence theory
Devolution
Distributive justice
Education inequality
Educational opportunities
Educational policy
Educational segregation
Educational tracking

Hate crimes
Human capital
Incarceration
Income inequality
Juvenile delinquency
Labeling or labeling theory
Latent functions/education
Magnet schools
Mainstreaming
Organizational crime
Penal reform
Public assistance
Public schools
Private schools
Privatization

Racial profiling
Rehabilitation
Repeat offenders
School desegregation
School voucher system
Special education
Social control
Social welfare
Voucher plans
Welfare policy
Welfare recipients
Welfare reform
Welfare state
White-collar crime

4

Non-Government-Related Social Institutions

Ιn this chapter, we discuss three non-government-related social institutions, their interaction with the political economy, and their impact on individuals and families. Like the social institutions discussed so far, they are important in the lives of social work clients.

Health Care

Health care is the social institution whose purpose is dealing with disease and injury and improving health, on both an individual and community level. Typically, in the United States, public health officials are concerned with issues of prevention, while medical practitioners are more concerned with treatment and cure, even though they might offer advice on healthy living.

Issues and Trends in Health Care

Access to Health Care.   Not long ago, patients in the United States used a *fee-for-service* system to access medical care. They themselves, or more commonly, their health insurance company, paid whatever the health care provider charged. Within the last 20 years a new system, managed care, has grown substantially. *Managed care* is a health care delivery system that sends patients to preselected care providers with prearranged agreements on what costs will be covered. *Health maintenance organizations* (HMOs), *preferred provider organizations* (PPOs), and other kinds of managed care programs also challenge the fee-for-service system by strict review of recommended treatments. These programs can require that patients receive prior approval before receiving treatment and can refuse to pay physicians or hospitals if they deem that the treatment was unnecessary. This helps to hold down health care costs.

Individuals can subscribe to group health care plans on their own, but more typically they are covered by their employers' plans (or under the family plan of a working spouse or parent). More than 43.6 million Americans (15.2 percent of the population) have no medical insurance coverage (Mills & Bhandari, 2003). The working poor comprise a large proportion of this group: 19 million of the uninsured hold full-time jobs.

Unlike other industrialized countries, the United States offers neither national health insurance nor guaranteed health services. The United States is one of the few industrialized nations where illness or injury can lead directly to financial catastrophe (Kilborn, 1997). Due to lack of money and insurance coverage, many Americans forego preventive care, putting their health at serious risk.

Bias in Medical Research.   Until recently, many medical scientists have performed research using exclusively male subjects to draw conclusions about humans in general. Studies on the effects of aspirin in reducing the risk of heart attacks and the effects of heavy coffee intake on heart attacks and strokes were conducted in the late 1980s. The huge numbers of subjects (i.e., 22,071 and 45,589 individuals, respectively) included *not a single female participant* (Ames, 1990). Increasing awareness of gender bias in medical research, along with pressure from various women's groups, has begun to spur changes, although research on diseases that affect primarily women (e.g., breast cancer, osteoporosis) is still funded at levels that are lower than research on those diseases that affect men equally or more. In the early 1990s, Congress mandated that women be included in large, long-term research studies (Guthrie & Wahberg, 2002).

Cure versus Care.   Many physicians are uncomfortable dealing with terminal illnesses. They feel that they have failed if a patient dies. This translates not only into prolonged suffering but also increased health care costs. Medicare expenditures on patients in the last year of life range from four to six times higher than Medicare expenditures for others in the same age groups; more than one-quarter of all Medicare expenditures are for last-year-of-life (LYOL) care (Centers for Medicare and Medicaid Services, 2003). The *hospice* movement, on the other hand, provides *palliative care* (i.e., comfort, pain relief) and "death with dignity." It focuses on quality of life for terminally ill people rather than triumph over disease. Social workers are likely to play a more significant role in hospice care than in hospital care.

Adults can express their preferences about various types of life-extending medical interventions, but also need to take legal steps to protect themselves from unnecessary medical intervention. By writing a *living will* and giving *durable power of attorney for health care* to a trusted friend or relative, they have the opportunity to exercise control over potentially painful and invasive but ineffective medical treatment at a time in the future when they are unable to speak for themselves.

Understanding the Health Care System

Functionalist Perspective.   Structural functionalists view illness as dysfunctional because it prevents individuals from performing their assigned roles. This point of view was articulated by James Buchanan Duke, the founder of the Duke Endowment. He explained his support for the expansion of health care facilities in the Carolinas in a newspaper interview in the 1920s, saying, "People ought to be healthy. If they ain't healthy they can't work, and if they don't work they ain't healthy. And if they can't work there ain't no profit in them" (Goulden, 1971).

A primary function of healthcare is to maintain a healthy workforce. The fact that the vast majority of those individuals who have health insurance coverage receive that benefit through their employer makes clear the link between financial support for health care and the needs of the political economy. Tax-supported insurance (e.g., Medicaid) for nonworkers tends to be stingy and often stigmatizing.

The Conflict Perspective.   The *medical establishment* includes health care providers, laboratories, clinics, pharmaceutical companies, hospitals, medical supply manufacturers, and insurance companies. Through its political and financial clout, the medical establishment has become the most lucrative business in the country. In theory, the supply-and-demand of a capitalist system should keep health care prices competitive, but in reality the members of the medical establishment, not health care consumers, determine the demand by deciding what kinds of medical services and supplies are needed and then providing them at the prices they set. Often there are inherent conflicts of interest, as when doctors have financial interests in labs, pharmacies, hospitals, and medical supply companies. It is difficult to know if a doctor has made a choice based on the needs of the patient or the needs of his or her pocketbook.

As the gatekeeper of the profession, the American Medical Association controls who can provide medical services by controlling who is licensed to diagnose and treat patients, and prescribe drugs, effectively eliminating some competitors (such as homeopathic healers) and controlling those who remain (e.g., nurses, social workers, and physical therapists). Early in the twentieth century, physicians expanded their practice opportunities by campaigning against midwifery. Using the power of the AMA, they persuaded many states to make it illegal for anyone but a physician to deliver babies.

Constructionist Perspective.   Both "illness" and "health" are culturally defined. An example is our understanding of pregnancy and childbirth. Pregnancy was once thought of as a normal part of a woman's life. Even though childbirth was often dangerous or even fatal, women delivered their babies at home with the help of female relatives or nurse-midwives. Physicians redefined pregnancy as a medical condition and delivery as a medical emergency that required the assistance of a specially educated person, usually meaning a male obstetrician. Both the patient and the physician socially reconstructed even routine births as medical crises requiring in-patient hospitalization. Other routine problems and processes that have been medicalized include short stature, menopause, and hair loss.

Other examples of the social construction of illness are addictions and behavior problems, such as overeating, phobias, and adolescent rebelliousness. These were once identified as personal weaknesses or eccentricities, but came to be defined as diseases or mental disorders. Once these problems were medicalized, physicians became the primary supervisors of treatment as well as gatekeepers to those applying for medical benefits. Contextual factors, such as family patterns, poverty, violence, trauma, and oppression, were seldom viewed as relevant in explaining or contributing to the disorders.

Relationship of the Health Care System to the Political Economy

Like other American social institutions, health care is highly integrated with the political economy. In contrast to most other countries, in the United States health care is not a right of citizenship, but a commodity that is delivered to consumers through the private market system. Conservative politicians and the medical establishment have always campaigned against proposals for government health care programs and also oppose government intervention in the delivery of health care services.

Sociologists (see Thio, 2000, pp. 388–389) argue that although medical care appears to be organized like any other business in the free market, it is quite different. Consumers do not have much input into purchasing choices because they cannot determine what they need. Sick or injured people are not in a strong position to question their doctor's choices. They rely on the medical establishment to tell them what to get and how much they must pay. Most have few incentives to "comparison shop" because they pay only a share (about one-third) of the costs directly.

Health care consumers would like to believe that physicians have their patients' interest as their primary concern. However, as mentioned, the profit motive may influence doctors' decisions about courses of treatment. Likewise, patients would like to believe that their HMO has their best interests at heart, but most people have learned otherwise. Like more traditional insurance programs, the goal of the health maintenance programs is to (1) make a profit for their stockholders and (2) to make sure the hospitals and doctors are paid if patients are too sick to work or if fees are more than patients can afford. In other words, the ultimate concern is for the financial well-being of the insurance company and the care providers rather than the health of the consumers. This is reflected in exclusions for "pre-existing conditions" or excessively high insurance rates for individuals who have serious or chronic illnesses.

Another example of the close ties between the health care establishment and the political economy is the change in legal restrictions that now allow pharmaceutical companies to market prescription drugs directly to the public. Between 1995 and 2000, the number of drug industry staff employed in doing research dropped slightly (from 49,000 to 48,000); during the same time, sales staff increased from 55,000 to 87,000 (Barry, 2002). The pharmaceutical industry spent $15.7 billion on advertising and marketing in 2000 (Sneyd, 2002). According to the National Institute for Health Care Management Research and Educational Foundation, spending on prescription drugs nationwide climbed 17.1 percent in 2001 (Sneyd, 2002). The drug industry is already by far the most profitable in America with revenues and returns three to eight times higher than the medians for other industries (Barry, 2002).

The Impact of the Health Care System on Individuals and Families

How the Health Care System Obstructs Well-Being.   The medical establishment focuses on micro-organisms to explain ill health but often does not consider the harmful effects of poverty. From the perspective of the members of the medical establishment, people in the lower economic classes contribute to their own poor health by eating the wrong foods and living in unsanitary conditions. They seldom question the reasons behind these "choices." By not taking context into account, the medical establishment reduces a societal level issue to an individual one (Macionis, 2001).

Scientific medicine has not done a good job of meeting the needs of women, people of color, poor people, and older adults. Women and members of racial and ethnic minorities are less likely than white males to receive aggressive and sophisticated health care and mental health care. (See Figure 4.1.) In a lengthy report mandated by Congress in the Minority Health Disparities Act of 2000, the Institute of Medicine, a unit of the National Academy of Sciences, concluded that there was overwhelming evidence of less adequate medical treatment provided for racial and ethnic minorities compared to whites, even when insurance, in-

---

FIGURE 4.1   *Inequities in Medical Treatment by Gender and Race or Ethnicity*

Studies suggest that race, ethnicity, and gender determine access and use of medical interventions for the following medical conditions:

Discrimination by Gender

- ❑ Renal transplant
- ❑ Blindness
- ❑ Pain treatment/management (undertreatment)
- ❑ Treatment of acute myocardial infarction
- ❑ Receipt of anti-retroviral therapies/HIV treatment

Discrimination by Race and Ethnicity

- ❑ Renal transplant
- ❑ Treatment for heart disease
- ❑ Access to invasive cardiac procedures (angioplasty)
- ❑ Blindness
- ❑ Pain treatment
- ❑ Influenza vaccinations
- ❑ Treatment for endometrial cancer
- ❑ Fewer limb-saving therapies for peripheral vascular disease
- ❑ Higher incidence of limb amputation in blacks with diabetes

---

Sources: Office of Research on Minority Health, 2000; American Medical Association, 2000.

come, age, and severity of the disease were the same (Schmid, 2002). The AARP reports that older adults are often denied preventive care routinely provided to others, they are less likely to be screened for life-threatening diseases, and they are "routinely overtreated, undertreated, or even mistreated by health care professionals with little or no training in geriatrics" (Pope, 2003, p. 7). They are also consistently underrepresented or excluded from clinical trials (Pope, 2003, p. 8).

Issues of lack of access to medical care were discussed above. The experiences of poor people in the health care system are quite different from those who are affluent or well-insured. The poor may use public health clinics and emergency rooms for primary care. They are unlikely to receive preventive care or adequate follow-up services.

How the Health Care System Promotes Well-Being.   Obviously, the American health care system has been effective in dealing with many health care problems. Immunizations have resulted in a great reduction or total elimination of some infectious diseases, and other advances in health care technology have produced artificial replacements for limbs and organs, innovative fertility treatments, and life-saving treatments for very low birth-weight babies. The public health system and occupational safety regulations have done much to reduce health risks from many sources (e.g., lead poisoning, asbestos, on-the-job injuries, and so forth).

Religion

Religion is the social institution that organizes a system of beliefs and practices related to aspects of life having to do with the supernatural. It involves the things that are sacred in people's lives—those that inspire awe and reverence—as opposed to everyday experiences. Religion as a social institution is not the same thing as denominational theology or personal spirituality. Social scientists are less interested in specific religious doctrines or beliefs than they are in religious groups and organizations, the behavior of individuals within these groups, and on conflicts between religious groups (Roberts, 1995, p. 28). In this chapter, we explore the influence of religion on American society.

Religions typically include three elements: beliefs, practices (rituals), and a community of believers (Durkeim, 1965/1912). Most formal religions also include norms or rules for how people should behave.

About 60 percent of Americans consider themselves members of some religious organization (National Opinion Research Center [NORC], 1999). The United States is home to more than 280 religious denominations (Thio, 2000, p. 320). Ninety-four percent of Americans report that they are Christian and 3.7 percent Jewish (Wright, 2002). Three faiths—Islam, Buddhism, and Hinduism—account for about half the people following other religions; the proportion of Americans in these religions grew by three- or fourfold between the 1970s and 2002, but their absolute numbers remain small (Smith, 2002).

Many of the religious denominations showing sudden growth in America reflect the arrival of refugees from Asia, the Middle East, and Latin America. The Roman Catholic Church, for example, is gaining members, primarily due to heavy immigration from Mexico and other Catholic countries. The fastest growing segment of Presbyterian and Methodist faiths are ethnic Korean congregations (Schaefer, 2000).

Generally the larger "mainline" Protestant churches (e.g., Disciples of Christ, Episcopal, United Church of Christ, United Methodist, Presbyterian, and Congregational) have lost members or are struggling to maintain the size of their membership roles. Many members of mainline Protestant faiths have been leaving them for churches that follow strict codes of behavior and rigid interpretations of Biblical teachings (Schaefer, 2000). Southern Baptists, Jehovah's Witnesses, the Church of Latter Day Saints (Mormons), the Church of God, Assemblies of God, Church of the Nazarene, the Church of God in Christ, Catholic Pentecostals, and Seventh-Day Adventists are among the fundamentalist groups enjoying significant growth (Stockard, 2000, p. 312).

Religion is linked to ethnicity and nationality in all parts of the world. Faith communities in America reflect a very high degree of racial and ethnic segregation (Schaefer, 2000). This pattern reflects each group's culture, not a history of forced segregation. Latinos are likely to be Catholic, as are people of Irish, Italian, and Polish descent; many people of Greek descent belong to the Greek Orthodox Church, and African Americans are likely to be members of the African Methodist Episcopal (AME) or black Baptist churches. Many Southeast Asian refugees from Vietnam, Cambodia, and Thailand are Buddhist. Recent Arab immigrants are likely to be followers of the Islamic faith (Muslims). Research studies show that the religious involvement of different ethnic groups within the same denomination varies considerably even though the church can be a powerful force for assimilation (Schaefer, 2000).

Patterns of religious affiliation are also strongly related to geographic region in the United States. This has implications for who might be considered a member of a "religious minority" in different parts of the country. Southern Baptists dominate in the Southeast, Catholics in the Northeast and Southwest, Lutherans in the upper Midwest, and Latter Day Saints (Mormons) in Utah. Jews once comprised fully one-third of the population of New York City. Many Jews have now left the urban centers of the Northeast to settle in the suburbs and in the Sunbelt states of Florida, Arizona, and California (Shapiro, 1999).

Today most Americans show an amazing tolerance for religious diversity. Nevertheless, many have little knowledge about faith traditions outside their own. The authors of this text believe that it is important for social work practitioners to have a basic understanding of the major religions. In some types of social work intervention, knowledge of religious culture can facilitate treatment (Rey, 1997). We recommend that students make an effort to expand their knowledge of different religious traditions.

Many theologians divide common world religions into two major groups, "Western" and "Eastern." The three major *Western religions* (Judaism, Christianity, and Islam) actually originated in what Americans call the Middle East. They are monotheistic religions (espousing belief in one god). Their followers form congregations and worship formally in groups at specific times and in specific places (i.e., in synagogues, churches, and mosques). Other characteristics of Western religious beliefs are a sense of conflict between the spiritual and the secular, the importance of sacred texts, a perception of time as linear, and a view of each person as a unique creation. Major *Eastern religions* (Hinduism, Buddhism, and Shintoism), on the other hand, have multiple deities and/or sub-deities. There is a belief in the harmonious duality or balance of spiritual and worldly elements, time is viewed as cyclical, and souls are believed to transmigrate between beings (reincarnation). Confucianism and Taoism, widely practiced in the Far East, are usually considered to be philosophies rather than religions.

The importance placed on *proselytizing* (actively seeking converts) varies considerably among religions. Followers of Eastern religions place much less emphasis on proselytizing than do Christians and Muslims. Hinduism, for example, makes no effort to change the beliefs of others but rather finds ways to integrate them under the great umbrella of traditions that comprise the Hindu faith. Judaism is non-proselytizing because to be Jewish typically involves not only a religious commitment but an ethnic heritage as well. (This is discussed further in Chapter 6.) Outreach programs are mostly limited to efforts by Reform Jews aimed at non-Jewish partners and children in mixed marriages (Schaefer, 2000).

Issues and Trends in Religion

Civil Religion. While many countries have an official "state religion" (e.g., Belgium, England, Iran, Ireland, Israel, Italy, Saudi Arabia, Spain, and Sweden) the United States, of course, does not. On the other hand, Americans do not practice the strict "separation of church and state" that many believe is constitutionally required. The government at many levels supports religion through tax policies, publicly supported chaplains, and invocation of God's presence at ceremonial occasions. Polls show that most Americans do not object to the inclusion of religion in the public realm as long as no particular denomination is favored (NORC, 1999; Wolfe, 1998). In fact, it is considered "un-American to be godless, or worse, to attack religion" (Thio, 2000, p. 329).

Sociologists describe the United States as having a form of *civil religion,* a kind of hybrid of religion and politics (Bellah, 1967; McGuire, 1997; Roberts, 1995). American civil religion promotes faith in a supreme being (however individuals choose to understand the deity) and the "American way of life," including individual freedom, patriotism, and the moral authority of elected leaders in times of crisis. Civil religion also has its rituals, including singing the national anthem at sporting events and displaying the flag as a sacred symbol on national holidays and other occasions. American presidents, beginning with Ronald Reagan, have concluded their speeches with "God bless the United States of America," which evokes the civil religion of the nation (Schaefer, 2000).

Fundamentalism. Some religious scholars (e.g., Hunter, 1991) believe that there is a new realignment of religious difference that is not based on doctrine or denomination; in fact, this realignment sometimes cuts right through the middle of a congregation or denomination. The dividing line is between conservatives/fundamentalists and liberals/interpretationists.

Fundamentalists in Western religious traditions accept the literal meaning of scripture; that is, they believe it is the "inerrant word of God." Their assumption is that a text means whatever it means to somebody who is reading it today (Helminiak, 1994, p. 25). Fundamentalists assert the absolute correctness of their own beliefs and reject religious pluralism. Typically, among Christian denominations, fundamentalism is associated with the evangelical tradition and includes members of Pentecostal, Southern Baptist, Seventh-Day Adventist, and Assembly of God congregations. In national surveys, 31 percent of American adults describe their religious upbringing as "fundamentalist" (NORC, 1999).

Interpretationists use a historical-critical approach to reading sacred texts (Helminiak, 1994, pp. 26–27). This approach is called "historical" because it requires that the text be put back into its historical and cultural context before deciding what it means. It is called "critical" because it requires careful thought and detailed analysis. Liberals/interpretationists are likely to be found among Unitarians, United Methodists, Episcopalians, Congregational-ists, and Presbyterians, as well as Reform Jews.

Despite expectations that religious fundamentalism and political conservatism go hand-in-hand, the reality is often more complex. Davis and Robinson (1996) found that although fundamentalism was correlated with conservative views on nontraditional families, feminist and gay causes, and prayer in school, they were not associated with attitudes on economic issues. Instead, the researchers found that people with fundamentalist beliefs were more likely than their liberal/interpretationist counterparts to support organized labor and believe that profits should go to workers rather than stockholders.

Religion-Related Controversies in Social Work.   Social workers often experience two different kinds of value dilemmas related to religion. In some agencies, they may feel pressure to use religious beliefs as a context for the provision of services. In other situations, they may find that their personal religious beliefs are in conflict with those of their clients or the profession.

In 2000, presidential candidate George W. Bush proposed the establishment of *faith-based social services* as an alternative to traditional social service programs. Supporters of this initiative believe that faith-based services supply the moral content that is lacking in secular nonprofit or government agencies (Karger & Stoesz, 2002). Nevertheless, when government-supported social service programs are imbedded in faith-based organizations, professional ethics dictate that social workers respect service consumers' religious preferences (or lack of religious affiliation).

Perhaps more commonly, some practitioners experience dissonance between their own religious beliefs and practices and those of their clients or the values of the social work profession. Typically these conflicts arise in the context of disagreements over gender roles (i.e., patriarchy), abortion, the physical discipline of children, and differing views on homosexuality.

Understanding Religion

Functionalist Perspective.   Functionalists believe that the social order is enhanced by the existence of organized religion(s) (Durkeim, 1965/1912) and civil religion (Schaefer, 2000). Religion encourages conformity by providing cultural norms or by *sacralizing* those norms that already exist (i.e., conferring supernatural legitimacy on the norms and laws of society) (Roberts, 1995). Religion unites people through shared symbolism and values. Civil religion expressly encourages patriotism and nationalism.

Conflict Perspective.   Although clearly religion has been used in many times and many places to justify persecution, violence, and even war, conflict theorists focus on how the institution of religion supports the existing social hierarchy and the interests of the ruling class. Historical examples include the Christian teaching of the "divine right of kings" in Europe during the Middle Ages, and support of the caste system by the Hindu religion in India. In this country, historically, religion has been used to endorse the status quo by legitimating the destruction of Native Americans, the slavery of Africans, and the oppression of women.

Many religions encourage people to focus on "another world to come" rather than working toward change in this one. The most famous critique of religion from a conflict perspective was offered by Karl Marx. In his statement that "religion is the opium of the masses," he meant that religion is like a drug that causes people to become complacent and docile even when they are exploited.

Constructionist Perspective.   Most religious people would argue that their beliefs are the result of divine inspiration, provided indirectly through prophets, clerics, and religious texts or perhaps directly to themselves individually. Social construction theorists say that people construct religious beliefs as a means of responding to life's uncertainties, tragedies, triumphs, and other great questions, trying to explain the unexplainable, find reason in the unreasonable, and perhaps gain the favor or assistance of supernatural forces. Organized religion is based on a shared construction of reality. Because they are matters of faith rather than fact, neither social workers nor scientists in any discipline can prove or disprove specific religious doctrines or beliefs.

The Relationship of Religion to the Political Economy

As noted in Chapter 2, Max Weber linked the development of capitalism to early Protestant beliefs. The "Protestant work ethic" continues to be touted as the basis of America's prosperity. Because American Catholics and Jews are also prosperous, and because capitalism is flourishing in non-Christian/non-Protestant countries such as Japan, Taiwan, and South Korea, Weber's theory probably is best used to explain the early emergence of capitalism rather than its continuing success.

   At the end of the twentieth century, the ideas flowed in the other direction as organized religion began borrowing marketing strategies from the business sector (Kroll, 2003; Lewis, 1996; Staples, 1998). Especially in the case of "megachurches" (those with memberships of 15,000 or more), congregations have become "the religious equivalents of Wal-Marts" in designing programs to meet the needs of their "customers" (Thio, 2000, p. 330–331). In 1970 there were just ten megachurches in the United States; today there are 740 (Kroll, 2003).

   While in principle the American people are committed to the "separation of church and state" (meaning a public policy of neutrality toward religion), in practice they not only permit but also insist on public manifestations of religiosity on the part of government officials (Pfeffer, 1970, p. 335). The power and grace of God (or "Providence," or "the Supreme Being") are regularly invoked. Political leaders may even use religion to shield their choices from criticism by saying that they prayed for divine guidance before reaching a decision, thus suggesting that questioning them is akin to questioning God.

   The government not only tolerates but also encourages religion in a variety of ways. These include its tax policies (exemptions for religious organizations and contributions to them), laws (including a 1954 law adding "under God" to the Pledge of Allegiance and a 1955 law requiring that "In God We Trust" appear on all U.S. currency), and practices (such as provision of funding for chaplains in Congress, the armed forces, and prisons; use of the Bible for rituals of "swearing in," and recognition of religious holidays). As noted, the George W. Bush administration supports the idea of faith based social services, which blurs the distinction between secular and religious agencies.

   Many have argued that Americans need to be concerned when those in power use their own religious point of view to interpret and judge the actions of others (Rosenblatt, 2001). The endorsement by public officials of a particular religious view, or even of religion in general, suggests that adherence to a religious creed is a prerequisite or an advantage to those seeking justice and fair treatment. "People who govern in the name of God attribute their own personal preferences to God and therefore recognize no limits in imposing those preferences on other people" (Center sues to remove monument, 2002). Organizations such as the American Civil Liberties Union (ACLU), Americans United for the Separation of Church and State, the Interfaith Alliance, and the Southern Poverty Law Center work to protect the interests of religious minorities and atheists from overly zealous judges and lawmakers.

The Impact of Religion on Individuals and Families

How Religion Obstructs Well-Being.   As mentioned earlier, the Bible has been used to justify slavery and racism (Hill & Cheadle,1996; Schaefer, 2000). The Christian faith to which slaves were introduced in America encouraged them to accept their inferior status, and many people believed that it exonerated the owners.

The beliefs, ritual expressions, norms, and organizational structures of organized religions routinely subordinate women (McGuire, 1997). Analyzing Christian teachings, for example, Stone (1978) reports that the Bible was written by men, edited by men, translated by men, and interpreted by men; until recently, most Biblical scholars were male. Thus one should not be surprised to see that men receive favorable treatment in Christian religious belief and practice. Traditional religions have placed women in exalted but protected positions. "Protected" often meant protected from becoming leaders (Schaefer, 2000, p. 156). Patriarchal views in sacred texts and contemporary religious practices continue to reinforce gender inequity (McGuire, 1997). Like other major religions of the world, the three Western religions (Judaism, Christianity, and Islam) are traditionally patriarchal. Orthodox Judaism, Roman Catholicism, and Islam continue to exclude women from the highest spiritual leader roles, although growing numbers of Protestant denominations, as well as Reform and Conservative Jews, allow women to lead congregations. Nevertheless, in many denominations, women are assigned to assistant clergy or co-pastor positions and find it more difficult than men to secure jobs in large, prestigious congregations (Schaefer, 2000).

Some religious denominations in America, especially those that are more conservative, promote homophobia (Helminiak, 1994; Hill & Cheadle, 1996). Although the message may be "hate the sin, love the sinner," their rhetoric supports an atmosphere of intolerance toward gay men and lesbians, which can encourage acts of violence.

Because America is a nation of Christians (although still not a "Christian nation" in an official sense), discrimination against members of minority religions and atheists is common. This may take the form of the obvious (such as pressure to participate in Christian prayers, or reluctance to make accommodations for non-Christian holy days or rituals) to the simply thoughtless (such as describing any generous or ethical person as an example of "a good Christian," forgetting that other faith traditions also promote moral behavior). Some Christians may ask, "Why can't we have prayer in school [or the Ten Commandments posted in the courthouse or a nativity scene in the public square]? After all, this country was founded on the principle of majority rule," forgetting that in this country religious beliefs and practices are matters of individual discretion and not matters to be decided by a majority vote.

Overly zealous proselytizing can be interpreted as a threat by members of religious minorities. For example, Raspberry (1999) reported that the Southern Baptist International Mission Board urged its denomination members to pray for the conversion of Jews: "Pray each day for Jewish individuals you know by name. . . . Love them as you would an unsaved relative." The president of the Union of American Hebrew Congregations, Rabbi Eric Yoffie, responded, "There's a kind of theological arrogance that pervades all of this, a certain willingness to play God, and an absence of awareness that these sorts of statements throughout history are associated with coercion, hatred and violence. . . . We'd like a little less love and a little more respect."

How Religion Promotes Well-Being.   Organized religion promotes the well-being of individuals, families, and society in many ways. First, religion establishes values of cooperation, altruism, and often social justice. Second, many congregations provide social services and support for individuals and groups. In addition, many religious organizations, and in particular black churches, have nourished social movements.

Most great cultures, and all the major religions, have obliged their people to help the less fortunate, including widows, orphans, the sick or disabled, and even traveling strangers (Morris, 1986). The history of social work as a profession is closely linked to Christian traditions of helping the poor (e.g., the Charity Organization Societies). The profession also draws heavily on the Jewish principle of *tzedakah,* which can be translated as a combination of charity and justice. The traditions of Judaism emphasize the goal of promoting self-sufficiency among recipients of charity, and in protecting them from embarrassment or stigma.

Many religious congregations provide information and referral to connect members and other community residents to social services, training opportunities, and jobs and sometimes grants or other funding. They also themselves provide some social services and limited financial support to people in crisis (often members of the congregation but also to other residents of the local community as well). Black churches have historically functioned as social service agencies in the African American community. Congregations often provide meeting space free of charge or for a very small fee for other social organizations within their community. Many denominations support hospitals, nursing homes and retirement centers, children's homes and residential treatment centers, adoption and foster care agencies, family life education programs, day-care centers for very young children and older adults, after-school programs and recreation programs for school children and adolescents, and refugee resettlement—if not with funding then with volunteers or gifts in kind (such as meeting space).

Religious organizations can provide continuity for immigrants to this country. The "ethnic church" performs multiple roles for racially and culturally distinct minorities, providing guidance, emotional support, and a broad range of social activities and outlets (Kim, 1999, p. 366). Churches, temples, and mosques help members retain a sense of identity by providing a place for religious and ethnic fellowship. People who are persecuted and discriminated against in other areas of life find inner strength and external social support in a wide variety of religious beliefs and practices. Religious organizations may offer one of the few welcoming "communities" for specific minorities. For example, the Metropolitan Community Church provides a safe haven and worship experience for gay men and lesbians.

African American churches served as a cradle for the civil rights movement and a training ground for the development of civil rights leaders. Religion can be the catalyst to those seeking social justice, inspiring individuals to break out of the limited roles prescribed for them by the society (McGuire, 1997). Black congregations continue this tradition of civic participation, frequently serving as platforms for collective mobilization. Religious congregations are especially successful in organizing residents for political action, in part because they "enjoy relations with other community institutions and congregations, larger religious bodies, and specialized, parallel religious organizations or private and public institutions" (Foley, McCarthy, & Chaves, 2001, p. 221).

Mass Media

The mass media manage the flow of images and ideas across society; they are a common source of information and a source of socialization. The mass media have the potential to present similar depictions of the world to tremendous numbers of otherwise different and un-related people (Turow, 1992). The depictions that the media deliver have the power to affect people's attitudes toward social issues, other people, and even themselves.

The mass media are what some sociologists call an "emerging social institution." They are relatively new in human history, dating from the invention of movable type in 1436. Not until the 1840s, with the invention of the telegraph, was long-distance communication sepa-rated from transportation (Croteau & Hoynes, 2003). One might note the contemporary irony that people who are immersed in a crisis that cuts off electric power may know much less about what is going on in their immediate vicinity than do media consumers hundreds, or even thousands, of miles away.

The development of newspapers, magazines, radio, movies, network television, cable TV, and the Internet and the ubiquitous presence of electronic devices have made the media an increasingly powerful and influential social institution. In 1950, only 9 percent of Ameri-can homes owned a television; by 1955, the percentage had jumped to 64.5 percent and by 1965, it increased to 92.6 percent (Television Information Office, 1985). Now more than 99 percent of American households have television sets and 66 percent have two or more. A 1999 national survey indicated that three of every five American children have a TV in their bedroom; nearly half of all homes with children have a VCR, video game equipment, and a home computer; and subscriptions to the Internet are nearly as common as subscriptions to the newspaper. Children spend more time sitting in front of a screen than they do in school.

Issues and Trends in Mass Media

Violence in the Media.   Probably the most notable issue related to the mass media is con-cern about the graphic portrayal of violence. The American Medical Association, the Ameri-can Academy of Pediatrics, and the American Psychological Association have gone on record reporting the negative effects of violence in the mass media, especially on television and in films, based on studies that show correlations between viewing patterns and aggressive behavior.

The Center for Media and Public Affairs analyzed television content on an average day in 1995 (CMPA, 1996). The study reported 1,738 scenes of violence, not counting 948 scenes in commercials and the "real" violence present in nonfiction programs, such as *Hardcopy, Inside Edition,* or the regular news. According to one educational video, *Media and the Cul-ture of Violence: The Killing Screens* (Gerbner, Kilbourne, & Jhally, 1994), violent acts in action films double or triple with each sequel, and the rate of violent acts portrayed in children's cartoons is 20 to 30 per hour. Many music videos also endorse violence, particu-larly against women. Because children imitate what they see, one can understand how vio-lence in the media may be particularly harmful to children when the aggressor is portrayed as attractive, when violence seems justified or goes unpunished, and when the suffering of victims is not shown.

Even local news programs tend to focus on violence. A study analyzing the content of 52 markets on March 11, 1998 found that 46 percent of the news was about crime, disaster, war, or terrorism (LaFayette, 1998). The newspaper axiom "If it bleeds, it leads" influences the electronic media as well. Sensational violent crimes make up less than one percent of all crimes, but they constitute a majority of crime coverage, leaving viewers and readers with a badly distorted picture of their world (Dyer, 2000, p. 87).

Diversity Issues. In the United States, the media are extremely powerful simply because they are unavoidable. Either from direct viewing or reading, or from secondhand reports, Americans obtain the vast majority of their knowledge and beliefs about life outside their direct experience from media sources (Lester, 1996, p. 6). Americans are becoming more comfortable with being a diverse nation, but minority cultures are increasingly defined by advertisers and scriptwriters rather than reflecting genuine ethnic heritage. For example, many Americans' exposure to Latino culture is limited to the images presented by Taco Bell. Unfortunately, portrayals that assume and reinforce negative stereotypes are common (Lester, 1996, p. 7).

Although the proliferation of cable channels has allowed for "niche marketing" and "narrowcasting"—programming directed at specific minorities (e.g., African Americans, Spanish speakers)—studies show that rather then encouraging cultural integration, this pattern may further segregate those populations from the mainstream. In other words, African Americans watch programs with predominantly black casts and whites watch programs with predominantly white casts. In 1998, the number one ranked show for black audiences was ranked 117th by white viewers (Richmond, 1998). Because ultimately the goal of the media is to generate profits, diversification to include underserved audiences is likely to occur only if they are identified as growing consumer markets (Turow, 1992).

New Technology/Computer-Mediated Communication. Television and newspapers continue to be the dominant sources of news. Media scholars are skeptical about the long-term impact of new media outlets, such as the Internet (Croteau & Hoynes, 2003). Even when they go to the Internet to seek news, most users look at the Web sites of major media organizations, such as CNN, the AOL News Channel, or large metropolitan newspapers. Rather than seeking original sources, users turn to the Internet simply to gain easier access to existing mass media news outlets.

It has been estimated that 107 million people worldwide use the Internet (Marriott, 1998). The majority of Web sites are based in the United States and 90 percent of the communication is in English (Kendall, 2001). Not surprisingly, young people make up the fastest growing segment of Internet users. An America Online spokesperson stated, "AOL literally lights up after school" (Henry & Schwartz, 1999, A1).

Changing Patterns of Ownership: Media Mergers. The decade of the 1990s witnessed a concentration of entertainment and news media ownership. Many of the same corporations own and operate television networks, radio stations, film studios, music studios, book publishing companies, video rental and movie theater chains, and magazine and newspaper outlets. Some of the largest corporations are AOL Time Warner, ABC/Disney, CBS/Viacom, and Fox/News Corporation. Currently, a half dozen global conglomerates control virtually all entertainment programming and news outlets (Bagdikian, 2000). The Federal Communications Commission [FCC], which was created to protect the public's interest in the nation's airwaves, has failed to block a growing monopoly of media power. In defending the policy of deregulation, the Bush-appointed chairman of the FCC, Michael Powell, noted, "The market is my religion" (Safir, 2003).

Understanding the Mass Media

Functionalist Perspective.   For most Americans, print, film, radio, music, television, and the Internet are central parts of daily life (Croteau & Hoynes, 2003, p. xvii). These media experiences have the social effect of creating a common frame of reference. For example, most people instantly recognize both the special meaning and the context of many otherwise obscure catch phrases that were delivered through the mass media: "the white Bronco," "yada, yada, yada," "Omigod, they killed Kenny!" "May the force be with you," "voted off the island," "Is that your final answer?" "You've got mail," and "Let's roll!" Functionalists would say that these catch phrase cues from the popular cultural have the effect of strengthening social bonds. Communication (disseminating information) and entertainment are clearly the manifest functions of the mass media. Although their function as an agent of socialization is sometimes manifest (as in programs like Sesame Street), often people are unaware of how television and other media continue to socialize not only children but also adults. They support mainstream cultural values (e.g., individualism, competition, and patriotism). Another function of the mass media is to promote commerce by marketing goods and services.

Conflict Perspective.   Conflict theorists argue that the mass media are controlled by the wealthy and powerful, who use them to mold public opinion and to help preserve their place of privilege. The messages put forth by the mass media reflect positions of the owners and managers. "Who gets depicted, what about them gets depicted, why, with what consequences, at what time, and in what situation" is determined in the corporate boardroom (Turow, 1992, p. 164).

Many groups in society are losing access to the public sphere through the media as a result of the conglomerations just described. This has limited the ability of sections of the community to voice their interests, their opinions, and their priorities and has prevented other groups from responding to, or even being aware of, these different voices (Curran, 1992, p. 102). There is a "fundamental contradiction between the ideal that public media should operate as a public sphere and the reality of concentrated private ownership" (Golding & Murdock, 1992, p. 23). McChesney (2000, pp. 29–30) argues that such a concentration of economic, cultural, and political power into so few hands—and mostly unaccountable hands at that—threatens the very basis of democracy.

Constructionist Perspective.   The messages that the mass media present play a central role in organizing the images and conversations through which people make sense of the world (Golding & Murdock, 1992, p. 15). A vast body of research has demonstrated that media content does not reflect the realities of the social world.

George Gerbner and his colleagues at the Annenburg Public Policy Center at the University of Pennsylvania have studied the mass media for many years. They are concerned about television's role as an "electronic storyteller," replacing traditional cultural sources and monopolizing the socialization process. Most of what we know (or think we know) comes from stories in our culture, not from direct personal experience. With the ever-present effects of the mass media, everyone in America views the same images and listens to the same dialogue, defining what is to be valued and what is to be discounted. There is a homogenization of culture, with much of it being presented for the "lowest common denominator" or, at least, at the level that will bring in viewers and attract sponsors. Gerbner's *cultivation theory* suggests that heavy viewers of television come to develop a common outlook on the world that is consistent with what they see on TV. Because images are similar across television channels, heavier viewers hold more stereotyped views of social groups than do light viewers (Gerbner, Gross, Morgan, & Signorielli, 1994); they are more sexist (Signorielli, 1993) and racist (Gerbner, Gross, Morgan, & Signorielli, 1982); and more likely to believe that the world is a violent and dangerous place (Gerbner et al., 1994).

Relationship of the Mass Media to the Political Economy

The media are often referred to as the "Fourth Estate" or the "Fourth Branch of Government." This designation reflects the idea that the media (originally print journalists or "the press") have an important role in overseeing government functioning, and in particular in revealing abuses of state authority (Curran, 1992). This "watchdog" role is supposed to override all other functions in importance. One might argue that the threat to individual freedom lies not so much with government abuse as with corporate oligopoly. One of the consequences of corporate control of the media is that reporters are less likely to investigate the actions of the conglomerates that pay their salaries (Curran, 1992).

Underwood (1993) reported that as marketing has become the focus of most newspapers, MBAs with a background in the business world began to replace people with journalistic experience in executive positions. The clear goal of media executives is to create steady profits. The easiest approach for audience maximization (and the advertising revenues that follow) is to create a light, entertainment-oriented product, even in news programming. Media analysts Neil Postman and Steve Powers (1992) argue, for example, that television news is primarily "entertainment fodder." Because advertisers, not consumers, are doing the most important buying, the principle product being sold by the media is the *audience,* not newspapers, magazines, or programs (Croteau & Hoyes, 2003).

In the 1990s, several sources (e.g., Jacobson & Mazur, 1995; Kerwin, 1992; Masterson, 1993) documented the often successful efforts of advertisers to get editors of magazines and newspapers to censor content that might reflect negatively on their companies or their products. For example, in 1993 Mercedes Benz, which spent an average of $14.5 billion a year on print advertising, instructed magazines that all Mercedes Benz ads would be canceled if anything of a derogatory nature about their cars, other German products, or Germany in general, appeared in their publications (Donaton, 1993). The automobile manufacturer was successful in securing compliance from over half of the magazines they contacted. Another powerful automobile manufacturer, Chrysler Corporation, went even further. In 1996 Chrysler sent a letter, through its ad agency, PentaCom, telling magazines that carried its advertising that they would need to be notified in advance of "any and all editorial content that encompasses sexual, political, social issues, or any editorial that might be construed as provocative or offensive" (Baker, 1997, p. 30). Although automakers "apparently lead the pack," manufacturers of packaged goods and large retail outlets are also touchy about the content of articles and editorials (p. 31). Some sponsors claim they fear reactions of activist groups despite evidence that consumer boycotts do little if any damage to sales.

Despite the disquieting trends noted above, the United States is one of very few countries where the general perception is that the media should be controlled exclusively by market forces rather than being responsible to the public well-being (Lazar, 1994a, 1994b). In fact, there has been increasing deregulation of American broadcasting, prompted in part by a proliferation of cable channels that supposedly allow the presentation of a wide variety of programming and opposing points of view on all topics.

Politics has become inextricably intertwined with the mass media, and in particular, with television. The medium of television has been accused of having negative effects on the American election process, in particular in relation to the increased cost of political campaigns and a focus on candidates' images rather than campaign issues (Perse, 2001). The soaring costs of modern election campaigns is a direct reflection of the price of air time. It is now virtually impossible to get elected to national or state office without an effective media campaign.

The media also detract from American politics by treating political life as a "spectator sport." The sports metaphor of "winning" and "losing" dominates media news and discussion (Croteau & Hoynes, 2003). Media coverage of campaigns focuses on the comparative electability of the candidates rather than where they stand on issues. In response to media pressure, candidates often are presented as personalities (created through a process called *packaging*). Instead of studying and taking a position on an issue, politicians may say something that simply reflects the results of a recent poll or focus group. Of course, citizens need more adequate information to make informed decisions in the voting booth.

The Impact of the Mass Media on Individuals and Families

How the Mass Media Obstruct Well-Being

Images That Hurt and Mislead.   A multitude of studies have been conducted to analyze how the media present people of different genders, sexual orientations, ages, social classes, physical (dis)abilities, and racial and ethnic backgrounds. A majority of viewers and readers believe that media messages, even advertisements aimed directly at them, have little impact. Media critic Jean Kilbourne (1999, p. 27) notes, however, that "the most effective kind of propaganda is that which is not recognized as propaganda."

Affluent white men have historically controlled the mainstream media, which helps to explain why some groups are virtually invisible and others are presented in a negative light. In fact, the pervasiveness of a white perspective in the media is one of its most powerful characteristics. The media do not talk about "white culture," or "the white community," as they do "Latino culture" or "the Black community," suggesting that whiteness is to be taken for granted and the norm against which all other groups are to be measured (Croteau & Hoyes, 2003).

Two questions need to be addressed in relation to vulnerable populations and the media. First, are they there? And second, what is the nature of the images presented? A study conducted in 2000 of television and theatrical roles showed that African Americans received almost 15 percent of all roles cast (which is larger than their proportion in the U.S. population). Latinos, however, and Asian Americans were badly underrepresented (4.9 percent and 2.2 percent, respectively) (Screen Actors Guild, 2001). Native Americans are virtually invisible outside of reruns of old Westerns.

Blatantly racist images—the bloodthirsty savage, or the shuffling, slow-witted black servant—now are rarely found in the media, although that was not always the case. Evidence of stereotyping is more subtle in contemporary media offerings. For example, African Americans accused of crimes are seen being handcuffed and taken into custody while white suspects are photographed standing in business suits next to their attorneys on the courthouse steps (Smith, 1992).

Ganje (1996) discusses a photo of an Anglo woman in a cowboy hat and a young man in traditional Indian dress found in a North Dakota tourist magazine. The picture is accompanied by a caption listing the woman's name, title, and hometown, and the name of her horse. No identifying information on the Native American is given.

Ganje (1996) suggests that the problem of objectifying Native people by using them as characterizations is further exacerbated by the common practice of using Native American images and titles for professional, college, and high school sports teams: Redskins, Braves, Warriors, and so forth. The mascots for these teams are often drawn as exaggerated Indian caricatures, in a fashion similar to the animals that represent their competition.

Not so subtle hurtful images of other minorities appear as well. They include the portrayal of Jewish children as fat and Jewish men as lusting after blonde Gentile women (Woodbury, 1996), the Irish as drunks (Ross, 1996), the Italians as members of the Mafia, Latinos as illegal aliens (Chavez, 1996), and Arabs, Muslims, and Middle Easterners as barbaric and cruel (Jackson, 1996).

The family and heterosexual relationships central to the plots of many films, music videos, and television programs ensure that women are regularly included in media roles (Croteau & Hoynes, 2003, p. 212). Nevertheless, there are about three times as many portrayals of men as women in main character roles; and on news programs, anchors, reporters, interviewers, and invited experts are overwhelmingly male (Huston et al., 1992).

As with other minorities, women in the media are often presented in terms of stereotypes (Kilbourne, 1999). Gender stereotyping is greater in advertising than in programming or feature articles. Ads feature pencil-thin female models with large breasts (often computer-enhanced) with implicit subtexts that suggest that women are subservient to men, if not obviously sex objects. Even images that magazines present of mothers mask the reality of women's lives. "No one tires, no one frets, no one sweats. Motherhood is presented as a series of appealing snapshots" (Schwartz, 1996, p. 78).

Subtle differences in the language that is used signify that a male perspective is the norm in American society. For example, coverage of women's events includes constant *gender marking:* announcers make clear it is the NCAA *Women*'s National Championship Game while the men's version is billed simply as the NCAA National Championship Game (Messner, Duncan, & Jensen, 1993).

As with African Americans and women, the number of portrayals of lesbians and gay men in the media has grown, and their portrayal has slowly become less stereotypical (Croteau & Hoynes, 2003). The first gay male lead of a situation comedy appeared in 1998 with the introduction of *Will and Grace.* That had been preceded, somewhat earlier, by the first lesbian lead character, *Ellen.* On the other hand, although gay characters may be clearly identified, they are not seen in intimate relationships in the same way that heterosexual couples are portrayed.

People with disabilities are largely absent from the media. When they are presented, their disability is the focus of the story. Persons with disabilities very seldom appear as simply another character, either central to the plot or incidental (Makas, 1993; Nelson, 1996).

Overwhelmingly, the society portrayed in American media is middle or upper class. Affluent images are the most obvious in advertising but they also are apparent in television programming (Croteau & Hoynes, 2003). In a content analysis study of media portrayals of the poor, Clawson and Trice (2000) found that African Americans were overrepresented, as were urban dwellers. They also found that the media underreported the proportion of poor people who are employed.

Public Health Issues.   The content of television programs and commercials may have a negative impact on viewers' health. Sports programming, for example, is flooded with soda, beer, pizza, fast food, and snack food commercials. Similar products, with the omission of beer and the addition of candy and sweetened breakfast cereals, appear in commercials in children's programs. Too often, children's distorted understanding of nutrition comes from Saturday morning television (Signorielli & Lears, 1992). Today teens drink twice as much soda as milk; this is the opposite of the pattern that prevailed a generation ago (Kilbourne, 1999, p. 46).

Alcohol and tobacco use are commonly associated with exposure to advertisements and to programs that present drinking and smoking as glamorous activities with no consequences (Perse, 2001). Alcohol is the most frequently advertised beverage in televised sports and the most common type of drink portrayed in programming. Tobacco ads were banned from the broadcast media in 1971; however, through print ads and clever product placement tobacco companies are able to effectively target not only adults but also children. In a recent study, more than one half of a sample of children's animated films featured smoking (Goldstein, Sobel, & Newman, 1999).

The mass media are also effective in promoting the idea that casual sexual activity brings no negative consequences (Lowry & Shidler, 1993). A 2002 study found that "two-thirds of all television shows airing between 7 a.m. and 11 p.m. had some sexual content, and roughly one in seven shows now includes a portrayal of sexual intercourse, either depicted or strongly implied" (Brown, 2002, p. A3). Heavy exposure to sexual content in the media may lead adolescents to believe that sexual activity is common among young people and that premarital sex and extra-marital sex is socially acceptable (Greenberg, 1994).

The Internet.   A threat of a different kind is found in the expansion of the Internet and its uncensored Web sites that not only dispense inaccurate information but also actively promote discrimination and violence against vulnerable groups. The Southern Poverty Law Center reported that there were 405 active U.S.-based hate sites on the World Wide Web in 2001 ("Hate group growth continues," 2002). The Pulitzer Prize winning columnist Thomas Friedman wrote

> because the Internet has an aura of "technology" surrounding it, the uneducated believe information from it even more. They don't realize that the Internet, at its ugliest, is just an open sewer, an electronic conduit for untreated, unfiltered information. Worse, just when you

might have thought you were all alone with your extreme views, the Internet puts you together with a community of people from around the world who hate all the things and people you do. (Friedman, 2002, p. A9)

How the Mass Media Promote Well-Being. Social learning theory suggests that children will imitate behaviors they observe. In addition to the negative effects noted above, studies have shown that young viewers of programs like *Mr. Rogers' Neighborhood* exhibit pro-social behaviors, such as being more cooperative and helpful and talking about their feelings (Friedrich & Stein, 1975).

One of the most positive aspects of the mass media is their potential to capture the nation's attention and support in the struggle against injustice or fraud. The civil rights movement of the 1960s was nurtured through media exposure (Perkinson, 1991). The investigative journalism of Bob Woodward and Carl Bernstein of the *Washington Post* led to the resignation of Richard Nixon when they exposed illegal activities related to the Watergate scandal. Seeing current film footage of the Vietnam War on the evening news was at least in part responsible for a growing antiwar sentiment that shifted public support.

Television offers a cheap source of entertainment for people who cannot afford to go out or are restricted for other reasons. It may be the only connection some older adults or other isolated individuals have to the world outside their homes. TV viewing may be the only activity that some families are able to share.

The importance of the communication function of the media becomes particularly clear during an emergency situation. Residents of communities that experience weather-related disasters (e.g., blizzards, hurricanes, floods, and tornadoes) rely on the media, especially radio and television, for up-to-the-minute information. Now many people across the country also turn to the Internet for breaking news; this was especially apparent on September 11, 2001. Media coverage may facilitate and reinforce societal cohesion, giving listeners and viewers a sense of connection to others who are sharing a common experience (Perse, 2001, p. 62).

Looking Ahead

In these last three chapters we have examined eight social institutions. Each social institution helps to organize social relations in a particular sector of social life.

A concept that describes the hierarchical relationships among people in different social status groups is social structure. We examine social structure as it relates to class, race and ethnicity, gender, gender preference, and disability in the next three chapters.

Key Points

- In the United States, health care is not a right of citizenship, but a commodity that is delivered to consumers through the private market system.

- The medical establishment focuses on microorganisms to explain ill health but does not consider the harmful effects of poverty.

- The forces of organized religion both serve and obstruct the causes of social justice.

- The significant differences among religious groups may lie more in where they fit on the fundamentalist continuum than in other doctrinal beliefs.

- The major trend in mass media for the last 20 years has been a consolidation of ownership within and across mediums.

- The society portrayed in the mass media is not an accurate reflection of reality.

Questions to Think about and Discuss

1. As a country, most of our health care dollars are invested in treatment rather than prevention. What are the implications of this for vulnerable populations and economic policy?

2. Do you believe the United States should provide universal access to health care services?

3. At one time, many religious denominations in this country supported slavery and later, segregation of the races. At the same time, others (e.g., Society of Friends, Unitarians) supported abolition and integration movements. Do you think that formal religion leads or follows social change?

4. In the last week, what stereotypes about race, gender, age, sexual orientation, and disability have you seen in the mass media?

5. What role does advertising play in your decision to buy particular products?

6. Do you think the media are doing a good job of investigating and reporting abuses in government and business?

Recommended Readings

Dershowitz, A. M. (1997). The dangers of the Christian Right—and their Jewish Allies. In A. M. Dershowitz, *The vanishing American Jew* (pp. 143–165). Boston: Little Brown.

Haynes, A. W., Eweiss, M. M. I., Mageed, L. M. A., & Chung, D. K. (1997). Islamic social transformation: Considerations for the social worker. *International Social Work, 40,* 265–275.

Hill, J., & Cheadle, R. (1996). *The Bible tells me so: Uses and abuses of holy scripture.* New York: Anchor/Doubleday.

Kilbourne, J. (1999). *Deadly persuasion: Why women and girls must fight the addictive power of advertising.* New York: The Free Press.

Lazar, B. A. (1994). Why social work should care: Television violence and children. *Child and Adolescent Social Work Journal, 11,* 3–19.

Lester, P. M. (Ed.). (1996). *Images that injure: Pictorial stereotypes in the media.* Westport, CT: Praeger.

Lincoln, C. E., & Mamiya, L. H. (1990). *The Black church in the African American experience.* Durham, NC: Duke University Press.

Norden, M. E. (1994). *The cinema of isolation: A history of physical disability in the movies.* New Brunswick, NJ: Rutgers University Press.

Rodriguez, C. E. (1997). *Latin looks: Images of Latinas and Latinos in the U.S. Media.* Boulder, CO: Westview Press.

Internet Search Terms

Charities	Home health care	Managed care
Fee-for-service	Hospice	Media
Health care	Long-term care	Religion

Part III

Introduction to Social Structure in American Society

Society refers to a group of people who occupy a defined territory and share a common culture. *Social structure* is "the framework that surrounds us, consisting of the relationships of people and groups to one another, which give direction to and set limits on behavior" (Henslin, 2001, p. 97). In explaining how sociologists study social structure, Grusky (1994) suggests that they look at several key concepts. One is how much inequality exists, and another is how rigid the system is, that is how easily individuals move from one level to another. (In this text, we will use the term *inequality* to refer to numeric differences, and *inequity* when inequality appears to be the result of economic or social injustice.) Another concern is how traits present at birth, such as sex, race, and ethnicity influence subsequent social standing. In this section, we discuss social structure in relation to social class, race and ethnicity, and other social statuses (gender, sexual orientation, and disability). The perspectives that were used to explain social institutions will be used again to contribute to a deeper understanding of social structure.

As noted in Chapter 1, a *niche* is defined as a "status occupied by an individual or family in the social structure"; Germain and Gitterman noted that our society is "studded with marginal, stigmatized, and destructive niches that denigrate human beings" (1995, p. 818). Of particular interest to social workers is the fact that some groups suffer from discrimination and oppression while others enjoy unearned privilege. Particular statuses, such as being poor, dark-skinned, female, gay or lesbian, or disabled, are characteristics of "populations at risk." Rather than just viewing these people as victims of oppression, we will identify the diverse strengths that they have.

Chapter 5 covers social stratification (social class). The impact of social class on individuals and families is discussed and special attention is given to the experiences of the poor.

In Chapter 6, we discuss racial and ethnic groups and their characteristics, beginning with the American mainstream (white, middle-class) values, and continuing with the cultural characteristics of various racial and ethnic minorities. We have tried to avoid stereotyping these groups, and readers should understand that no brief, general description applies to all individuals in a population. Also, students should not expect to become "culturally competent" practitioners based on reading a few paragraphs in a HBSE text. In particular, students and practitioners need to remain aware of the *diversity within diversity* of many racial and ethnic groups. In other words, there may be as much variability *within groups* as among them. A list of recommended readings is provided at the end of Chapter 6 to help readers get started in expanding their insight into the experiences of specific racial and ethnic groups.

In Chapter 7, we discuss other social statuses, beginning with gender and sexual orientation, and ending with persons with disabilities. Again, experiences of inequity are presented.

Many beginning social work students feel overwhelmed by the issues of social injustice brought to their attention in Human Behavior courses. Our intention is to make you critical thinkers, not to lead you to despair. As students, as social workers, and as citizens, you will have many opportunities to advocate on behalf of vulnerable populations.

5

Social Stratification

Social Classes in America

Sociologists have yet to reach agreement on how many social classes there are in America and what principal "fault lines" should be used to define them (Grusky,1994, p. 4). Of greater interest to social workers, perhaps, are the issues of how the lifestyles, attitudes, and person-alities of individuals are shaped by their class "locations," and what types of social processes and public policies serve to maintain or challenge discrimination (Grusky, 1994, p. 5).

The idea of social class is one way to describe the inequalities that are present in Ameri-can society. To be a part of a *social class* is to rank with others in terms of wealth, power, and prestige. This ranking separates people into different groups that experience different oppor-tunities in life and different ways of looking at the world. In fact, sociologists argue "no as-pect of life goes untouched by social class" (Henslin, 2001, p. 270).

Inequality is most clearly observed in the amount of wealth held by people in different social classes. *Wealth* refers mostly to real estate and stocks and bonds, including unearned income, such as capital gains and executive bonuses, while *income* reflects salary and wages. Inequality in wealth is much greater than inequality in income. Most of the very rich (those whose net worth is in the hundreds of millions) derive their wealth from inheritance; it is very difficult to become rich simply by working hard.

Class distinctions are often difficult to describe. The following section will explore the most common criteria: wealth, occupation, and education.

At the very top of the *upper class* are the members of the "upper-upper" class, some-times call the "blue bloods," "aristocracy," "old money," or "high society." They comprise less than 1 percent of the total U.S. population. The matter of birth and inheritance separates the "upper-uppers" from the "lower-upper" class, which is also described as "new rich," the "working rich," or the "corporate class." Most of these families have enormous wealth. The "new rich" (about 4 percent of the population) may achieve their status through entrepreneurship, as one of the rare star athletes or entertainers who command exorbitant salaries or as winners of the lottery.

The *middle class,* comprising 40 to 45 percent of the U.S. population, is the one most shaped by education. It also can be broken down into two groups, the "upper middle" and the "average middle." The upper-middle class is comprised of the "elite" professionals, such as physicians, lawyers, and upper-level managers. The average-middle class, on the other hand, is composed of members of the "minor" professions, such as social workers, teachers, and nurses, as well as middle managers and small business owners. The middle class is dependent on salary income rather than inherited wealth and their employment is the source of their status.

We have combined the *lower-middle class* and the *working class* because the distinctions between them are often blurred. People in this class may be skilled laborers, firefighters and police officers, and clerical personnel. Lower-middle-class people who may have been well-paid factory workers now find themselves downsized and working several part-time service jobs in order to maintain their lifestyle. This group constitutes almost one-third of the population.

The *working poor* make up about 16 percent of the population. These are people whose income falls below the official poverty line even though they have jobs, at least part of the year. Their jobs are unskilled and include work such as house cleaning, seasonal farm work, and fast-food service. These workers typically receive minimum wage and no employee benefits.

The *underclass/permanent poor* may be found in isolated rural areas or concentrated in urban centers. They have little or no connection with the job market. Those who are employed typically have temporary positions doing menial labor. Public assistance is their main source of support. About 4 percent of the population falls into this class.

Poverty as a Special Concern of Social Workers

Social workers are particularly interested in the people at the bottom of the socioeconomic scale—those who suffer from poverty. Because of the profession's commitment to social justice, the needs of the poor are a major focus of change efforts.

Deciding what poverty is, is a problem in itself. Americans think of hunger and homelessness as indicators of the existence of poverty. Clearly most people in the world today, and especially people in the United States and other industrialized countries, do not experience deprivation in the same way that the vast majority of people in the world experienced in past centuries or as some people experience today in a few areas of the world. Nevertheless, there are millions of people in this country who do not have enough to eat or adequate shelter. We call this *poverty as deprivation.*

Another view of poverty is *relative poverty* (called *subjective poverty* by some sociologists). This is the sense of deprivation experienced when people compare themselves to others who have more of a society's resources. In other words, it is the everyday experience of inequality.

There are many misconceptions about who "the poor" are. One of the most common is that the poor are primarily people of color and single mothers and their children. Whereas these groups constitute a disproportionate number of those living in poverty, they are not the majority.

As the heads of poor families, women are overrepresented in poverty. This *feminization of poverty* is related to increases in the rates of divorce, separation, and out-of-wedlock births; fathers not paying child support; and a reduction in government benefits. Even when women are employed, they are more likely to live in poverty than male heads of households because they are more likely to be employed in the secondary labor market.

Although whites make up the majority (50.1 percent) of people living in poverty in the United States, people of color are overrepresented among the poor (see Table 5.1), and they are more likely to be among the extremely poor (Dalaker & Proctor, 2000). More than 8 percent of Latinos and more than 10 percent of African Americans had incomes under 50 percent of the poverty line. Asian American households, on the other hand, are underrepresented among the poor, but this reflects the fact that they often have many income earners living together in extended family households.

As a distinct age group, American children are more likely to be poor than adults or the elderly. This holds true across racial and ethnic groups, although poverty rates are higher for African American children and Latino children (approximately 1 in 3) compared to white children (about 1 in 7). Poor children are more likely to die in infancy, to be malnourished, to have health problems, to drop out of school, to be involved in criminal activities, and to have babies while they are in their teens—thus perpetuating the cycle of poverty (Henslin, 2001, p. 278).

Social Mobility

There is an almost universal belief in America that social mobility—getting ahead—is possible for anyone (Tropman, 1989). Nevertheless, despite "rags to riches" stories, mobility within a single generation (change in individual social standing) is usually rare. Most mobility involves movement *within* one class rather than movement *between* classes (Duncan et al., 1998). Social mobility is closely linked to educational attainment.

Historically a woman's social ranking was equated with her husband's. Women also had less opportunity for upward mobility than men because they were limited to occupations

TABLE 5.1   *Poverty by Racial Group Compared to the Proportion in the General Population, 2000*

	Percentage Living below Poverty Line	*Percentage of U.S. Population*
African American	22.1%	12.3%
Nonwhite Hispanic	21.2%	12.5%
Native American	25.9%	0.9%
White	7.5%	75.1%

Source: U.S. Bureau of the Census. *Current population survey: 2001.*

that offered little opportunity for career advancement. When marriages end in divorce, women commonly experience downward social mobility.

White women have gained more from equal opportunity laws and affirmative action programs than have people of color. A loss of manufacturing jobs and other unfavorable economic conditions has slowed down the social mobility of many minority groups.

Although generally one thinks of upward social mobility as a good thing, individuals who change their social class, even through the support and sacrifices of their families, may find themselves painfully alienated from their parents and cut off from their cultural roots (Sennett & Cobb, 1973). For people of color who succeed, there may be additional expectations of "payback" to relatives and communities left behind that make the transition even more difficult (McClain, 1986).

Structural mobility occurs when significant changes in society propel many people up or down the social class ladder at the same time. Generally the trend since 1900 has been toward upward mobility, due to the expansion of the economy and a dramatic increase in average educational attainment. One recent change has been the downward mobility of many middle-class and blue-collar workers due to elimination or exportation of manufacturing jobs (discussed in Chapter 2).

Understanding Social Stratification

Functionalist Perspective

Functionalists believe that an unequal class structure is necessary for a successful society (Davis & Moore, 1945). According to this view, people will work hard only if they receive rewards commensurate with their skills and education. Thus, in order to fill the most important positions in society, the system has to provide exceptional rewards to draw talent away from less important and easier work. Poverty is also "functional" in this view, because it keeps up the demand for low-wage jobs and ensures that the "dirty" work of society gets done, as well as providing a market for cheap goods.

The "rags to riches" myth—the idea that anyone can make it in America—is functional for society because it encourages people to strive for success. It also places blame for failure on the individual.

Conflict Perspective

Conflict theorists argue that inequality is the result of oppression. Social class involves prestige and power, as well as economic inequality. Typically, those with the most prestige, power, and wealth want to protect their privileges, while those without try to get more.

Karl Marx, who developed conflict theory, believed that social class was the primary factor in understanding human behavior. He said that capitalist societies were composed of two classes: the *bourgeoisie,* who owned the means of production, and the *proletariat,* who sold their labor to the owners. Marx saw great inequality in wealth and power arising from the exploitation of the proletariat, which, he argued, made *class conflict* inevitable. Marx predicted that inequality would result in revolution. Contemporary Marxists believe that a lack of class consciousness precludes this revolution.

Constructionist Perspective

Constructionism is about subjective understanding. Americans have a different understanding of social class than do Europeans. One does not see a strong class consciousness in the United States, particularly among laborers. Workers think of themselves as middle class (or aspire to being middle class) and hence lack a sense of shared interests with other low-income people. Vanneman and Cannon, in their 1987 book, *The American Perception of Class,* suggest the problem is that the United States has no leftist political party to organize the lower classes and express their interests.

In contrast to Euro-Americans, who see social status as rooted in wealth and prestige, some minorities may have a different understanding of social class. For example, African Americans view class as detached from income and based instead on identified middle-class behaviors. These behaviors would include maintaining good family relationships, participating in the community, and dressing appropriately (Vanneman & Cannon, 1987, p. 227). Some occupational roles, such as teacher or clergyperson, also contribute to a valued class position. These are examples of how a vulnerable group can set internal community standards for evaluating worth, separate from those of the larger society.

The Impact of Social Stratification on Individuals and Families

Human needs can be divided into several categories. The effects of social class are experienced in all these.

Addressing the Concerns of Daily Life

Housing.   Shelter is a basic human need. Home ownership is the bedrock of the "American dream." The good news is that nationally, levels of home ownership have increased among both white and nonwhite populations. Home equity is an important source of financial security for low-income and minority households. On the other hand, it is difficult for low-income people to pay rent and save for a down payment at the same time. Stocks of affordable housing have declined and rents have gone up. For many of the working poor, housing shelter costs constitute more than 50 percent of their budget. The Department of Housing and Urban Development considers housing affordable if costs do not exceed 30 percent of a family's income. A worker would have to earn $15.21 an hour—$31,637 a year—to afford the average cost of a typical two-bedroom apartment in this country (Armas, 2003). The federal minimum wage is $5.15 an hour.

Many of the working poor are consigned to live in crowded, dilapidated units that may lack insulation, central heat, functional plumbing, and adequate wiring. The ranks of the homeless are increasingly filled with families rather than single adults; more than one-third of the homeless are families with children (U.S. Conference of Mayors, 2000).

Health.   Although white people generally enjoy better health than people of color, the reason appears to be related to socioeconomic status rather than genetic factors (Kiel et al., 1992). There is a negative correlation between health status and economic class; the lower a person's class, the less likely it is that he or she will enjoy good health, at any age. For the very young, the disparity is particularly notable. In the United States, the children of the rich can look forward to a healthy childhood, while those who are poor are as vulnerable as those in many developing countries. The 1999 infant mortality rate for the United States was 7.1 deaths per 1,000 births. Even though this was the lowest rate ever recorded, it was still higher than at least 20 of the other industrialized countries in the world, including Singapore and the Czech Republic (Wright, 2002).

Infant mortality rates within the United States vary considerably from one region to another and among racial groups. At 14.6 deaths per 1,000 births, infant mortality rates for African Americans are more than double the 6.0 rate for whites (Wright, 2002). There may be many reasons for this discrepancy but an important factor is the quality of medical care received by people of different socioeconomic groups.

Clearly, this is associated with being one of the many children in this country who are raised in a poor community or a poor family. "The life chances and quality of survival of infants born in poverty are a reflection of the value that a society places on social justice" (Newman & Newman, 1999, p. 121). Research indicates that negative effects of childhood poverty on well-being continue into adult life (Reynolds & Ross, 1998). (See Figure 5.1.)

Poor people cannot afford to buy fresh fruits and vegetables and other sources of high-grade, low-fat nutrition. Diets high in fat and sugars contribute to various health problems, including obesity, high blood pressure, high cholesterol, and diabetes. And it may be more than a matter of having the cash available for groceries. A study cited in the *New York Times* (Epstein, 2003) reported that there were four times as many supermarkets in white neighbor-

---

FIGURE 5.1 *Infant Health and Well-Being in the United States*

❏ In 1999, 7.6% of infants born in the U.S. were low birth weight, the highest percentage since 1973.

❏ The low birth weight rate for white infants has risen from 5.6% in 1990 to 6.6% in 1999.

❏ The low birth weight rate for black infants was 13.2% in 1999, nearly twice the white rate.

❏ In 1999, 6.4% of Hispanic infants were born with low birth weight.

❏ Research shows that mothers who live in poverty, lack health insurance, and do not receive adequate prenatal care are more likely to give birth to low birth weight babies.

❏ Low birth weight is the factor most closely associated with infant mortality, accounting for 64% of infant deaths.

❏ Although infant mortality rates have dropped for all groups over time, racial and ethnic disparities remain.

    ✔ Among whites, the infant mortality rate was 5.8 per 1,000 births in 1999.

    ✔ Among blacks, the infant mortality rate was 14.6 per 1,000 births.

Sources: Centers for Disease Control and Prevention (2001); National Center for Health Statistics (2001). *Health topic: Infants and children.*

hoods as in black ones, and three times as many bars in poor neighborhoods as in rich ones. Fast food and cigarettes are abundant in inner-city areas, and healthy alternatives are limited.

South Africa and the United States are the only two industrialized countries that don't have some form of national health insurance (DiNitto, 2000, p. 263). The nonpoor usually are insured through group policies with their employers. The working poor are an exception: They are frequently not covered by health insurance at work, yet they earn too much to qualify for Medicaid and not nearly enough to be able to afford to buy insurance on their own. The poor are largely covered by the federal/state Medicaid program; unfortunately Medicaid reimburses providers at such a low rate that many clinics will not accept Medicaid patients.

Many poor people do not have an ongoing relationship with a personal physician. They delay treatment as long as they can, often until there is a crisis, and then must use the emergency room where there are likely to be long waits and no follow-up.

Mental Health.   As is the case with physical health, the lower classes also suffer more from mental health problems. Anxiety and depression are the two most common illnesses. While these often have a genetic component, they are profoundly influenced by the person's social class (Mirowsky & Ross, 1989). Clearly stress is related to mental illness. While the well-to-do also experience stress, they have more resources (e.g., money, staff, time, access to professionals) available to deal with it. People of lower socioeconomic status not only experience obvious stressors, but also must contend with a subjective experience of lack of control over many elements of their lives. A real or perceived sense of control over one's life may be the most important factor in reducing risk for mental illness (Mirowsky & Ross, 1989).

Mental health services are covered less frequently and less adequately by health insurance than are services related to physical needs. Access to private mental health practitioners is correlated with economic status. People with Medicaid are seen in public clinics, often by inexperienced staff or student interns.

Transportation.   Many Americans are dependent on their automobiles because their communities do not provide adequate alternatives. Lack of transportation seriously limits the poor in their efforts to seek and maintain employment. The working poor generally cannot afford cars; even if they can buy a used vehicle, they cannot afford to keep up with insurance and maintenance expenses. They must rely on public transportation, which is nonexistent in rural areas, and offers only limited service in many cities and suburbs. With jobs moving from the center city to the suburbs, the urban poor are even more constrained in their efforts to be self-supporting.

Finances.   No matter what problems people have, access to money makes it easier to cope. Many problems "go away" if funds are available to fix them—paying for car or plumbing repairs, for example, or retaining an attorney, hiring a housekeeper, or scheduling a "mental health getaway." People who have disposable income can focus on making investments and finding tax shelters. The very wealthy are able to live on the interest income from their investments, and never touch the principle or have to work for a salary (Odendahl, 1990).

Most people in the middle class have some money in savings. Many have enough equity in their homes to be able to borrow against it in case of emergencies. They have access to reliable transportation; usually the household owns at least one car. Middle-class parents expect their children to attend college and provide them with "enriching" experiences, such as music lessons or summer camp, and family trips to museums, historic sites, and other educational places.

Most people in the lower-middle class/working class don't have savings accounts. They live paycheck to paycheck. An illness or injury or temporary layoff (or even a car repair or broken-down major appliance) constitutes a financial crisis. They pay 15 to 20 percent more for most goods and services than do the better off, because instead of paying cash, they charge them on their credit cards and then pay interest and late fees. The Federal Reserve estimates that American families owe an average of $12,000 in consumer debt. If a family started with a $10,000 balance at 18 percent interest and made only minimum monthly payments, it would take 56 years to pay off the debt and the interest cost would total $28,079.

The working poor may be described as living on an "economy budget" (approximately 155 percent of the poverty level). They can afford basic necessities if purchased at the lowest possible cost, but must forego the simple pleasures that members of the middle class enjoy: cable TV, babysitters, eating out in a restaurant, going to the movies, vacations that involve staying at a motel, professional haircuts, special lessons or camp or even weekly allowances for the kids (Schwarz & Volgy, 1992).

Typically, members of the underclass/permanent poor have no cash reserves and a negative credit history. They rely on friends and relatives, then title loans and pawn shops for help with short-term financial needs. They may pay interest rates as high as 300, 400 or even 700 percent to get "immediate" tax refunds or to borrow against anticipated paychecks. Often they must rely on in-kind trade-offs (an hour of babysitting in exchange for a ride to the clinic) to make ends meet. Even if they receive a windfall, they cannot get ahead financially because they feel they must help out those who have helped them in the past (Stack, 1997).

Crime.   There is an inverse correlation between income and victimization. The most likely crime victims live in households with incomes under $7,500 (Wright, 2002). For example, low-income women are at higher risk of being physically assaulted by an intimate partner than are women in higher socioeconomic statuses. A shelter worker estimated that 85 percent of her clients returned to battering relationships because of difficulties in finding housing and employment (ACLU, 2001).

A common cliché is that "justice is blind"; the reality, however, is that one's chances of getting arrested, convicted, and sent to prison are significantly shaped by class membership.

> *For the same criminal behavior* [italics in original], the poor are more likely to be arrested; if arrested, they are more likely to be charged; if charged, more likely to be convicted; if convicted, more likely to be sentenced to prison; and if sentenced, more likely to be given longer prison terms than members of the middle and upper classes. (Reiman, 1998, p. 102)

When lower-class status is accompanied by membership in a minority group, the probabilities increase.

Of course the reality is that the rich and powerful also commit crimes. In comparison to the crimes committed by the poor (those included in the FBI Index), white-collar crime is more costly and probably more widespread (Reiman, 1998, p. 111). As noted in Chapter 3, *white-collar crime* is defined as crime committed by people of high social position in the course of their employment or financial affairs (Sutherland, 1940). Examples of white-collar crime are bank embezzlement, business fraud, and antitrust violations. It is estimated that such crime costs the country between $200 billion and $400 billion per year (Henslin, 2001). Reiman (1998) suggests that the criminal justice system often fails to define the unethical and dangerous acts of those who are well off as crimes. He adds that while poverty contributes to crime by creating need, wealth can contribute to crime by unleashing greed (p. 29).

Access to Technology.   In 1999, more than 40 percent of U.S. households had computers (Alter, 1999). Several groups are less likely than others to be Internet users. Race and income are associated with Internet access. As of 2001, 68 percent of Latinos and 60 percent of African Americans did not have Internet access. Three-fourths of households with incomes lower than $15,000, and two-thirds of households with incomes between $15,000 and $35,000 lacked Internet access. The relative disadvantage of children who do not have access to computers and the Internet in a technology-based society will continue to grow. And even when computers are provided in schools, computer proficiencies are not sufficient when basic reading and critical thinking skills are not being taught well because of overcrowded classrooms and inexperienced teachers.

Belongingness and Connections

Family Life and Child-Rearing.   People of similar background tend to intermarry. This is most true for the "upper-uppers." The trend in America in the twentieth century was for religion to become a less important criterion for spouse selection and level of education to become more important. Divorce is more common for members of the lower social classes due to the stresses of job insecurity and unreliable income (Coontz, 1992).

There are significant differences in child-rearing patterns across social classes. According to Kohn (1977), lower-class parents expect their children to conform and comply. Middle-class parents, on the other hand, encourage creativity and independence in their children and tolerate more individuality.

When parents cannot provide child care themselves, upper-class families may hire live-in nannies. Middle-class families use day-care centers. In lower-middle-class and working-class families, spouses seek employment on different shifts to meet child care needs and/or rely on kin to take care of their children.

Connections to the Community and Beyond.   Upper- and middle-class people often socialize with colleagues and coworkers, sometimes using their contacts to advance their careers. Middle-class friendships involve shared interests and leisure pursuits. Working- and lower-class people tend to spend their free time with relatives. Rubin describes these extended family contacts as "the heart of working class social life" (1976, p. 191).

Members of the upper class, particularly wealthy women who are supported by their husbands, may be involved in volunteer work for various nonprofit organizations; in addition to the value of their contribution to the larger community, these activities build important alliances and interpersonal networks (Ostrander, 1980). Higher-income people seem inclined to participate in all kinds of voluntary organizations, including religious ones. For many, religious participation may be an activity used to gain social respectability (Johnston, 1996). Middle-class people are likely to be involved in additional community activities that relate to their children's interests: Scouts, PTA, soccer, neighborhood organizations, and so on.

The volunteer armed forces is disproportionately comprised of members of less affluent classes (Crumbo, 2003). Young people enlist seeking opportunities for employment and education and a chance to move away from communities that offer them limited futures. Some argue that the burden of fighting wars falls unfairly on those who don't have the economic advantages of middle- and upper-income Americans.

Values and Attitudes

There persists a belief that the poor differ from other Americans in the values that they hold. Probably the most notable proponent of this view was Oscar Lewis (1966) who believed that it was the values that the poor embraced that kept them in their lower-class status. According to Lewis, those living in this *culture of poverty* were unable to delay gratification or plan for the future, and these deficiencies were passed from generation to generation. While Lewis blamed the poor for their poverty, other theorists point to structural reasons for their plight. William Julius Wilson (1996), for example, holds that lack of opportunity rather than lack of motivation is the cause of poverty.

Many people believe that poverty is the *result* of negative attitudes and behaviors. Research, however, indicates that poverty may be the *cause* of values and behaviors typically associated with lack of success in American culture. When they have resources available, previously poor people share the same attitudes that other members of society espouse. Even when they are destitute, the poor tend to have the same dreams as the middle class. In his classic 1967 study of "street-corner" men, for example, Elliot Liebow found that his African American male study participants had internalized the values of the majority culture. It was their impoverished environment that prevented their acting on these values.

Looking Ahead

Social class remains a topic that is not easily acknowledged or discussed. By keeping it invisible, the effects of inequality can be attributed to other causes. Americans worry about crime, drug abuse, and family dissolution. It would be a major step toward social justice if the nation's concerns turned to poverty and a host of other problems directly traceable to racism and economic marginality. In Chapter 6, we discuss discrimination based on race and ethnicity, and in Chapter 7, as it relates to gender, sexual orientation, and disability status.

Key Points

- No aspect of life in America is unaffected by social class.

- Women and people of color are overrepresented among the poor.

- Despite a belief in "rags to riches," significant social mobility in America is rare.

- The life chances of an infant born in poverty are a reflection of the level of social justice in any society.

- A recent sociological trend in America has been the downward mobility of many middle-class and blue-collar workers.

• Low-income people share the same aspirations and values as members of the middle and upper classes.

Questions to Think about and Discuss _____

1. Why are poor people in the United States poor?

2. Is socioeconomic inequality an inevitable feature of human life?

3. Is class consciousness a good thing?

4. Think of a problem that could affect people in all walks of life (a kid gets into trouble with the law; a seriously ill family member needs full-time care at home); in what ways does having money make the problem easier to deal with?

5. Discuss why poor families are more likely to be charged with child neglect than wealthier families.

Recommended Readings _____

Allison, D. (1992). *Bastard out of Carolina*. New York: Penguin Books.

Ehrenreich, B. (2001). *Nickel and dimed: On (not) getting by in America*. New York: Metropolitan Books.

Fine, M., & Weis, L. (1998). *The unknown city: Lives of poor and working-class young adults*. Boston: Beacon.

Lind, M. (1995, June). To have and have not: Notes on the progress of the American class war. *Harper's Magazine*, pp. 35–47.

MacDonald, M. P. (1999). *All souls: A family story from Southie*. New York: Ballantine Books.

McClain, L. (1986). The middle-class black's burden. In C. Page (ed.), *A foot in each world: Essays and articles by Leanita McClain* (pp. 12–15). Evanston, IL: Northwestern University Press.

Nelson, M. K., & Smith, J. (1999). *Working hard and making do: Surviving in small town America*. Berkeley: University of California Press.

Newitz, A., & Wray, M. (Eds.). (1998). *White trash: Race and class in America*. London: Routledge.

Internet Search Terms _____

Class structure	Social inequality	Social stratification/mobility
Poverty	Social justice	Social welfare
Privilege	Social status	Socioeconomic status

6

American Society and Cultural Diversity

The United States as a Multicultural Society

Clearly, the United States has a majority, dominant, or mainstream culture, but it supports various minority or subdominant cultures as well. Whereas America has been called a *melting pot,* meaning that different immigrant cultures become blended into a uniquely American culture, it really is more like a tossed salad, where diverse groups retain and share their distinctive subcultural flavors while living together in a larger society. Another term for this pattern is *cultural pluralism.*

Obvious elements of culture are those one can directly observe, such as language, clothing, hairstyles, body adornment, music, dance, or architecture. Culture includes shared beliefs as well as behaviors; culture promotes a sense of group solidarity. It is more than simply the history, language, and traditions of a people, however. "It involves a form of self-conceptualization that the individual assumes or others assign" (Lukes & Land, 1990, p. 155).

Identifying the *majority* or *dominant culture* in America is not just a matter of counting members of different racial and ethnic groups. The dominant culture is a reflection of the power of its members as well as their numbers. The dominant culture is supported by a society's social institutions (discussed in Chapters 2, 3, and 4). For example, the need to learn and use the dominant language (English) is demanded in public schools and by most employers (acting as agents of the political economy). These are powerful forces of socialization and control.

Cultural patterns set some members of society apart from the mainstream. Typically, when we think of *cultural minorities,* recent immigrant groups with distinct languages and traditions come to mind. Mass migration to the United States in the last 30 years, largely from non-European countries, has made America far more multiethnic and multicultural than ever before. But cultural minorities also include groups that have lived here for hundreds of years, such as the African Americans whose ancestors arrived in the holds of slave ships. Native Americans have been living here for thousands of years, long before any of the "majority" population arrived. Because of their physical characteristics (interacting with the forces of discrimination and oppression), these racial minority groups have not been fully assimilated into the mainstream and have instead retained many unique cultural features.

If culture is about a perception of difference, of separation from the mainstream, of shared language, values, norms, and experiences, then there are gay and lesbian cultures and a disability culture as well. From this perspective, the notion of homosexuality or disability is one of group belongingness and distinction from other groups who do not share that identity (Cruikshank, 1992; Gilson & DePoy, 2002). We explore this topic further in the next chapter.

Many minority cultures have recognized *communities*.[1] The community protects the social identity of its members in the face of stigma. Many minorities, including gays, lesbians, and people with disabilities, as well as racial and ethnic minorities, are enriched by their connections to their identificational community and its shared traditions.

The Council on Social Work Education (the body that sets the standards for accreditation of social work schools and programs) requires that content on minority cultures be included in the curriculum. It is important that social worker practitioners not only tolerate or accept differences, but also that they celebrate *diversity* as a source of strength for individuals, families, and our society as a whole.

In the United States, social workers are likely to be professionally involved with individuals and families not only from a variety of social classes, but also with individuals, families, groups, and communities from different ethnic and cultural traditions. Knowledge of these differences and skill in applying it (referred to as *cultural competence*) is a prerequisite for professional practice. There are many implications of cultural differences for social work assessment (Anh, 1994), counseling (Chao, 1992; Falicov, 1998), intervention, and community organization efforts. What is considered normal or even preferred in some cultures may be frowned on or condemned in others. (For example, many Asians find the common dominant American cultural pattern of isolating infants and small children in beds and rooms of their own shocking.)

New Arrivals

According to the 2000 U.S. Census, America's foreign-born population stands at 31 million, an increase of 57 percent over 1990. The proportion of foreign-born is 11.1 percent, or one in nine. Latin Americans and Asians were more than three-quarters of those newcomers.

In addition to cultural differences brought with them from their country of origin, racial and ethnic minorities also differ in terms of the conditions of their arrival and the length of time they have been in the country. There are three categories of new arrivals: immigrants, refugees, and undocumented aliens. *Immigrants* come more or less voluntarily, responding to both "pull" and "push" factors. Sometimes the "pull" factor—dreams of joining relatives and achieving success in a new country—is stronger. At other times, the "push" factor—escaping from squalor and starvation—is stronger. Examples include the Irish fleeing the potato famine in the nineteenth century, or Haitians or Dominicans escaping the pervasive poverty of their island in the twentieth century. *Refugees,* on the other hand, are forced out of their home countries by war or other extreme political conditions. Their lives or liberty would be endangered if they returned. Examples include the "boat people" and other refugees who fled Southeast Asia at the end of the Vietnam War in 1975. Other large groups of refugees have included eastern Europeans, Afghans, Ethiopians, Cubans, and Salvadorans. As a result of their experiences, many refugees suffer from posttraumatic stress disorder. *Undocumented aliens* are, typically, unskilled laborers who are in this country illegally trying to find work.

Although the United States makes the largest financial contribution of any nation to worldwide refugee assistance programs, many nations much smaller than the United States host many more refugees (U.S. Committee for Refugees, 1996). Some groups are not welcomed. For example, although they claim to be fleeing persecution, most Haitians are classified as economic migrants rather than refugees and thus denied asylum and admission to the United States. On the other hand, since the 1950s, the United States has had a tradition of accepting refugees leaving communist nations, such as Hungarians, Cubans, and Southeast Asians, in numbers greater than regulations would ordinarily permit (Schaefer, 2003).

Light-skinned newcomers have the advantage of "blending in" with the majority group in America, at least in terms of appearance, so that they have greater freedom of choice in becoming members of the dominant culture. Beside physical appearance, other factors that make assimilation easier are youth, education, bilingualism, the degree of similarity of the background culture to the mainstream culture, and the availability of cultural mentors (Queralt, 1996, p. 67).

The result of successful efforts to blend is called *cultural assimilation* (also referred to as *acculturation*). Cultural assimilation means being able to function on equal terms with the rest of society by understanding and following cultural norms. Achieving a higher level of integration is called *structural assimilation,* which means being fully accepted into the institutions and social circles of the mainstream group. Some sociologists argue that *marital assimilation* (high rates of intermarriage between members of different groups) is the highest level of integration. Nevertheless, there are many instances of intermarriage (such as U.S. servicemen bringing home Korean brides) that do not reflect evidence of full acceptance of a minority group into the majority society.

The price of full assimilation is the disappearance of the ethnic group. Some people instead choose to be *bicultural,* meaning that as individuals they are able to successfully negotiate more than one culture, usually the dominant one plus their own. Typically these individuals are first exposed to socialization within their minority cultural group and later to significant experiences with the majority culture. This is common for children and adolescents of first-generation immigrants and refugees. Another example is the way African American parents and other caretakers prepare their children to deal successfully with the negative encounters they will be exposed to in the majority culture (see, for example, Carothers, 1990).

Ethnicity and Race.   *Ethnicity* differs from race (and class) in that it is characterized by cultural distinctions—language, customs, values, beliefs, holidays, music, food, dress, and so on. These are characteristics shared by people with a common history, and at one time, a common geographic location. First generation immigrants often live in *ethnic enclaves,* such as Chinatown, the Barrio, Little Havana, or Little Saigon that help them preserve their ancestral culture (Min, 1990).

Religion is often closely tied to ethnicity (see Chapter 4). Membership in a non-Protestant religious group (e.g., Catholic, Eastern Orthodox Christian) has helped to define and preserve the distinctiveness of many white ethnics, such as the Italians, Irish, Poles, and Greeks (Min, 1990; Schaefer, 2003).

Many social workers and sociologists use the term *people of color* to refer to "Americans whose ancestors or who themselves came from non-European areas of the world and who can be identified through the color of their skin" (Stockard, 2000, p. 59). This sounds simple enough, but defining "white," either legally or culturally, has been a lengthy, controversial, and often logically inconsistent process in this country (Nguyen, 2000).

The broad categorizations of "white" and "nonwhite" people is a variant on the questionable practice of identifying and designating different human races (Close, 2000). Even the U.S. Census Bureau struggles with the notion of race; its instructions to citizens say that they are to classify themselves by race as it "reflects common usage not an attempt to define biological stock." The 2000 census gave Americans the opportunity, for the first time, to identify themselves as belonging to more than one race. The majority of Americans (97.6 percent) still chose a single category (Wright, 2002). The most common choice for mixed race was white/American Indian or Alaska Native, followed by white/Asian. A total of 410,285 respondents identified themselves as being a member of three races.

It wasn't until European explorers began encountering people who looked quite different from them that the idea of human *races* developed (Begley, 1995). Generally, racial categories are based on physical characteristics, such as hair texture, facial features, skin color, and body build. At first glance, the categories appear to be self-evident. Nevertheless, when scientists try to categorize people by various other biological factors, such as blood type or biochemistry, they come up with quite different arrangements. For example, using blood type, Germans would be in the same category as New Guineans; using lactose tolerance, Norwegians would be lumped together with the Fulani of Nigeria (Begley, 1995). This, and the fact that race is differently defined in different cultures, suggests that racial categories as people use them every day are social constructs rather than biological realities. Many of the nations of Central and South America, for example, have complex systems of placing people in a myriad of racial groups using a *color gradient* along a continuum from light to dark (Schaefer, 2003). The majority of anthropologists today agree that using the concept of race to distinguish among different populations of humans is meaningless. In fact, most scientists (and many social work students) would argue that there is but one "human race."

On the other hand, biological arguments to the contrary do not keep Americans from using race as a kind of mental shorthand to categorize and stereotype large populations. In fact, being perceived as members of particular races has very real consequences for everyone in American society today. Especially for people of color, race shapes their daily experiences in ways that whites seldom appreciate. The stresses or hassles associated with being a member of a minority group make getting through the day more difficult for many people.

Stress is accentuated by poverty. The dual influence of race or ethnicity and socioeconomic class status is called *ethclass* (Queralt, 1996, p. 3). Ethclass suggests that an individual's life chances, lifestyle, and behaviors are influenced by the interaction of class and race/ethnicity. For example, the life experiences of an African American physician differ substantially from those of an African American nursing home aide.

Inequity and Privilege

A *minority* is a population group that shares a distinctive identity and is subjected to stigma, prejudice, discrimination, and oppression. Minority does not necessarily connote small numbers, but rather refers to a subordinate position in society. For example, women make up a slight numerical majority of the population but are in a subordinate position and therefore are considered a minority. Even when, as a whole, they outnumber whites (as is predicted to occur in this century), people of color will continue to be a minority in the United States.

A *stigma* refers to any physical or social attribute that so discredits or devalues a person's social identity that it disqualifies that person from full social acceptance in the minds of others (Goffman, 1963). One might argue that having dark skin, kinky hair, and a broad, flat nose is still a stigma in American society. In the case of gay men and lesbians, stigma results from a violation of the mainstream cultural norm of heterosexism. In the case of persons with disabilities, stigma results from a violation of mainstream cultural norms of appearance and ability. Using food stamps or a wheelchair is stigmatizing in this society.

Prejudice is a negative *attitude,* often based on an irrational generalization about an entire group of people. A prejudice biases someone against another person simply because the second person is identified as a member of a particular group. An example of prejudice is the belief that all Arabs are likely terrorists.

Discrimination is an unfavorable *action,* or unfair treatment, directed toward members of a minority group. An example of discrimination is refusing to hire someone with a disability even though that disability is unrelated to job requirements. *De jure discrimination* is discrimination that is supported by the law; an example is the practice of segregation that was enforced in southern states before the civil rights movement brought legislative and judicial changes. *De facto discrimination* is discrimination that is the result of institutional discrimination—customary, legal behaviors and policies—that yields discriminatory outcomes, such as segregated neighborhoods and schools. Discrimination can be a reaction to many characteristics, including not only race or ethnicity, but also religion, national origin, gender, sexual orientation, disability, age, and appearance. *Oppression* is "a form of discrimination that is long term, systematic, and institutionalized, (i.e., embedded within key social structures such as the educational system, the health care system, and the criminal justice system)" (Queralt, 1996, p. 171).

Inequalities of status and opportunity are probably inevitable in most societies. *Privilege* is a special advantage or benefit enjoyed by a group or population. When some people are oppressed, others enjoy privilege, regardless of whether they actively support or take part in acts of oppression either collectively or individually. This is an idea that makes many privileged individuals uncomfortable.

Peggy McIntosh (whose work is included in the Anderson and Collins book recommended at the end of this chapter) has listed 46 situations and describes how her experience is "privileged" because of her white complexion. For example, "I can swear, or dress in second-hand clothes, or not answer letters, without having people attribute these choices to the bad morals, the poverty, or the illiteracy of my race. . . . Whether I use checks, credit cards, or cash, I can count on my skin color not to work against the appearance that I am financially reliable" (McIntosh, 1992, p. 80).

Insensitivity to privilege is common in the mainstream culture. Tropman (1989) notes "the belief that one earns one's status is an important value within American society" (p. 7). To deny the effects of race, to espouse *color blindness,* works only if one assumes that being white is no different from being any other color (Kincheloe, Steinberg, Rodriguez, & Chennault, 1998). Whiteness is a socially constructed and hence entirely arbitrary category; nevertheless, to be white is to escape the real and entirely non-arbitrary prejudice, discrimination, and oppression experienced every day in this country by people of color.

Exploring Mainstream and Minority Cultures

It is difficult to describe the commonalities of large populations without oversimplifying. We caution readers to be aware that any discussion of cultural values and practices does not imply that every individual in that culture fully subscribes to its values or norms. It is important to remember that there is much *within-group variability* and that *between-group differences* are often exaggerated. Particularly for social work practitioners, it is important to explore with the individual client the meaning that culture holds for him or her rather than making assumptions based on group membership.

We will now discuss cultural characteristics, beginning with "mainstream" values. Although a number of mainstream social values were identified and described over 40 years ago (Williams, 1957), discussion of white, middle-class values in American social work texts is a relatively recent development. The earlier omission reflects the arrogance of the white middle class in assuming that while other groups were different, their own ways were already understood and accepted as the norm and the best model for successful life in America, with no further need for elaboration. Many whites don't think of themselves as having race or ethnicity. Because the majority of social work students and instructors were white and middle class, this assumption was not questioned.

We believe that even white, middle-class students need to be given the opportunity to reflect on the characteristics of mainstream culture. A discussion of minority cultures follows, with groups listed in alphabetical order.

Mainstream American Values

The mainstream or dominant culture in the United States is usually associated with the white, middle class. Historically, this group has been further defined as white, Anglo-Saxon Protestants (WASPs)—generally understood to be immigrants from Great Britain. The choice of English as the official language of the country and the predominance of Protestantism as the majority religion, as well as the adoption of a legal system based on English law, reflect the power and influence of early English, Welsh, Scottish, Scotch-Irish and Irish Protestant settlers. The dominance of WASPs in this country is "most evident in the widespread use of the terms 'race' and 'ethnicity' to describe everyone but themselves" (Macionis, 2001, p. 368). Gradually immigrant groups from other parts of Europe have joined the WASP majority. (Some students might be surprised to learn of the historic reluctance of WASPs to accept "undesirable foreigners," such as Germans or Irish Catholics, much less Poles, Italians, or Slavs.)

Much of the core of the mainstream American value system has remained intact through its history and continues to receive widespread support (Prigmore & Atherton, 1986) even though some of the values are inconsistent with each other or even contradictory (Achenbaum, 1983; Tropman, 1989; Williams 1957). What is thought of as traditional

American culture is the legacy of white, middle-class Euro-American descendants of immigrants from Great Britain (England, Scotland, and Wales), Ireland, and Germany, with somewhat less influence from immigrants from other countries in Western and Eastern Europe and the Mediterranean coast. Because of their white skin color, similar religious background (Christianity), and frequent intermarriage, members of these immigrant nationalities quickly adopted the mantle of the dominant group (Achenbaum, 1983; Queralt, 1996), shaping and refining U.S. mainstream culture. Among the values that characterize this culture are (1) work; (2) achievement—especially as it is reflected in economic success and material comfort; (3) self-reliance, independence, freedom, individualism, and competition; (4) equality before the law; (5) science, logic, progress, efficiency, and practicality; (6) geographic mobility; (7) informality and directness in personal relationships; (8) moralism; (9) time awareness; and (10) youthfulness and an orientation to the future. (The descriptions that follow are true for many white, middle- and upper-class Americans, but readers should be aware that there are many variations within this group, just as there are among members of minority/nondominant groups. There are also urban/rural differences as well as regional differences [see, for example, Escott & Goldfield, 1991].)

1. The American **emphasis on work** is derived from a Puritan heritage that valued work for its own sake. The *Protestant work ethic* is recognized as the moral basis for the American capitalistic economic system and policies in social welfare. Work for economic gain is considered the way to success, a sign of personal morality, and a moral obligation (see detailed discussion in Chapter 2). Many Americans, for example, feel uneasy in contemplative or meditative activities and prefer to keep busy and "work hard" even in their leisure pursuits. Only paid employment is considered "real" work; for example, lack of respect for the home-making responsibilities of stay-at-home mothers is reflected in welfare reform policies that require poor mothers to leave their young children in day-care centers and seek jobs outside the home.

2. Although education and occupational status are important, **achievement** and success in America are often measured in terms of income and wealth. *Conspicuous consumption*—the purchase of showy automobiles, large houses, fashionable clothing, flashy jewelry, and expensive electronic goods, whose primary purpose is not utilitarian but to impress others—is a modern American characteristic. This trend toward ostentation is a cultural trait promoted even further by a continual stream of media advertising that tells potential customers "you are what you own."

3. Linking the values of work and individualism is the American myth of **self-reliance.** The tendency of Americans to overestimate what they have accomplished on their own and deny how much they owe to others began with the fiction that colonial Europeans built a land of plenty out of nothing. In reality, however, the abundant concentrations of game and edible plants they found were not natural but had been developed by the stewardship of Native Americans (Kehoe, 1999). Recent research demonstrates that as they moved westward across the continent, American pioneers were dependent on a large network of kin, neighbors, religious institutions, and government programs (especially the availability of free or low-cost land).

Belief in the importance of **individual rights** over those of the family, the collective, or community life is a particularly American characteristic (Martin & O'Connor, 1989), although its roots can be found in the emergence of capitalism in seventeenth century Europe. Neither contributing to the group's well-being nor placing the group's well-being first are fully appreciated in American mainstream culture; this contrasts markedly with cultures where the extended family or group is more valued than the individual, as is common in many minority communities (Ewalt & Mokuau, 1996).

Closely linked to the values of achievement and individualism is the American value of **competition.** This competition occurs not just between sports teams or business enterprises, but also among individuals in groups and even within families. Americans tend to have a dichotomous point of view: If you are not a winner, you must be a loser. There is little sense that with less competition and more cooperation, everyone could "win."

4. The Constitution of the United States was written by men who deliberately rejected the traditional social stratification of Europe; consequently, Americans have a formal **commitment to equality** before the law (Prigmore & Atherton, 1986). Over time, this concept has been extended to mean an equality of opportunity for social and economic rewards. Nevertheless, for many years, rewards not resulting from achievement, such as those associated with being white or male, were considered the natural order of things. Unfortunately the continuing prevalence of sexism, heterosexism, institutional racism, and other group superiority themes mars the American societal ideal of true equality.

5. Perhaps because they live in a relatively young society, Americans tend to value **science, logic, progress, efficiency,** and **practicality.** Technical efficiency tends to be valued for its own sake, rather than for what it serves to accomplish (Prigmore & Atherton, 1986). Aesthetics, sentimentality, spirituality, mysticism, rituals and ceremonies, and reverence for the past are often viewed with skepticism. There is a belief that all problems can be solved by science, eventually if not right away.

6. Americans have always valued geographic **mobility.** Historically, they pressed toward new frontiers. Now individuals and families move far away from home to take advantage of educational or career opportunities, or simply to seek adventure and change. Adults are often separated from their families of origin by thousands of miles. Even married partners sometimes work and live in different communities or even different states.

The profusion of private automobiles reflects a uniquely American obsession with being able to go where and when one wants, without having to rely on or to consider anyone else. In the 1950s and 1960s, public financing in America was gradually redirected from the streetcars and trolleys that served urban and poor families and used instead to provide new roads for suburban commuters and their cars, promoting urban sprawl, traffic congestion, and pollution. (This is discussed further in Chapter 8.)

7. Americans prefer **informality** and **directness** in personal relationships. With its emphasis on equality, American society downplays the use of honorifics and formal titles ("your majesty," "your lordship"). Americans often ignore both age and occupational or social status, addressing relatives, close friends and distant acquaintances, or even strangers by their first names. Direct confrontations about misunderstandings and frank discussion of feelings are not uncommon. There is a sense that "honesty" in relationships is more important than diplomacy.

8. As a group, mainstream Americans have traditionally expressed their **morality** by responding promptly to calls for help and giving generously to victims of disease and natural disasters. Typically, this humanitarianism is expressed in organized and impersonal ways through large charities, such as the Red Cross or the United Way. To most Americans, humanitarianism means private support for those who are in trouble "through no fault of their own" (Prigmore & Atherton, 1986).

On the other hand, many members of the American mainstream are quick to blame chronically poor people, minorities, and other client populations for causing their own problems and are reluctant to support them through government programs or direct subsidies, even though the country as a whole possesses enormous wealth (Jansson, 1993; Prigmore & Atherton, 1986; Ryan, 1976). The American cultural obsession with self-reliance and independence may come at a significant cost to others in the family, group, organization, or community. A narrow Puritanism that seeks reasons for disapproval of others leads to viewing the dependent state of the chronically poor and unsuccessful as *immoral* rather than simply unfortunate. The core value of individual responsibility exonerates society and confirms personal failure for those who cannot or do not reach success (Day, 1996).

9. The American mainstream group puts a **premium on time,** which they schedule, regulate, and measure exactly (Queralt, 1996, p. 76). In fact, involvement in friendships, and religious or other community activities are often evaluated in terms of the time investments they require. (Minority groups in American tend to be much more flexible in their use of time.)

10. Whereas minority groups in the United States value and respect the aged, mainstream America has had a long-standing **infatuation with youth.** In a quickly changing society, the aged often have not been appreciated for their wisdom and experience.

African Americans

African Americans are the now the second largest minority group in the United States (ranking just below Hispanics/Latinos in the 2000 census). There are more blacks here than in any African country except Nigeria (Wright, 2002). The ancestors of most African Americans came to this country not as immigrants or refugees but as slaves. Scholars disagree about the relative impacts of the cultural practices of their West African homelands, the slave experience, and more recent oppression as victims of institutional racism, on their current condition. Recent black immigrants have come from Haiti, Jamaica, Trinidad, and Tobago in the Caribbean and from Nigeria, Ethiopia, Ghana, and Kenya in Africa.

Beginning in 1910 and lasting through the 1920s, there was a *Great Migration* of African Americans from the rural South to northern industrial cities, such as Chicago, New York, Philadelphia, St. Louis, and Detroit (Walker, 1999), where they were employed in meatpacking, auto-making, and steel-manufacturing plants. Nevertheless, the majority of African Americans still live in the South.

Scholars disagree about how much African culture survived the slave experience, although clear vestiges of folklore, religion, language, and music remain (Schaefer, 2003). Strong kinship bonds are the most enduring cultural strength that black Americans brought with them from the African continent (Hill, 1999). African Americans are more likely than whites to care for children and older adults in an extended family network. Data show that grandparent caregivers are most commonly African American grandmothers (Fuller-Thompson, Minkler, & Driver, 1997; Wilhemus, 1998). The African American family remains a resilient and adaptive social institution despite threats of poverty and discrimination (Billingsley, 1992).

After the family, religion is the most important aspect of the lives of most African Americans (Sudarkasa, 1997). African Americans are more likely than whites to attend church, with most of them being members of Baptist or Methodist congregations (Schaefer, 2003). For more than 300 years, African American churches have served as community centers, promoting the rights of black Americans and providing both informal and formal social services (Walker, 1999). A variety of non-Christian groups have also exerted a great influence on African Americans. About 30 percent of regular participants in U.S. mosques (Muslim houses of worship) are African Americans.

In addition to the values discussed above, Hill (1999) has also made a strong case for both achievement and work orientation being central to African American culture. He argues that the majority of low-income African Americans prefer work to welfare, and that black parents at all income levels hold high educational aspirations for their children. Schaefer (2003) reports that working-class blacks indicate a greater desire for their children to attend college than do working-class whites and that poor blacks are more likely to be working and have more than one wage earner in a family.

As with all minority groups, one has to consider the effects of class as well as race in understanding African American culture. In his book *The Declining Significance of Race,* sociologist William Julius Wilson (1978) stated that while racism remains an important factor, social class is becoming more central to understanding the African American experience. He suggests that there are two quite different African American worlds: one that is located in the inner city where joblessness and violence define everyday life and the other, located in the middle-class suburbs where good jobs, good schools, and opportunity prevail (1996). We would add another category of experience: African Americans living in rural areas of the South, where school districts have few resources and jobs are disappearing.

Arab Americans

There have been several waves of Arab immigration to the United States, the first beginning around 1875. Arab Americans trace their ancestry to more than a dozen countries in the Middle East. Most Arab countries are predominantly Muslim, but not all people from the Middle East are Arabs, nor are all Arabs Muslims.[2] An Arab American is a person descended from people whose native tongue was Arabic and who lived by Arab cultural traditions and values; a Muslim is a follower of the Islamic religion and may or may not be Arab (Banks, 1997).

The U.S. Census Bureau doesn't use an Arab American classification. In terms of racial classification, the government has at different times considered Arab immigrants to be Asians, "other Asians," Caucasian, white, black, or "colored" (Suleiman, 1999); socially, Arabs are treated as "honorary whites" or "white but not quite" (Samhan, 1999). They are not considered a minority for purposes of employment or housing. Most Arab Americans identify themselves by national origin rather than by ethnicity. Because there is so much diversity among Middle Eastern immigrants, they lack a sense of solidarity (Walbridge, 1999).

There are about three million Arab Americans in the United States ("100 questions and answers about Arab Americans," 2001). Many live in metropolitan areas in or near Los

Angeles, Detroit (Dearborn), New York (Brooklyn), and Chicago. On average, Arab Americans are better educated and have higher median incomes than other Americans (Suleiman, 1999).

Asian Americans and Pacific Islanders

Asian women married to American service men account for a large proportion of Asian immigrants since 1950. The Immigration Act of 1965, which came into full effect in 1968, abolished discrimination based on national origin and ended 40 years of Asian exclusion. Min (1995a) reports that the proportion of immigrants from Asia increased from 9 percent in 1960 to 25 percent in 1970, and then to 44 percent in 1980. In fact, the majority of Asian Americans (except for those of Japanese descent, and a smaller proportion of Chinese and Filipino Americans) are foreign-born immigrants.

According to the 2000 census, Asian Americans are the fastest growing minority in the United States. In the 1980 census, 3.4 million Americans identified themselves as Asians and Pacific Islanders. This was a doubling of the 1970 census figures due primarily to the influx of Southeast Asian/Indochinese refugees (Vietnamese, Laotians, and Cambodians [Kampucheans]) after the fall of Saigon in 1975. By 1990, the numbers had doubled again, due largely to high rates of fertility (Gold, 1999). The major nationality groups of Asian Americans are: Chinese, 24 percent; Filipino, 21 percent; Asian Indian, 13 percent; Vietnamese, 11 percent; Korean, 10 percent; Japanese, 10 percent; and other, 10 percent (Lee, 1998).

Asian Americans are probably the most internally diverse American minority group, representing immigrants from many different nations and cultural traditions. Unlike Latinos, the majority of whom are Catholic and Spanish-speaking, Asian Americans represent a wide variety of religions and languages. Asian Americans also experience diversity related to generational differences (Min, 1995a). Japanese Americans, for example, distinguish among the *Issei* (first generation), the *Nisei* (second generation), the *Sansei* (third generation), and the *Yonsei* (fourth generation) and their experiences in this country (Nishi, 1995; Schaefer, 2003). Koreans distinguish the *ilchomose* or "1.5 generation"—the middle-aged, bilingual and bicultural adults who accompanied their parents to the United States when they were young (Schaefer, 2003).

South Asians—people from India, Pakistan, Bangladesh, and other South Asian countries—are culturally similar to one another and distinct from other Asian groups (La Brack, 1999; Min, 1990). South Asians experienced British colonization and thus many of these immigrants grew up speaking English, at least in school. Typically, those who arrived in America since 1995 are educated, wealthy, and urban; many are professionals in the health care field, although others are employed in service industries as cab drivers, motel managers, and convenience store clerks (La Brack, 1999; Mogelonsky, 1995). Most South Asian immigrants share a religious identity either as Hindus or as Muslims (Min, 1990).

The most recent wave of Asian arrivals—the Southeast Asian/Indochinese refugees—included not only Vietnamese, Cambodian [Kampucheans], and Laotian nationals, but also many ethnic Chinese from all three countries and various highland tribal peoples, such as the Lao Hmong and Yao and the Vietnamese Montagnards. These refugee groups had a wide range of educational and economic backgrounds and a variety of languages and cultural traditions. Unlike immigrants who move voluntarily, most of the Indochinese refugees survived a stressful, frightening, and often traumatic escape to freedom. Whether they left by sea or by land, the casualty rate en route was high; this was followed by months or even years of waiting in overcrowded refugee camps in Thailand or Malaysia. Many of those who had education and high-status occupations in their native countries had to accept menial jobs in their new American home due to language difficulties or lack of professional credentials. Those whose background was agrarian also had to struggle to adjust to modern American society.

An additional difficulty for this refugee population resulted from their initial dispersal across every state in the country. They were spread out because they had no previous family ties, there were no established ethnic communities, and per federal policy, they had to be "matched" with the congregational sponsors who agreed to take responsibility for them. Refugees later moved on (*secondary migration*) to areas where the climate was more familiar and other members of their nationality had gathered. Thus, many Indochinese are now found in California, where more than half of Vietnamese Americans, Cambodian Americans, and Hmong Americans live (Gold, 1999). There are also settlements of Vietnamese in Texas and adjoining states. On the other hand, many refugees remained closer to their original sponsors; for example, there are large groups of Cambodians in Massachusetts, Rhode Island, and Washington, and Hmong in Minnesota and Wisconsin.

Many of the cultural values of immigrants from East Asia (i.e., people from China, Japan, and Korea) are derived from Confucianism. This philosophy promotes filial piety and other strong family-centered values. For example, one value is to bring honor to the family, or at least to avoid bringing it shame—in fact, this is a central tenet of Asian cultures (Ho, 1987). Confucianism also teaches the importance of maintaining social harmony. Harmony in interpersonal relationships is accomplished through tact, delicacy, and politeness. Contributions to unity and harmony are more valued than are competitive success or self-satisfaction. Confucianism emphasizes a hierarchical or vertical ordering of society on the basis of age, gender, and social position, specifically in the relationships between father and son, husband and wife, older brother and younger brother, "ruler" (e.g., teacher, employer) and "subject" (e.g., student, employee). These prescribed roles suggest formal styles of interpersonal interaction and contribute to the smooth interaction of individuals in different social roles.

Although they have many cultural similarities, because of the brutal acts of occupying Japanese forces in Manchuria and Korea before World War II, Chinese and Korean Americans tend to limit their contact with the Japanese American communities (Min, 1995a). Also, because most Korean Americans are Christians, their communities are often united through congregational connections, unlike Chinese Americans who are more likely to follow traditional Asian religious practices.

Many Confucian values are shared by refugees from Vietnam, Laos, and Cambodia. Buddhism has also shaped Asian values across the centuries. Buddhism stresses the values of self-control, humility, generosity, mercy, and of cultivating a correct lifestyle. People from many Asian backgrounds are exceedingly reluctant to brag, or even to claim individual credit for their accomplishments. Westerners may be surprised at this level of humility.

Asian Americans are often called the *model minority* since they seem to have succeeded economically, socially, and educationally without significant confrontations with the white majority. They have the lowest divorce rate of any racial group in the United States (3 percent), the lowest unemployment rate (3.5 percent), the lowest rate of teenage pregnancy (6 percent), and the highest household family income (Schaefer, 2000).

Some sociologists contend that the economic success of Asian Americans can be attributed to cultural values: self-discipline, an emphasis on formal education, and a strong entrepreneurial spirit. Asian Americans are well-represented in professional occupations and in the small business sector (Min, 1995b). Many new Asian immigrants have accepted menial jobs and lived as groups in tight quarters until they saved enough to buy a small business such as a gas station, green grocery, convenience store, laundry, or restaurant where all members of the family helped out. Although family income for Asian Americans is higher than that of whites, this reflects larger household size and the fact that more family members are employed.

Pacific Islanders were first recognized in the United States census in 1980; they were listed separately from Asians in the 2000 census (Wright, 2002). The largest subgroup is the native Hawaiians, followed by Samoans, Guamanians, and Tongans (Kitano & Daniels, 1988). There were fewer than one million people who identified themselves as at least part Hawaiian or Pacific Islander, and fewer than 400,000 who identified themselves as being only Hawaiian or Pacific Islander in the 2000 census (Wright, 2002). Most Pacific Islanders live in Hawaii or in cities on the west coast of the United States (San Francisco, San Diego, Seattle, and Los Angeles). As with many other minority cultures, there is a common theme of group affiliation, collective effort, and commitment to family (which is broadly defined, and may be as large as a whole village) (Mokuau & Tauili'ili, 1992).

Filipinos are the second largest Asian American group in the United States (Schaefer, 2000). The Philippines is the most Westernized country in Asia (Min, 1995a). A Spanish colony beginning in the middle of the sixteenth century, the Philippines came under the control of the United States in 1898, after the Spanish-American War. The earliest Filipino immigrants arrived as American nationals. In 1934 the islands gained commonwealth status and gained full independence in 1946, but residents lost their unrestricted immigration rights. Filipinos learn English in public schools and immigrants to the United States adjust easily because of the strong American cultural influence in their homeland.

Latinos

According to the Census Bureau, as of July, 2001, Latinos outnumbered African Americans in the United States, making them the largest minority group (Armas, 2003). This increase was due to high immigration and birth rates. Latinos now make up 13 percent of the population and Blacks make up 12.7 percent.

Latinos can be divided along lines of class, race, and culture. The dominance of the Spanish language, however, as well as a growing political awareness, is a unifying force among Latinos. About 85 percent of Latinos in the United States speak Spanish (Wright, 2002); others speak Portuguese, French, Dutch, English, and Native American languages, such as Quechua, Mayan, Aymara, and Guarani, and Creole dialects (Castex, 1994).

Hispanic is the term that has been used by the federal government for this minority group since 1978. The term *Latino/a* is preferred by most academics. It is geographically more accurate because it refers to people from Central and South America rather than to people from Spain. It is more politically correct because it affirms Latinos' native, precolonial identity. Neither Latino nor Hispanic is a racial classification. Latinos may identify themselves racially as white, Native American, Black, or a mix of two or more of these. Latinos usually don't refer to themselves as Hispanics or Latinos, but rather identify with their country of origin (e.g., *Cubano, Mejicano*) (Schaefer, 2003). The term *Chicano/a* is commonly used in the West and Southwest for Latinos of Mexican descent who were born in the United States. *La Raza* (which literally means "the people") connotes pride in pluralistic Spanish, Native American, and Mexican heritage (Schaefer).

Between 1980 and 2000, the Hispanic/Latino population in the United States more than doubled from 14.6 million to 35.3 million, according to Census Bureau data (Wright, 2002). The majority (58.5 percent) trace their roots to Mexico. The next most numerous in terms of national origin are Puerto Ricans (9.6 percent) and Cubans (3.5 percent). (These proportions are quite different in different parts of the United States; for example, persons of Cuban origin account for nearly 70 percent of all Latinos in the greater Miami area and 30 percent of Dade County's population [Grenier & Perez, 1999]). There has also been an erratic flow of Latinos from Central America, fleeing wars and economic hardship in El Salvador, Nicaragua, Guatemala, and Honduras (Duignan & Gann 1998; Jones & Rhoades, 2001).

The largest numbers of Latinos live in California and Texas, where they make up almost a third of the population (Wright, 2002). Other states that have high proportions of Latinos in their populations include New Mexico (42 percent), Arizona (25 percent), Colorado (17 percent), Florida (16 percent), New York (15 percent), New Jersey (13 percent), and Illinois (12 percent) (Wright, 2002). Overall, they are a young population, with 30 percent of Latinos being under the age of 15.

The majority of Latinos now living in this country have come in the last century, with most arriving since World War II. The pattern of immigration for the major Latino groups differs considerably. More immigrants have come to the United States from Mexico than from any other country in the world (Maciel & Herrera-Sobek, 1998). Nowhere else in the world do two countries with such different standards of living share a relatively open border; the proximity of Mexico encourages immigrants to maintain strong cultural and social ties with their homeland (Schaefer, 2000, p. 297). All Puerto Ricans are U.S. citizens and as such move back and forth freely between their island and cities on the U.S. mainland. More so than other Latinos, they sustain multiple familial, economic, and social relations that span geographic borders (Falicov, 1998, p. 40). Most Cuban Americans came to this country as refugees, either as a result of the Cuban Revolution in 1959, during the program of "freedom flights" between 1965 and 1973, or as part of the Mariel boatlift in 1980. They were cut off from their culture of origin for a long time, but that is changing now.

The church is the most important formal organization in the Latino community (Schaefer, 2000, p. 318). A growing number of Latinos in the United States are joining Protestant churches, especially conservative evangelical or Pentecostal denominations (Falicov, 1998; Schaefer, 2000). Many of the churches are small—often with Spanish-speaking leadership—and offer a strong sense of community (Schaefer, 2000). Nevertheless, the vast majority of Latinos (more than four out of five) remain committed to Catholicism, and Latinos account for over a third of Roman Catholics in the United States (Duignan & Gann, 1998; Feagin & Feagin, 1999). Traditional Catholic rituals continue to be practiced in Latino homes. A particular focus of devotion is the Virgin of Guadalupe, the patron saint of Mexico. Falicov (1998, p. 146) describes her as "the perfect fusion of indigenous Aztec and Catholic European elements, the only brown-skinned virgin who validates the promise of Catholicism for indigenous persons [throughout Latin America]. In fact the Virgin of Guadalupe has many Indian names. "

Most Latinos embrace *familism,* or pride and closeness in their families. Familism is generally seen as a good thing, as extended families provide support throughout an individual's lifetime. On the other hand, it may have the negative effect of discouraging youths from taking advantage of opportunities that would separate them from their families (Schaefer, 2003).

Latino immigrants contribute much to the U.S. economy (Maciel & Herrera-Sobek, 1998). Undocumented workers in particular take jobs that are unattractive to most American citizens. Their work is critical to American agriculture, and they also contribute to the construction, restaurant, and textile industries. The American rich probably benefit most from Latino immigration through the services of underpaid gardeners, maids, cooks, and nannies. Undocumented Latino workers pay local and federal taxes for which they will never claim any benefits (Maciel & Herrera-Sobek, 1998, p. 6).

Latinos have earned a reputation as employees who are hardworking and less likely to complain about poor working conditions or low wages than native-born workers (Engstrom, 2001). The commitment of Latinos to work differs from that of middle-class Anglos who are likely to be motivated by individual achievement. Latinos are more likely to toil because they firmly believe they have to for the survival and well-being of their children and other loved ones. On behalf of their families, they are willing to work overtime and/or moonlight, and accept grueling, exploitative working conditions (Falicov, 1998, p. 124). Although some people have expressed concern about *remittances* (monies that immigrants send back to their country of origin, which measure in the tens of millions of dollars), they probably represent "a small price to pay for the human capital that the United States is able to utilize in the form of the immigrants themselves" (Schaefer, 2000, p. 123).

Native Americans

In this text we will use the term *Native Americans* to refer only to those indigenous peoples who are native to the North American continent. (Thus Native American Indians and Alaskan Natives are included, while Hawaiians, and natives of Guam and Samoa, who also are indigenous peoples, were covered under the Pacific Islander category). Although some Native Americans prefer the term *American Indian* (Lewis, 1995), because of the many legitimate objections to its use (see Herring, 1999) we will use the former term. Other terms sometimes used for this population include *First Americans* or *Original Americans* (Herring, 1999), and *First Nations* (Kehoe, 1999). The federal Bureau of Indian Affairs defines a Native American as a person whose "blood quantum" (i.e., proportion of native blood) is at least one-fourth (LaFromboise & Graff Low, 1998). Native Americans tend to identify as members of a nation first, and then as members of a tribe (Herring, 1999). The term *tribe* is usually a designation for a kin-based group without political institutions (Smith, 1986). A *nation* has a political organization (Winthrop, 1991).

At the time of their arrival in the Americas, European immigrants confronted hundreds of Indian tribes speaking over 700 different languages (Schaefer, 2003). Many of the indigenous cultures were quite advanced, incorporating agricultural practices such as irrigation and crop rotation, ceramic and metallurgical crafts, networks of roads and bridges, and democratic forms of governance (Bruchac, 1991; Creamer & Haas, 1991; Day, 1996; Pascua, 1991; Stuart, 1991). Because of a lack of natural immunity to European diseases, as well as the genocide perpetrated by European invaders, their numbers were reduced to about one-twentieth of the original population, yet more than 300 distinct Native American tribes survive in the lower 48 states and more than 200 in Alaska (Lewis, 1995). There are over four million U.S. citizens who identify themselves as at least part Native American or Alaskan native (Wright, 2002). Almost half of these Native Americans live in the West. Native Americans make up about 8 percent of the population of Oklahoma, and 6 percent of the population in Arizona and Montana (Kehoe, 1999). Nevertheless, because almost half of Native Americans live in rural areas and one-third in just three states (Oklahoma, California, and Arizona), most citizens are hardly conscious of a Native American presence in the United States (Henslin, 2001).

Native Americans are a heterogeneous population. They vary in terms of their language, residence (rural, urban, reservation), level of acculturation, and socioeconomic status (Herring, 1999).

Even though there are differences among tribes, including the degree of acculturation to the mainstream, there are some common characteristics of most Native American cultures. For example, Native Americans, like many other minorities, take a more collective view of society than the mainstream culture. That includes emphasis on the importance of the family, group primacy, and noncompetitiveness. Individual achievement is not valued. Other important Native American values include sharing, cooperation, noninterference, harmony with nature, a present—and cyclical rather than linear—time orientation, and a deep respect for elders (Herring, 1999, p. 72).

Although many Native Americans have been converted to Christianity, many still continue to embrace elements of their traditional religions as well. Native American religious beliefs have been misrepresented and oversimplified as "worship of Mother Earth." In fact, First Nations peoples had many prophets and philosophers and fairly complex cosmologies that generally conceptualized a female reproductive power gifted to women and plants (Kehoe, 1999). Native American groups have tried without success to limit tourist access to numerous sacred sites that lie on public lands, such as the Grand Canyon, Zion, and Canyonlands National Parks (Schaefer, 2000).

Native Americans, like other minority groups, are reasserting pride in their ancestry. This is reflected in a surge in self-identified membership (almost quadrupling between the 1960 and 1990 censuses) and interest in restoring native languages to daily use (Kehoe, 1999). Although it has meant the loss of better educated Indians from the reservations, the movement of Native Americans to urban areas has contributed to the development of intertribal networks. *Pan-Indianism* refers to intertribal social movements in which several tribes unite in common identity (Schaefer, 2003). *Powwows,* featuring dancing, singing, and competitions, are organized events that celebrate Native American culture and educate the general public (Parfit, 1994).

White Ethnics and Jews

The term *white ethnics* refers to immigrants from Europe whose language and culture have differed from white Anglo-Saxon Protestants. About half the U.S. population falls in this category, although many of the earlier arrivals have intermarried and now describe themselves as having a mix of ethnic/national backgrounds—or simply as "white" or "American." Many early European immigrants (the Dutch, Germans, Scandinavians, and Scotch Irish) spread out across the frontier and became farmers and landowners. Later immigrants were more likely to stay in large cities, where the first generation or two remained in ethnic "enclaves" with people from similar backgrounds. There are still high concentrations of Poles in the Chicago and the Milwaukee areas, for example (Pacyga, 1999). Even with the movement of white ethnics to the suburbs, full assimilation into the mainstream culture was curtailed by the revival of ethnic pride in the 1970s (Radzilowski & Radzilowski, 1999).

Schaefer (2003) reports that the ethnicity currently embraced by English-speaking whites is typically *symbolic*. Symbolic ethnicity does not influence what people do or say, or whom they befriend or marry. It may, in fact, be more a result of experiences in the United States than practices brought from the home country. Some "ethnic" foods and "ethnic" celebrations actually began in the United States. Participating in boisterous St. Patrick's Day parades and drinking green-colored beer, for example, is not how March 17th is observed in Ireland.

Jews are considered by some sociologists to be another white ethnic minority group. They entered America in several waves, beginning before the Revolution, peaking with the immigration of German Jews between the 1820s and 1870s, and again with Jews from Poland, Russia, Romania, and other parts of eastern Europe between 1880 and 1924 (Shapiro, 1999). Despite a long history of anti-Semitism in Europe, most Jews who migrated to the United States came voluntarily until the early 1930s when the tyranny of the Third Reich in Germany drove many from Germany, Austria, Poland, and Hungary (Schaefer, 2003). In the 1960s and 1970s, many Jews came from Israel, the Soviet Union, and Iran. From the beginning, Jewish immigrants settled in eastern port cities, including Newport, Philadelphia, Charleston, and Savannah. In the early twentieth century, approximately half of America's Jews lived in New York City (Shapiro, 1999). Another wave of immigration, particularly from Eastern Europe, occurred after World War II.

The United States ranks first among nations in the number of Jewish citizens, accounting for 46 percent of the world's Jewish population (Schaefer, 2003). Jewish organizations report that there are 5.8 million American Jews; it is estimated that only 3.8 million of these are religiously observant (Wright, 2002). There are three major divisions of Jews in the United States: Orthodox (the most traditional), Conservative, and Reform (the most liberal). Differences are reflected in how traditional rituals are accepted and practiced. Most Jews tend to identify themselves as a cultural or ethnic minority rather than as a religious one (Lipset & Raab, 1995). They express their identity through a variety of political, cultural, and social activities (Schaefer, 2003). For observant Jews, acts of fasting, eating permitted foods, and the study of the Torah and the Talmud assume more importance.

The acculturation pattern of Jews has been an exception to the general American pattern of success of partnering with conservative political values. Although on the whole Jews are prosperous, they are politically liberal rather than conservative (Shapiro, 1999). This political orientation may derive from their own long history of oppression that leads them to empathize with other disadvantaged groups. Another explanation is the Jewish religious principle of *tzedekah*, the obligation of the fortunate to help individuals and communities in difficulty.

The tendency of young Jews to marry outside their faith community, and the reluctance of their non-Jewish partners to convert are contributing factors to the numeric decline of this ethnic group (Lipset & Raab, 1995, p. 44.) This trend is also hastened by low birth rates. The fertility rate of Jewish women is 10 percent less than the level needed for population replacement (Goldstein, 1993). Nevertheless, the Jews' sense of family, community, and heritage remains strong.

Understanding Race and Ethnic Inequity

Discrimination against minorities is no longer legal in this country. While overt expressions of blatant racial and ethnic prejudice diminished considerably in the last half of the twentieth century, prejudice has not disappeared. Modern prejudice is more subtle, more diplomatic, less conscious (Myers, 1999). It may be that people are trying to suppress unpopular, unwanted thoughts (Devine, 1995) or that they have learned when and where prejudicial talk is not acceptable (Southern Poverty Law Center, 1995).

Myers (1999) summarizes how social psychologists explain prejudice using *social identity theory.* A number of experiments have supported the basic assumptions of this theory: (1) we find it useful to put people into categories, (2) we associate ourselves with certain groups (*ingroups*), and (3) we compare our groups to other groups (*outgroups*) with a built-in bias favoring our own groups. When resources are scarce and people feel insecure and frustrated, prejudice and discrimination toward outgroups is more common. Members of outgroups may be *scapegoated* for negative social and economic conditions over which they have no control, because it is safer to blame them than to confront people in power.

Functionalist Perspective

Functionalists believe that society works smoothly when everyone shares the same culture. Particularly in times of scarcity or external threat, a sense of "we-ness" (ingroup membership) promotes social solidarity. Functionalists therefore are apt to support strict limits on immigration and encourage minorities to pursue cultural assimilation. That is, they encourage minorities to adopt the dominant group's language, values, and norms and stifle their own.

The functionalist perspective emphasizes how the parts of society are structured to maintain its stability. Schaefer (2003, p. 16) notes that, from a functionalist point of view, racist ideologies provide a moral justification for maintaining a society that routinely deprives certain groups of their rights; racist oppression discourages subordinate people from questioning their lowly status; racist myths encourage support for the existing order; and racist beliefs relieve the dominant group from having to address the economic and educational problems faced by subordinate groups. Functionalists are not necessarily in favor of inequality; but their perspective helps to understand why such systems exist.

Conflict Perspective

The conflict perspective is often used to examine relationships among racial and ethnic groups because it readily accounts for the presence of tensions and competition (Schaefer, 2003, p. 17). Conflict theorists argue that powerful people use prejudice and discrimination to hold onto their status in society by exploiting minorities. This is especially true in economic arenas. Elites benefit when intergroup racial or ethnic prejudices keep nonelites from recognizing the interests they share in common. Capitalists exploit racial and ethnic strife to produce a *split labor market,* that is, workers are divided by race and ethnicity across job statuses (Bonacich, 1972). For example, in some places, higher status (and cleaner) jobs, such as driving trucks or other pieces of equipment, are reserved for whites, while people of color pick up the trash, spread the asphalt, or shovel the dirt. There is an implied threat, held over the heads of white workers, that should they strike, minority workers would be called on to fill their positions. The consequence, according to conflict theorists, is that the working class is divided, and white workers perceive the source of their insecurity in minority workers rather than in the capitalist owners of the company.

Portraying the problems of racial and ethnic minorities as their fault rather than recognizing the role of the dominant majority in developing and/or maintaining the system is sometimes listed as an example of *blaming the victim* (Ryan, 1976). Conflict theorists remind policy makers that the ultimate responsibility for social problems must rest with those who possess the power and authority to change them (Myrdal, 1944; Southern, 1987).

Some conflict theorists also are concerned about the role of the United States in promoting a *brain drain,* or the immigration of skilled technicians and professionals away from their homes in developing nations where their talents are desperately needed. In addition, when immigrants from other countries are recruited to fill prestigious and financially rewarding positions in America, the United States can continue to ignore native-born members of subordinate groups who could be trained to enter these fields (Schaefer, 2003).

Constructionist Perspective

Our discussion about the difficulty of defining "race" should make clear the role of social construction in race and ethnic relations. Constructionists focus on how labels produce prejudice. Labels lead to *selective perception* or *filtering*; that is, they cause people to pay attention to certain things and ignore others. For instance, if you believe that all Asian American students are good at math, you may fail to take note of one who excels in art.

"Racial and ethnic labels are especially powerful. They are a shorthand for emotionally-laden stereotypes. The word 'nigger' is not a neutral term"(Henslin, 2001, p. 331). Neither is "chink," "spic," or "kike." (Scornful terms also applied to other minority groups: "femi-nazi," "fag," "cripple," and "retard" are examples of hurtful labels). Such words arouse powerful emotions and get in the way of rational discourse.

Constructionists stress that people are not born with prejudices. Instead children are socialized to be prejudiced through interaction with others, particularly those who hold strong prejudices themselves. Americans live in a society where racial and ethnic stereotypes abound.

American Society and Experiences of Racial and Ethnic Inequity

All racial and ethnic minorities have been victims of discrimination and oppression at some time in American history. This continues today, most notably in underrepresentation in elective office, discrimination in housing and employment, lack of access to medical care, overrepresentation in the criminal justice system, and everyday hassles. Historically the experiences of minority groups may have been different, but all suffered tremendously. Social cohesion within these groups, including the development of mutual aid organizations and advocacy groups, has greatly facilitated their advancement in American society. The groups are presented below, roughly in chronological order in relation to when they arrived in North America.

The Experience of Native Americans

Although the United States never had an official policy of deliberate extermination of Native Americans, use of the term *genocide* is not inappropriate in describing the actions of many white settlers (invaders) and their government that decimated the populations of indigenous people on the North American continent (Henslin, 2001; Kendall, 2001; Macionis, 2001). The nature of the violence perpetrated against Native Americans (see Bordewich, 1996) as well as the total disregard for human life might bring one to question which people were more deserving of the label "savage." The U.S. government broke treaty after treaty as it forced Indian nations to move westward to clear land for white settlers. Over half of the Cherokee Nation died on the *Trail of Tears,* the path of their forced removal from the southeastern United States to Indian Territory (Oklahoma). According to the Bureau of Indian Affairs, today Native Americans control only 2 percent of the country's land area. Native Americans were not granted U.S. citizenship until 1924 and could not vote in Arizona or New Mexico until 1948. Until 1930, Native American children were separated from their families and sent to special Indian boarding schools where they were forced to wear Anglo-style clothing and punished when they used their native languages. Many schools serving Native American children today fail to meet their needs; there are few Native American teachers and the curriculum is presented from a Euro-American perspective. Underenrollment is a problem at all ages, from elementary school through college. *Internal colonialism* is the term used to describe treatment of subordinate groups like colonial subjects by those in power (Schaefer, 2003, p. 176).

Native Americans are the most disadvantaged minority in the United States. They rank behind others in income, employment, housing, nutrition, and health, and ahead of others in alcoholism, school dropout rates, infant mortality, delinquency, and mental illness (Atkinson, Morten, & Sue, 1998; Henslin, 2001; Kendall, 2001; Thio, 2000). Native American men living on reservations have an average life expectancy of less than 45 years and women less than 48 (Churchill, 1994). Although tourism and the sale of crafts are important sources of employment on many reservations, they do not improve the tribal economy significantly (Schaefer, 2003, 187). Many Native Americans work for the government, especially in the Bureau of Indian Affairs, but also in state and local governments and for the military.

The Experience of African Americans

Between 1619 and the 1860s, more than 500,000 Africans were brought to America as slaves (Walker, 1999). At the beginning of the Civil War, only 10 percent of blacks in America were free. Although not all slaves were brutally treated, most lived under barely subsistence conditions, and it was not uncommon to separate slave families at the auction block. The slave family had no standing in law; marriages between slaves were not legally recognized. *Slave codes*—laws developed to restrict the rights of slaves—varied from state to state, but there were common themes (Schaefer, 2003, pp. 205–206). Violators were whipped, mutilated, or killed. It was against the law to teach slaves to read or to give them a book, including the Bible.

Slavery ended in the South with the Emancipation Proclamation in 1863. The Thirteenth Amendment to the Constitution, ratified in 1865, permanently abolished slavery and the Fourteenth Amendment, ratified in 1868, further protected the rights of former slaves. Nevertheless, African Americans soon lost ground. In 1896 the Supreme Court ruled in *Plessy v. Ferguson* that "separate but equal" treatment was acceptable. *Jim Crow* laws in the South enforced segregation in housing, employment, education, and all public accommodations and severely limited independent African American economic initiatives. *Lynching* (killing someone without a legal trial, usually by hanging) was a mechanism of terror used to keep black citizens from challenging the status quo. There may have been as many as 6,000 lynchings in this country between 1892 and 1921 (Feagin & Feagin, 1999). Another mode of control was arbitrary arrest and imprisonment; often black convicts were used to provide free labor for both public and private enterprises. African Americans were denied the right to vote through a series of quasi-legal obstacles, such as poll taxes and literacy tests.

Although they have always participated in the defense of this country, African Americans have not received equal treatment in the military until relatively recently. The first casualty of the American Revolution was a black man, Crispus Atticus. Five thousand African Americans served continuously during the Revolutionary War; African Americans made up 10 percent of Union forces and 25 percent of the Union navy in the Civil War and some 500,000 African Americans served overseas in World War II (Walker, 1999). Ironically, African Americans in the U.S. military were assigned to segregated units until the middle of the twentieth century.

In 1954 in *Brown v. the Board of Education,* the Supreme Court voted unanimously that "separate but equal" was unconstitutional under the Fourteenth Amendment. The following year, blacks in Montgomery, Alabama, launched a boycott against that city's segregated bus system, led by Dr. Martin Luther King, Jr. Largely in response to the massive demonstrations, marches, sit-ins, and boycotts that followed, Congress passed the Civil Rights Act of 1964, the most far-reaching legislation to protect the rights of African Americans since the abolition of slavery.

Although legally protected from discrimination, African Americans still suffer from the effects of prejudice. Examples of mistreatment include the deliberate burning of African American churches and *racial profiling* (individuals targeted for unfair treatment by law enforcement personnel because of the color of their skin). As noted in Chapter 4, African Americans receive less adequate medical care than do whites. Some argue that stress resulting from racism and suppressed hostility exacerbates hypertension among African Americans, a critical factor in higher mortality rates from heart disease, kidney disease, and stroke (Schaefer, 2003). When elected to office, African Americans serve predominantly black districts and communities; they hold a disproportionately small share of elective and appointive offices in the United States (Schaefer, 2003, p. 256).

The Experience of Asian Americans

More than 300,000 Chinese migrated to California between 1850 and 1880, where most performed manual labor for the railroads and for farmers and miners (Yung, 1999). As "aliens" and persons of color, they had no legal rights and could not become citizens. They were often the target of mob violence—beaten, burned, shot, and lynched (Day, 1996; Yung, 1999). Racism, and fears on the part of white laborers that they would lose their jobs to Asian immigrants, led to the passage of the Chinese Exclusion Act in 1882 (Yung, 1999). This legislation was repealed in 1943, probably because the Chinese were American allies in World War II.

The need for cheap laborers was soon filled with Japanese immigrants, who began coming to the West Coast somewhat later than the Chinese. As they became more successful, they faced similar legal restrictions on their rights. In 1922, the U.S. Supreme Court ruled that foreign-born Japanese could not become American citizens because they were not Caucasians. Early in World War II, Japanese Americans, including many who were born in this country, were rounded up and moved to ten *internment camps* located in remote rural areas in seven states, taking only what they could carry with them (Tamura, 1999). All people on the West Coast of at least one-eighth Japanese ancestry were taken to assembly centers for transfer to evacuation camps; two-thirds of the evacuees were U.S. citizens (Schaefer, 2000). This has been described as "one of the most vicious forms of discrimination ever sanctioned by U.S. laws" (Kendall, 2001, p. 323). Italian Americans and German Americans faced no similar persecution, even though the United States was at war with Germany and Italy as well as Japan. The Japanese internment camps were closed in 1946. Four decades passed before the American government issued an apology to these Japanese Americans and their descendents and paid $20,000 to each internment camp survivor, beginning in 1990 (Takaki, 1993).

Asian Americans remain greatly underrepresented in politics, far below the level for blacks and Latinos. Outside of Hawaii, there is no congressional district where Asian Americans make up the majority of voters (sometimes due to discriminatory apportionment schemes) (U.S. Commission on Civil Rights, 1992, p. 159). Although in comparison to other groups, Asian Americans appear to be doing well financially, there are several arguments that this is not an accurate reflection of their true economic status. They are concentrated in large cities such as San Francisco, Los Angeles, New York, and Honolulu, where living expenses are much higher than in the rest of the country on average. Min (1995b) reports that individual income is lower for Asians when compared to whites with the same level of education, and that they are "severely underrepresented in high-ranking executive and administrative positions" in corporations and government (pp. 42, 48).

The Experience of Latinos

Mexican immigrants were able to move freely across the border until 1924 when the U.S. Border Patrol was created. Being concentrated in the Southwest, Latinos were isolated politically and therefore fell victim to exploitation by landowners (Jansson, 1993). Employers often played on the fears of undocumented workers that they would be found and deported in order to stifle protests against harsh working and living conditions. Cesar Chavez successfully developed and led the United Farm Workers in the 1960s to demand legislation that would protect farm workers, including their right to unionize.

Increasing numbers of Spanish-speaking immigrants and their growing political, social, and cultural visibility has led to a resurgence of anti-Latino sentiment. This has been reflected in welfare reform legislation at both the national and state levels that led to drastic cuts in benefits previously available to immigrants, as well as efforts to make English the "official language" in many states (Gutierrez, 1999).

Persistent patterns of discrimination and the restructuring of the U.S. economy both have contributed to the low economic position many Latinos occupy in American society. Recent research indicates that the gap between the average earnings of Mexican immigrants and native workers is growing (Gutierrez, 1999). This negative trend appears to apply also to comparisons of the income of native-born American citizens of Mexican descent to that of whites.

The Experience of White Ethnics and Jews

The country experienced a surge of immigration from Europe between 1880 and 1914; most immigrants settled in large Eastern and Midwestern cities. They comprised 40 percent of the population of the 12 largest cities in the country, and another 20 percent were second generation descendants; 60 percent of the industrial labor force was foreign born (Brody, 1980). Living conditions were abysmal: Wages were below subsistence level, working conditions were hazardous, crowded tenements were firetraps, and food poisoning was common (Jansson, 1993).

Although most were fair-skinned, immigrants from Ireland, Italy, Greece, Russia, and Eastern Europe faced discrimination based on their religions (Catholicism, Eastern Orthodoxy, and Judaism). Strong anti-Catholic sentiment had already developed in the mid-1800s when roughly one and one-half million Irish peasants immigrated to America to escape the 1845–1848 "potato famine" in their homeland. Indigenous Americans believed they were being overrun, and anti-Catholic, anti-Irish, and anti-immigrant sentiment often emerged (Jansson, 1993). *Nativism* refers to beliefs and practices that favor native-born citizens over immigrants (Schaefer, 2003, p. 107). By the 1850s, nativism, especially in opposition to Roman Catholics, became an open political movement in America.

Both Irish Americans and Italian Americans have been subjected to institutionalized discrimination in employment, with "swarthy" Italians being perceived as "not white" (Gambino, 1975; Sensi-Isolani, 1999). Mob violence directed against Catholic individuals and their property was common across the country between 1834 and 1854 (Schaefer, 2003). More than 30 Italians were lynched in the South between 1890 and 1910 (Sensi-Isolani, 1999). Anti-Catholic suspicion was clearly still an issue in the 1960 presidential election when John F. Kennedy ran for office. Hostility expressed toward white ethnics is often taken less seriously than is racism. For example, "Polish jokes" are less likely to be challenged than are anti-black remarks.

The civil rights of Jews were affected by the "blue laws" enacted by states and cities forbidding a variety of activities on Sunday. (Jews celebrate the Sabbath from sundown Friday to sundown Saturday.) Eastern European Jews who immigrated in the early twentieth century were associated with Marxist politics and hence faced discrimination on that account. Jews were excluded from many premier colleges and universities, as well as clubs, hotels, and some residential neighborhoods (Thio, 2000). They also faced discrimination in employment (Selzer, 1972). Prejudice and discrimination against Jewish people is called *anti-Semitism.* The most virulent and overt anti-Semitism in the United States occurred in the 1920s and 1930s. Well-known American leaders, such as Henry Ford and Charles Lindbergh, contributed to anti-Jewish sentiment by lending credence to fraudulent conspiracy theories (Schaefer, 2003).

For nearly 2,000 years, various Christian groups argued that all Jews share in the responsibility of the Jewish elders who condemned Christ to death and have used that to justify anti-Semitism (Schaefer, 2000, p. 388). Nevertheless, much anti-Semitism has more to do with negative attitudes related to stereotypes of Jews as overly clannish and financially shrewd (Wilson, 1996). In past centuries, Jews were often used as scapegoats and blamed for all kinds of problems, including plagues; at one time they were expelled from the nations of Spain, France, and England.

The *Holocaust* refers to the state-sponsored systematic persecution and annihilation of Jews by Nazi Germany and its collaborators. Between 1933 and 1945, two-thirds of Europe's total Jewish population was killed, including 90 percent of the Jewish population of Germany, Austria, and Poland (Schaefer, 2000, p. 390). Several European governments and leading financial institutions collaborated in hiding assets that had been stripped from Jewish citizens (McGeary, 1997). Despite irrefutable evidence and the testimony of eyewitnesses and survivors, a very small but vocal group of people called *Holocaust revisionists* claim that the events of the Holocaust never happened. Jews have been, and continue to be, targeted by the Ku Klux Klan and neo-Nazi skinheads. The *Anti-Defamation League of B'Nai B'rith* tracks reported anti-Semitic incidents, which include harassment, threats, assaults, and vandalism.

The Experience of More Recent Arrivals

The most common problems facing many immigrants and refugees in the United States today are language barriers, lack of employment opportunities and/or labor market exploitation, lack of educational attainment, lack of access to health care, cultural differences, and racism. Those who lack immigration documents (illegal aliens) are particularly likely to experience problems.

Many Middle Eastern immigrants and American citizens of Middle Eastern descent experience unwarranted prejudice, suspicion, and discrimination (McCarus, 1994). More than a third of Arab Americans report that they or their family members experienced discrimination because of their ethnicity, both before and after the events of September 11, 2001 (Telhami, 2002). Soon after the tragedies, at least five individuals were killed just because they appeared to be Arab or Muslim[3]; and another 1,000 physical and verbal attacks on Middle Easterners and South Asians were reported in a period of eight weeks (Ahmad, 2002). This was accompanied by government acts of racial profiling of "Muslim-looking" individuals at airports and detention or deportation of immigrants from Muslim countries.

Negative media portrayals of Arabs and Muslims and omissions or inaccuracies in history and social science texts in North American schools have contributed to perceptions of these peoples as inferior, uncultured, threatening, anti-American, anti-Christian, anti-Semitic, greedy, cruel, and barbaric (Banks, 1997; Muscati, 2002). Apparently, it is socially acceptable in America to feel hostile toward Arab Americans (Majaj, 1999).

Looking Ahead

While members of ethnic and racial minorities often grow up in supportive communities, members of other minority populations do not have that advantage. In Chapter 7, we will examine the experiences of women, sexual minorities, and persons with disabilities. Each of these populations has found ways to cope and succeed despite experiences of discrimination and oppression.

Key Points

- The United States is a pluralistic society.

- The dominant culture reflects the power of the majority group.

- A *minority* is a population group that shares a distinctive identity and is subjected to prejudice, discrimination, and oppression.

- Many members of minority cultures have learned how to function successfully in both their own and the majority culture; this is called *biculturalism.*

- Although there is little biological evidence to support the idea of different human races, the consequences of socially constructed racial categories are very real.

- American mainstream values emphasize work and individualism.

- Members of minority cultures have strong kinship bonds. They are more likely than members of the mainstream culture to emphasize collective goals that support the well-being of the family and the community.

- All racial and ethnic minorities have been, and many continue to be, victims of discrimination and oppression.

Questions to Think about and Discuss

1. Of the six questions answered by everyone for the 2000 U.S. census, two were about race and ethnicity. Do you think the government should continue to classify people by their race and/or ethnicity? Why or why not?

2. Describe the oppression and/or privileges you experience. Which are easier to talk about?

3. How would your life be different if your skin were significantly lighter or darker?

Recommended Readings

Abrahamson, M. (1996). *Urban enclaves: Identity and place in America.* New York: St. Martin's Press.

Alba, R. D. (1990). *Ethnic identity: The transformation of white America.* New Haven, CT: Yale University Press.

Anderson, M. L., & Collins, P. H. (Eds.). (1992). *Race, class and gender: An anthology.* Belmont, CA: Wadsworth.

Angelou, M. (1993). *Wouldn't take nothing for my journey now.* New York: Random House.

Begley, S. (1995, February 13). Three is not enough: Surprising new lessons from the controversial science of race. *Newsweek,* pp. 67–69.

Brodewich, F. M. (1996). *Killing the white man's Indian: Reinventing Native Americans at the end of the twentieth century.* New York: Doubleday.

Chow, E. N., Wilkinson, D. & Zinn, M. B. (1996). *Race, class & gender: Common bonds, different voices.* Thousand Oaks, CA: Sage.

Close, E. (2000, September 18). What's white anyway? *Newsweek,* pp. 64–65.

De Anda, R. M. (1996). *Chicana and Chicanos in contemporary society.* Boston: Allyn & Bacon.

Dershowitz, A. (1997). *The vanishing Jew.* Boston: Little, Brown.

Espiritu, Y. L. (1997). *Asian American women and men: Labor, laws, and love.* Thousand Oaks, CA: Sage.

Flores, W. V., & Benmajor, R. (Eds.).(1997). *Latino cultural citizenship: Claiming identity, space, and rights.* Boston: Beacon Press.

Gabaccia, D. R. (1998). *We are what we eat: Ethnic good and the making of America.* Cambridge, MA: Harvard University Press.

Gambino, R. (1975). *Blood of my blood.* New York: Doubleday/Anchor.

Gates, L. (1996). *Colored people: A memoir.* New York: Alfred Knopf.

Geha, J. (1990). *Through and through: Toledo stories.* St. Paul, MN: Graywolf Press.

Golden, M., & Shreve, S. R. (1995). *Skin deep: Black women & white women write about race.* New York: Anchor Books.

Gutierrez, D. G. (Ed.). (1996). *Between two worlds: Mexican immigrants in the United States.* Wilmington: Scholarly Resources Publishers.

Haines, D. W. (1997). *Case studies in diversity: Refugees in American in the 1990s.* Westport, CT: Praeger.

Hein, J. (1995). *From Vietnam, Laos and Cambodia: A refugee experience in the United States.* New York: Simon and Schuster.

Hong, M. (Ed.). (1993). *Growing up Asian American: An anthology.* New York: William Morrow.

Kadi, J. (Ed.). (1994). *Food for our grandmothers: Writings by Arab-American and Arab-Canadian feminists.* Boston: South End Press.

Kumar, A. (2000). *Passport photos.* Berkeley: University of California Press.

Liu, E. (1998). *The accidental Asian: Notes of a native speaker.* New York: Random House.

Mahler, S. (1995). *American dreaming: Immigrant life on the margins.* Princeton, NJ: Princeton University Press.

McCunn, R. L. (1988). *Chinese American portraits.* San Francisco: Chronicle Books.

Min, P. G., & Kim, R. (Eds.). (1999). *Struggle for ethnic identity: Narratives by Asian American professionals.* Walnut Creek, CA: Altamira Press.

Nguyen, A. (2000, July 31). The souls of white folk. *The American Prospect,* pp. 46–49.

Riley, P. (1993). *Growing up Native American: An anthology.* New York: William Morrow and Company.

Stack, C. (1974). *All our kin: Strategies for survival in a black community.* New York: Harper & Row.

Tatum, B. D. (1997). *Why are all the black kids sitting together in the cafeteria? and other conversations about race.* New York: Basic Books.

Weatherford, J. (1988). *Indian givers.* New York: Faucett.

Weatherford, J. (1991). *Native roots.* New York: Crown.

Internet Search Terms

Acculturation	Ethnocentrism	Population distribution
Assimilation	Ethnocultural diversity	Pluralism
Biculturalism	Individualism	Privilege
Cultural competence	Immigration policy	Race
Cultural diversity	Immigrants	Racism
Cultural pluralism	Legal/illegal alien distinctions	Refugees
Discrimination	Melting pot	Social group identity
Diversity	Migrant workers	Social inequality
Ethnic identity	Minority groups	Social justice
Ethnic relations	Multiculturalism	Undocumented immigrants
Ethnicity	Multiracial	

Endnotes

1. There is a confusion that derives from two common uses of the word *community,* one as a town or neighborhood, and one as "sense of community" or a social network among people who share some interest about a social issue, personal characteristic, or organizational/associational tie. The latter, *identificational communities,* are mental constructs. Often, identificational communities develop in response to experiences

of discrimination and oppression. The boundaries of identificational communities may or may not be consistent with neighborhood boundaries where minorities live.

2. The majority of Arab Americans, and almost all of those whose families have been in this country a long time, are not Muslim, but Christians whose ancestors came from Lebanon or Syria (Waldbridge, 1999). Recent Arab immigrants are more likely to be Muslim. Islam is the second largest religion in the United States (after Christianity), but only about one-fourth of the Muslims in the United States are Arabs (Banks, 1999). Many American Muslims come from countries in South Asia (Pakistan, Indonesia, and Malaysia) (Telhami, 2002). There is also a large and growing number of African American Muslims in this country.

3. Two of the victims were Sikh Indians, one was an Indian Hindu, one was Pakistani, and one was an Egyptian Coptic Christian (Ahmad, 2002).

7

Other Social Status Groups

In this chapter, we introduce the concept of social status and examine how it applies to three disadvantaged groups: women, gay men and lesbians, and people with disabilities. Social workers often join with these populations in advocacy efforts toward social justice.

Social Status

"A *status* is a socially defined position in a group or society characterized by certain expectations, rights, and duties" (Kendall, 2001, p 163). The term *status* is commonly associated with high or prestigious positions in society, but sociologists use the term to describe any specific position. For example, each year students preparing for professions begin internships with different organizations. They are expected to be prompt, dress appropriately, pay attention to their supervisor or mentor, and bring what they learn back to the college classroom for discussion. The status of "student intern" is similar across many disciplines. While "student intern" is a temporary status, many other social statuses are long term or permanent.

    Ascribed statuses are social positions that are conferred at birth or assigned later in life, based on characteristics over which an individual has little or no choice. Sex and race are good examples of ascribed statuses. Other kinds of statuses are more within the control of the individual; they are assumed voluntarily as a result of personal choice or direct effort (Kendall, 2001). These are called *achieved statuses*. Being a college graduate is a good example of an achieved status. Some statuses in American society carry more power and privilege than others. These include being white, male, heterosexual, and nondisabled. Other valued statuses are afforded to those people who belong to "mainline" Christian religious denominations, are youthful, attractive, tall and slim, well-educated, professionally employed, articulate, wealthy, or famous.

The concepts of prejudice, discrimination, oppression, and privilege that were discussed in relation to race and ethnicity in Chapter 6 also apply to the ascribed statuses of gender, sexual orientation, and disability. Nevertheless, the experiences of women; gay men, lesbians, bisexuals, and transgendered (GLBT) persons; and people with disabilities may be quite different from those of racial and ethnic minorities. Members of racial and ethnic minorities have the advantage of being part of families and communities that can help them in the process of developing a positive self-identity and in negotiating the demands of the dominant culture (Carothers, 1990; Lukes & Land, 1990). It is highly unlikely, on the other hand, that a gay man or a person with cerebral palsy will grow up in a family and community made up of other gay men or people with cerebral palsy. For these individuals, the first part of the socialization process will come from the dominant culture, complete with negative stereotypes. They are not isolated from society, but they are isolated from each other. Although there are supportive identificational communities of sexual minorities and people with various types of disabilities, most individuals must seek them out as they become adults. (The deaf community is an exception, as you will see later in this chapter.)

The situation for women, for the most part, is even more complex. They live in a society that is *patriarchal*—meaning that men hold the power to make formal decisions and determine policies. Although women may join together for support and advocacy, the majority of them owe at least a part of their social standing to the efforts of fathers and husbands. Just as homosexuals must interact with heterosexuals and people with disabilities must interact with the nondisabled, women interact daily with males, both in formal situations and also in intimate relationships as partners and caregivers, as daughters, sisters, wives, and mothers.

Gender

The terms *sex* and *gender* are often used interchangeably. In our discussion, *sex* will refer to biological differences, and *gender* will refer to those differences that are culturally constructed and socially transmitted.

Among the real biological differences between the sexes are chromosomal and hormonal differences that determine primary and secondary sex characteristics (such as reproductive organs, breast size, and facial hair). Additional biologically supported differences include sex differences in three behavioral domains: physical aggression, visual-spatial ability, and sexual behavior (Lippa, 2002).

Although biology determines many aspects of sex-related behaviors, society and culture define gender. "Gender is a human invention, like language, kinship, religion, and technology; like them. . . . Gender organizes social relations in everyday life as well as in the major social structures, such as social class and the hierarchies of bureaucratic organizations" (Lorber, 1994, p. 6).

Children are socialized by their families, schools, peers, and the mass media to conform to culturally approved gender expectations (*gender roles*). Even in this age of increasing attention to gender equality, girls are still encouraged to look pretty, nurture others, play cooperative games, and be "nice." Boys are encouraged to be tough, competitive, independent, and achievement-oriented.

It is often difficult to separate out what is biological from what is cultural. No human being has ever been raised without the presence of gender socialization and therefore purely biological influences on behavior cannot be isolated for study. While the possibility for a biological explanation of some behaviors cannot be ignored, these behaviors are always expressed in a social environment (Unger & Crawford, 1996).

Research on sex and gender differences is still being conducted; what is clear, however, is that the context of women's lives is different from that of men's. As already noted, America (like virtually all other societies) is patriarchal (Pratto, 1996). Just as racial and ethnic minorities experience inequities in a society that is dominated by whites, women experience inequity in a society dominated by males. Possible explanations for this are explored in the next section.

Understanding Social Stratification and Gender

Functionalist Perspective.   From a functionalist perspective, a division of labor between men and women, particularly in the family, is the natural order of human society. A complementary set of roles, with men providing economic support and making decisions, and women providing care and emotional support, ensures that important societal tasks will be fulfilled (Parsons & Bales, 1955). Conservative politicians and their supporters promote this traditional interpretation of "the family" as essential to the stability of American society. Despite the growing presence of women in the labor market, the ideology of patriarchy continues to operate in many spheres.

Conflict Perspective.   Conflict theorists remind us that, in most societies, differences exist between men and women in the areas of physical, economic, and political power. A colleague of Karl Marx, Friedrich Engels (1884/1902) said that capitalism intensifies male domination because it creates more wealth, which in turn gives greater power to men as owners of property or primary wage earners. Evidence of male domination in contemporary society is reflected in economic and political-related inequities, and gender-related violence.

Constructionist Perspective.   As noted above, gender is socially constructed. Language and concepts of gender are intertwined. For example, not long ago the term *mankind* was used to refer to all members of the human race—leaving many women feeling excluded. The use of *inclusive language* is now encouraged in professional writing and public discourse. Many formerly sexist terms have been replaced (e.g., the traffic caution sign "Men Working" now reads "People Working," and "postman" has been replaced by "mail carrier"). While some people consider this overly zealous political correctness, language does shape our view of reality.

The social construction of appropriate gender roles has been in flux over the past 30 or 40 years in this country. Especially as more women have entered the paid workforce, assumptions about women's capabilities have changed dramatically. Also, a perception that only men were "family breadwinners" and women were working by choice (i.e., just for supplemental income) has changed.

American Society and the Experience of Gender Inequity

Although not a numerical minority, women are considered a minority in the sense that they exercise less power than men in American society. In the past, laws prevented women from holding property, establishing credit in their own names, serving on juries, voting, and entering certain professions, while other laws subjugated them to the control of their fathers and husbands. Whereas this is no longer the case and much progress has been made, there remain significant areas of gender inequality.

Gender-segregated work refers to a pattern of employment wherein men and women are found in different occupations (Reskin & Padavic, 1994). Examples would be nurses, secretaries, and flight attendants (female dominated) and physicians, executives, and airplane pilots (male dominated). These occupational choices reflect gendered expectations—that women will nurture and provide assistance and men will take charge and make decisions.

Women typically hold lower-status, lower-paying jobs than men with similar educational backgrounds. Cross-cultural and historical research has shown that the status given an occupation is higher when most jobs in it are filled by men and lower if those same jobs are filled by women. For example, 100 years ago, most secretaries were men and the job had relatively high prestige. Now that 98.6 percent of all secretaries are women (U.S. Department of Labor, 2000), the job is accorded low esteem. In short, it is not the work that provides the prestige, but the gender with which the work is associated.

A majority of women in contemporary American society actually fill two roles, as paid and unpaid workers, and are easily exploited in both. Reskin and Padovic (1994) suggest that the burden of the second shift will probably preserve women's inequity at home and in the workplace for another generation. The *second shift* refers to the child-care and housework responsibilities that women assume after returning home from their paid employment. Women still do roughly three times more housework than men; they are more likely to perform time-consuming and routine household tasks, such as cooking and housecleaning, whereas men's chores involve fixing things and yard work (Coltrane, 2000).

Even when women hold the same positions as men and have comparable skills and training, they tend to earn less. Women in year-round, full-time executive, administrative, and managerial positions earn only 61 percent of what men are paid in the same positions (Wright, 2002). Among industrialized countries, the United States ranks below most other countries and above only Japan in the gender salary gap (United Nations, 1994).

Sexual harassment was defined by the U.S. Supreme Court in 1993 as any sexual conduct that makes the workplace environment so hostile or abusive to the victims that they find it hard to perform their job. Sexual harassment has come to be understood more recently as an abuse of power (by a person of either sex) to force unwanted attention on a subordinate. In 1979 Catharine McKinnon published a book on sexual harassment that presented the argument that sexual harassment is not a personal problem but rather one that is built into the very structure of business.

Employment is not the only area where men exercise power over women. Sexual violence should be understood as a dimension of gender stratification; it is fundamentally about power, not sex (Herman, 2001). The violence perpetrated against women by their partners is a reflection of a sexist, patriarchal society that treats women as if they were property. Women are seven to fourteen times more likely than men to report that an intimate partner beat them up, choked them or tried to drown them, or threatened them with a gun or a knife (ACLU,

2001). *Date rape/acquaintance rape* is relatively common but underreported on most college campuses. About 3 percent of college women are sexually assaulted during a typical college year (South Carolina Coalition Against Domestic Violence and Sexual Assault, 2002).

Women are also victims of violence in their own homes. Outside of the police and military, according to sociologists, the family is the most violent social institution in the United States (Macionis, 2001; Thio, 2000). Spouse abuse involves physical force ranging from a slap or push to the use of a weapon; it can also include psychological abuse, such as intimidation, threats, public humiliation, and intense criticism (Unger & Crawford, 1996). In a recent national survey, 64 percent of women who reported being raped, stalked, or physically assaulted after the age of 18 had been victimized by intimate partners (ACLU, 2001). Only relatively recently in this country have laws been changed to allow a woman to legally charge her husband with sexual assault.

Male power is also demonstrated in the pornography industry. Feminists define *pornography* as sexually explicit material presented in images or words that appear to endorse, condone, or encourage sexual abuse or degradation. They suggest that the objectification and control of women's bodies portrayed in pornography contributes to violence against women, in part by reinforcing rape myths (e.g., that women secretly want to be raped). Pornography is not limited to adult bookstores; it is a big business that includes Internet sites easily accessible to children. Music videos, while not legally pornographic, commonly include content that is misogynistic (demeaning of females).

Men also experience issues of gender inequity. The gender roles under which men labor are much more constraining than those available for women. For example, a man is expected to be the family's "breadwinner"; being a "stay-at-home father" may bring social ostracism. Men are also expected to hide their feelings and, in comparison to women, to have a less nurturing relationship with children and friends. Perhaps the most noteworthy inequity is the societal expectation that males go into combat when needed.

Sexual Orientation

Sexual orientation is defined as a person's preference in terms of partners in emotional-sexual relationships: same sex, other sex, or both sexes (Lips, 1993). Homosexuality (attraction to members of the same sex) and heterosexuality (attraction to members of the other sex) are not mutually exclusive; sexual orientation lies on a continuum rather than being a dichotomy (either/or). This understanding of sexual orientation leads us to other categories of sexuality, which include bisexual and transgendered individuals. *Bisexuality* refers to sexual attraction to people of either sex. *Transgendered* refers to people who feel they are one sex, even though biologically they are the other (Gagné, Tewksbury, & McGaughey, 1997).

It has always been difficult to get accurate information on the number of people who are members of sexual minorities. One of the few researchers who made an effort was Alfred Kinsey (1948, 1953), who estimated that 4 percent of males and 2 percent of females are exclusively homosexual. Nine percent of men and 4 percent of women ages 18 to 59 in America report some homosexual activity in their lives (Laumann et al., 1994). It should be noted that homosexual activity or experiences are not the same thing as homosexual identity. Many heterosexuals have had homosexual encounters.

Many research studies have linked homosexuality to biological factors, such as brain structure, hormonal influences, and genetics (Hamer & Copeland, 1994). Others suggest that sexual orientation is a product of society (Foucault, 1990), both society and biology (Golden, 1987; Weinrich, 1987), or simply a personal choice.

Sexual Orientation as Community and Culture

Generally, gay men and lesbians find large urban centers to be more hospitable to sexual diversity than rural areas. In some cities, there are identifiable gay neighborhoods, such as the Castro district in San Francisco, neighborhoods in other large cities, and even smaller cities such as Key West, Florida, Provincetown, Massachusetts, and Santa Fe, New Mexico. As noted in the last chapter, however, there are also gay and lesbian communities that are not geographically anchored (Cruikshank, 1992).

The creation of these gay and lesbian identificational communities resulted from both experiences of discrimination and a sense of commonality. Without a strong gay community, the gay liberation movement would not have come into existence; the existence of that movement, in turn, helped to expand gay communities (Cruikshank, 1992). Stigmatization and social rejection prompted a sense of solidarity in response to isolation from mainstream American society, but Queralt (1996) argues that there would be a gay community even without elements of oppression.

"Even if sexual minorities do not have a culture in the traditional sense, in the process of accepting a homosexual identity, they are socialized into a new set of norms and values" (Lukes & Land, 1990, p. 156). Not all gay men and lesbians belong to or participate in an identifiable culture related to their sexual orientation; nevertheless, there are elements of a common cultural experience that include pairing behavior; definitions of family; the time, place, and reason for celebrations; and religious services (Lukes & Land, 1990, p. 156). Cruikshank (1992), argues that, in its broadest terms, the essence of gay and lesbian cultures is self-determination. "To follow a different path openly and wholeheartedly rather than furtively, [lesbians and gay men] have created a culture in which homosexuality is the norm" (p. 139).

Understanding Social Stratification and Sexual Orientation

Functionalist Perspective.   Because functionalists assume a complementary set of roles for men and women, they do not see a legitimate place for gay men and lesbians in society; in fact, they would perceive them as a threat to traditional family arrangements. This perspective tends to support the status quo, and the view that a stable society is one wherein members share a common set of values, beliefs, and behavioral expectations. Thus, there is an absence of widespread support for civil rights for gay men and lesbians. Although gay men and lesbians have advocated for themselves and experienced success in a variety of venues, they continue to be marginalized by society.

Conflict Perspective.   The existence of gay and lesbian lifestyles is considered by many to be a threat to the institution of marriage and the family. Gays are routinely oppressed in American society. Social conflict theorists believe that, in defense of their idea of "the family," conservatives are willing to sacrifice the individual rights of gay men and lesbians in order to preserve their own social standing.

An example of efforts to restrict the rights of gay men and lesbians can be found in the customary use of sodomy laws. Sodomy laws (making anal and oral sex illegal) were on the books in 13 states until struck down by a U.S. Supreme Court decision in June 2003. They were rarely enforced and when they were, they were mainly used to criminalize sexual activity between men. Sodomy laws also were cited in denying custody to gay and lesbian parents, in keeping gay or lesbian couples from adopting children, and in justifying employment discrimination because all gay men and lesbians were considered "potential felons" (Madden, 2003).

Constructionist Perspective.   Just as gender is a social construction, so are sexual orientation and socially approved sexual relationships. A variety of sexual expressions have been found in almost all societies, but different cultures tend to privilege one orientation (usually heterosexism) over others. While in the United States homosexuality is often viewed as a deviant lifestyle, other countries and cultures are or have been more accepting of same-sex attraction (Gramick, 1983). Canada, Denmark, Holland, Norway, and Sweden have all legalized same-sex marriages. In ancient Greece and Japan, male-male relationships were held in higher esteem than male-female relationships (Gramick, 1983; Greenberg, 1988). By labeling homosexual behavior a "sin," and gay men and lesbians "sinners," religious conservatives impose a moral judgment that justifies and encourages discrimination against this group of people.

American Society and the Experience of Inequity Related to Sexual Orientation

Homophobia is the unreasonable fear of homosexuals and homosexuality. *Heterosexism* is the view that heterosexuality is normal and that any other pattern of intimate interpersonal relationship is inherently abnormal or wrong. Unlike racism and sexism, heterosexism is widely tolerated in our society, legally supported under most circumstances, and even encouraged in some sectors. It was not until 1973 that homosexuality was eliminated as a mental disorder from the *Diagnostic and Statistical Manual of Mental Disorders* (DSM) of the American Psychiatric Association.

Gay men and lesbians experience a wide range of discriminatory practices. These include denial of employment benefits generally granted heterosexuals couples, such as health insurance coverage for partners and paid leave when grieving the loss of a partner; denial of immediate access to a partner in case of accident or other medical emergency; inability to share health, auto, and homeowners' insurance policies at reduced rates (as generally offered to married couples); lack of job security; restrictions on adoption and foster parenting; restricted access to housing; absence of validation from many religious communities; and inability to serve in the military without hiding one's identity. "Civil unions" of gay men and lesbians are recognized in some states, but conservative politicians at both state and national levels have introduced legislation to ban "gay marriage."

Gay men and lesbians may be accused of seeking "special" rights when, in fact, they simply want the same basic civil rights and liberties available to all other citizens. The question of legal protection for gays under the Fourteenth Amendment has not been ruled on by the U.S. Supreme Court, and there is no federal law prohibiting discrimination in the workplace on the basis of sexual orientation. Nevertheless, 13 states, the District of Columbia, and several hundred municipalities and counties have legal protections in place for public and private employees (Kershaw, 2003).

Gay men and lesbians may face ridicule or social ostracism when they live with a partner and do so openly, express affection toward a partner in public, or talk about their weekends, vacations, or other social events without disguising the gender of their partner. Recent national surveys have documented strong negative attitudes toward gays; 48 percent of Americans believe that homosexual relations between consenting adults is morally wrong (Lacayo, 1998) and 46 percent believe that homosexuality is a sin (Leland, 2000).

These homophobic prejudices may be particularly difficult for adolescents who are gay or lesbian. In a 1997 survey, 46 percent of gay, lesbian, and bisexual youth in one state's high schools reported they had attempted suicide in the previous year (Peyser & Lorch, 2000). A 17-year-old adolescent gay activist interviewed for a *Newsweek* story noted, "If you're in a society that tells you you are an abomination, right or wrong, it's what you believe." (Peyser & Lorch, 2000, p. 56).

Of more serious concern than simple harassment is physical violence against gays. Now that the FBI identifies specific hate crimes, evidence of such criminal activity is widespread. In 1996, there were 1,016 reported sex-bias crimes (Carlson, 1998). There is concern that negative rhetoric from conservative religious and political leaders may encourage these crimes (Lacayo, 1998). As of December 1999, 23 states and the District of Columbia had hate crime laws that addressed sexual orientation (Leland, 2000).

Disability

There are 48 million Americans with one or more physical or mental disabilities that may affect their opportunities for employment (Kendall, 2001). The vast majority of individuals with disabilities were not born that way, but were injured in an accident or war, or suffer from the effects of an illness (Kendall, 2001). The proportion of persons with disabilities is greater now than in previous decades because of advances in medical technology that keep at-risk infants and accident victims alive and allow people to live longer, even though they have more impairments as they age.

Asch and Mudrick (1995) have interpreted disability statistics as follows. Disability is more prevalent among poor people, those who are poorly educated, and those who are single. African Americans have a higher prevalence of disability than do other racial groups. Not surprisingly, the probability of disability increases with age. Disability is not usually experienced as a single impairment, but rather one that coexists with other impairments.

While there are many definitions of disability, they essentially fall into two major categories: (1) those that locate disability as internal to the individual and (2) those that situate the problem in the interaction between the disabled person and the social environment.

The first category is the one that social workers are most likely to encounter in their dealings with other human service and health professionals. According to the 1990 Americans with Disabilities Act (PL 101-336), disability means "with respect to an individual, a physical or mental impairment that substantially limits one or more of the major life activities of such individuals, a record of such an impairment, or being regarded as having such an impairment." With these definitions, professionals are looking for a cure, or at least a way to rehabilitate the individual. These professionals may expect the person with the disability to be compliant and passive.

The second category of definitions establishes disability not just as a personal problem but also as a challenge to society to change attitudes and remove barriers (Karger & Stoesz, 2002, p. 94). This latter view sees the person's inability to function as the result of a handicapped environment, and disability as an element of human diversity (Gilson & DePoy, 2002).

Disability as Community and Culture

All who consider themselves disabled are potential members of the disability community. According to Linton (1998),

> we (disabled people) are bound together, not by . . . (a) list of our collective symptoms but by the social and political circumstances that have forged us as a group. We have found one another and found the voice to express not despair at our fate but outrage at our social positioning. (p. 4)

Linton (1998) goes on to describe "the cultural stuff of the disability community" as being

> the creative response to atypical experience, the adaptive maneuvers through a world configured for nondisabled persons. The material that binds us is the art of finding one another, of identifying and naming disability in a world reluctant to discuss it, and of unearthing historically and culturally significant material that relates to our experience. (p. 3)

The construction of disability as a community and culture constitutes a range of understandings. One noteworthy position on this continuum is that of the deaf community. People in the deaf community perceive deafness not as a disability, but as a minority culture (Luey, Glass, & Elliott, 1995; Padden & Humphries, 1988). Perhaps because children who are deaf are routinely separated from their families to attend special residential schools for the deaf at an early age, they are more likely to develop a unique and bicultural orientation to the world than are people with other kinds of disabilities. Among communities of disabled persons, the deaf community stands alone in having its own language, American Sign Language (ASL). The use of ASL is usually dominant in residential schools; fluency in ASL has the effect of cementing the culture and creating a different worldview, particularly for those who grow up with it (Luey, Glass, & Elliott, 1995; Wax, 1995).

Understanding Social Stratification and Disability

Functionalist Perspective.   The functionalist perspective uses a medical model to explain the role of disability in society. A medical model suggests that pathology resides within the individual. (This contrasts with the social work understanding of person-in-environment, wherein disability may be viewed as a lack of fit between the individual and his or her environment.) From a functionalist perspective, people with disabilities are restricted to the role of chronic patient. They are perceived as being unable to work or at least unable to work as productively as the able-bodied.

Conflict Perspective.   Conflict theorists argue that people with disabilities belong to a minority group that is kept in a subservient position and exploited by the health care industry (Albrecht, 1992). People with disabilities are treated as second-class citizens. Categorizing them as "deserving poor" (see Chapter 3) and giving them subsistence-level grants does little to bring them to full inclusion in society. Restrictions of opportunities for schooling, employment, and housing continue to limit their options.

A *caste system* is a form of social stratification in which one's status is lifelong and unchangeable. Szymanski and Trueba (1994) argue,

> the difficulties faced by persons with disabilities are not the result of functional impairments related to the disability, but rather are the result of a castification process embedded in societal institutions for rehabilitation and education that are enforced by well-meaning professionals. (p. 12)

For example, federal policy related to disability benefits forces recipients to choose between a limited grant along with Medicaid and a job with an income that will threaten their eligibility for health care coverage. Vocational rehabilitation agencies, with pressures of high caseloads and limited resources, also keep persons with disabilities locked into their low status by referring them to sources of employment that are easily available, such as dishwashing and custodial work (Mackelprang & Salsgiver, 1999).

Constructionist Perspective.   The social construction of disability is a process that has for the most part marginalized people with disabilities. People with disabilities, especially persons with mental retardation or mental illness, are sometimes perceived as dangerous when there is a proposal to move them into a group home in a residential neighborhood. They are more often thought of as helpless, dependent, incompetent, and tragic figures, or even as "perpetual children" (Mackelprang & Salsgiver, 1999, p. 6). The response to this construction is a patronizing stance that may result in their exclusion from activities or places that are considered to be suitable only for adults, including those arenas where they could effectively advocate for themselves.

When not perceived as victims, people with severe disabilities are sometimes portrayed as heroes who miraculously overcome all obstacles to lead a "normal" life. This image is also misleading. Linton (1998) points out that persons with disabilities are

> not only the high-toned, wheel chair athletes seen in recent television ads, but the gangly, pudgy, lumpy, and bumpy of us, declaring that shame will no longer structure our wardrobe or our discourse. We are everywhere these days, wheeling and loping down the street, tapping our canes, sucking on our breathing tubes, following our guide dogs, puffing and sipping on the mouth sticks that propel our motorized chairs. . . . Our symptoms, though sometimes painful, scary, unpleasant, or difficult to manage, are nevertheless part of the dailiness of life. They exist and have existed in all communities throughout time. What we rail against are the strategies used to deprive us of rights, opportunities, and the pursuit of pleasure. (pp. 3–4)

American Society and the Experience of Inequity Related to Disability

The issue of ascribed status is an important one for people with disabilities. Sociologists use the term *master status* to describe a perceived social status that dominates all the other statuses a person holds. Historically, occupation has been a master status for many men, and the most common master status for a woman was her role in the family as wife or mother (Kendall, 2001). Being very rich or poor can be a master status, as well as being a member of a minority race or ethnicity in a society where discrimination is the rule. For many individuals, disability becomes a master status. For example, when individuals must use wheelchairs, their disability may override all other statuses they might enjoy, such as educational achievement or occupational success. The master status concept is often apparent in the media. Most television portrayals of people with disabilities highlight the disability; television and film directors are reluctant to insert an individual with a physical disability into a minor role where the disability is irrelevant to the story (Makas, 1993).

The built environment is probably the most potent symbol of exclusion of people with disabilities from society. Mark Johnson, a disabilities activist (quoted in Shapiro, 1993, p. 128) notes that whereas African Americans fought for the right to sit at the front of the bus, persons with disabilities have had to fight for the right to *get on the bus*.

The current prevalence of "handicapped" parking places and bathroom stalls may lead the casual observer to believe that most public places are easily accessible to persons with mobility problems. Nevertheless, many amenities are inadequate or poorly designed or limited in their applicability. For example, trendy brick pavers may cause people using walkers to trip; sometimes a freight elevator at the back of the building may be the only available means of ascent. Public address announcements in airports are barely intelligible to people with normal hearing, much less to those with hearing impairments. Most signs and signals in our built environment are purely visual; Braille labeling is provided in elevators but rarely in other public areas. The lack of convenient and accessible public transportation is a major impediment for many persons with disabilities.

Organized political activity by people with disabilities and their families was rewarded in 1990 with the signing of the Americans with Disabilities Act. The ADA extends to people with disabilities civil rights similar to those made available on the basis of race and sex through the Civil Rights Act of 1964 (Karger & Stoesz, 2002). Nevertheless, stigma and oppression are ongoing problems for people with disabilities. As long as disability is viewed as an individual affliction rather than as a deficit in the physical or social environment, people with disabilities will continue to be an oppressed minority. If one accepts the assumption that stigma is a major barrier to full citizenship for people with disabilities, then advocacy for civil rights, in addition to the provision of social services and income maintenance, is the appropriate response (Hahn, 1991).

Looking Ahead

The chapters in Part III addressed social structure and its impact on vulnerable populations. In Part IV, we discuss social settings as contexts for human behavior. Social justice issues will be a continuing theme.

Key Points _____

- *Ascribed statuses* reflect characteristics over which an individual has little or no choice. Sex and race are examples.

- America is a patriarchal society. Gender inequity contributes to rape and domestic violence.

- Sexual orientation is a continuum rather than a dichotomy.

- Gay men and lesbians lack the legal protections afforded other minority groups.

- For many individuals, disability constitutes a *master status* that dominates all others.

- In spite of the gains made under the ADA, many people with disabilities continue to experience stigma and oppression.

Questions to Think about and Discuss _____

1. Why is it that in the twenty-first century women continue to be so underrepresented in elective office? What do you perceive to be barriers to electing a woman president?

2. What are your feelings about legalization of domestic partnerships ("gay marriage")?

3. Can you give an example that you have observed of a presumption of incompetence in relation to a person with disabilities?

4. Sometimes people without disabilities are called the "temporarily abled." What are the implications of this term?

Recommended Readings _____

Anderson, M. L., & Collins, P. H. (Eds.). (1992). *Race, class and gender: An anthology*. Belmont, CA: Wadsworth.

Chow, E. N., Wilkinson, D., & Zinn, M. B. (1996). *Race, class & gender: Common bonds, different voices*. Thousand Oaks, CA: Sage.

Cohen, L. H. (1994). *Train go sorry: Inside a deaf world*. New York: Houghton Mifflin.

Fries, K. (Ed.). (1997). *Staring back: The disability experience from the inside out*. New York: Plume.

Handler, L. (1998). *Twitch and shout: A Touretter's tale*. New York: Plume.

Mairs, N. (1996). *Waist-high in the world: A life among the nondisabled*. Boston: Beacon Press.

Pratt, M. B. (1991). My mother's question. *Rebellion: Essays 1980–1991* (pp. 111–124). Ithaca, NY: Firebrand.

Tannen, D. (1990). *You just don't understand: Women and men in conversation*. New York: Morrow.

Internet Search Terms _____

Discrimination	LGBT (Lesbian, gay, bisexual,	Sexual orientation
Gender/gender relations	transgendered)	Sexual harassment
Gender studies	Master status	Societal roles
Handicapped/disabled	PFLAG (Parents and Friends of	Stereotypes
Heterosexism	Lesbians and Gays)	Status
Homophobia	Sex role identity	Temporarily abled

Part IV

Introduction to Social Settings

Drawing upon an ecosystems perspective, in Part III we discussed various *niches* in the social environment (Germain & Gitterman, 1995).

> The physical and social settings of community, workplace, school, and so on constitute the *habitat* [of human beings]. . . . Physical settings such as dwellings, buildings, rural villages, and urban layouts must support the social settings of family life, interpersonal life, work life, spiritual life, and so on in ways that fit the lifestyles, age, gender, and cultural patterns of the residents. (Germain, 1991, p. 45)

Traditionally, social work texts have not paid much attention to aspects of the physical environment, but that is changing gradually with the awareness of how environmental issues affect individuals and communities. On the other hand, "It is the understanding of *the person as a social being* [italics in original] that constitutes the main area for the contribution of the social work profession" (Chess & Norlin, 1991, p. 26). Thus social systems and social settings (e.g., families, groups, organizations, communities, and so forth) have long been the focus of attention of social work curricula. These social systems are studied both as entities per se within a larger environment and as contexts for smaller systems.

In Chapter 8, we discuss communities as geopolitical systems, that is physical and social entities and settings (in contrast to the identificational communities described in Chapters 6 and 7). We look at the reasons for the decline of central cities and the accompanying growth of suburbs and the implications for community well-being. In Chapter 9, we draw on the large body of literature on organizational theories and assess their applicability to human service agencies and to the workplace as a social setting. In Chapter 10, we discuss a special type of organization, residential institutions. We provide an overview of the history of institutional care in this country and discuss the impact of institutional settings on the people who live in them.

Oppression of vulnerable populations occurs not only in residential institutions, but in organizations and communities as well. The profession's commitment to social justice suggests that this should be an area of concern.

In Chapter 11, we present formed groups and social movements. Both are arenas for coordinated action to work toward goals and can have a significant impact on members and participants, organizations, communities, and society.

In addition to being the contexts for understanding human behavior, communities, organizations, institutions, groups, and social movements also are settings for social work practice. Knowledge of how these collectivities operate will contribute to your professional effectiveness.

8

Locational Communities

"Next to the family, communities are the most basic and necessary social systems" (Bruggemann, 1996, p. 5). The profession of social work has its roots in community practice. Early social workers in settlement houses adopted communities as the arena for their interventions. These early social workers worked to improve housing and neighborhood conditions, and to establish day-care centers, educational programs, recreational opportunities, and job-training and referral services. Early efforts of the profession were an attempt to make neighborhoods more inhabitable for immigrants. Community context continues to be critical for certain vulnerable groups, particularly for those who cannot move about easily, such as children, older adults, people with physical disabilities, and often poor families. Knowledge of community is essential for good social work at any system level, and community practice reflects the profession's commitment to social and economic justice.

Defining Community

Even within social work, the term *community* is often used to mean different things. In Chapter 6, we introduced the concept of identificational communities; here we restrict the use of the term to mean locational or geopolitical communities. There are three essential elements of locational community: geographical area, social interaction, and common ties (Hillery, 1955). Locational community is where person and environment meet. Community residents interact with each other, share common interests, use many of the same resources, and access many of the same services. This interdependence among residents and between residents and their community environment is basic to the concerns of social work.

Communities are also social systems. Unlike organizations, which we will discuss in the next chapter, the relationships in communities are not based on formal, contractual expectations, but rather on mutual benefits. Communities usually do not have formal goals, but goals can be identified by examining the common needs and problems of people who share the same geographical space.

Types of Communities

Types of communities are defined in relation to population size or location or function. A *metropolis,* for example, is a city of 50,000 or more people. A *suburb* is a residential urban area beyond the political boundaries of a city. An *edge city* is a business center some distance from the downtown but close to the intersection of major highways: typically it is a mix of corporate office buildings, medical centers, shopping malls, fast-food franchises, hotels, and entertainment complexes. (See Garreau, 1991 for examples of edge cities.) The occupancy of the suburb peaks at night while the occupancy of the edge city peaks during the day. A relatively new term is *megalopolis,* which refers to one or more cities and their surrounding suburbs whose boundaries have converged; an example is the Boston to Washington, DC, corridor.

Neighborhoods are important subsystems of cities. Fellin (1995, p. 77) defines *neighborhood* as a "geographical area which includes dwellings where people reside. . . . [Some also] contain nonresidential buildings such as schools, churches, stores, service buildings, police stations, fire stations, and offices." The boundaries of a neighborhood may be politically set, as with voting wards, school districts, or church parishes. Social factors may also be used in the definition of neighborhoods. For example, the *Social Work Dictionary* says neighborhood inhabitants "share certain characteristics, values, mutual interests, or styles of living" (Barker, 1995, p. 252). Often neighborhoods are occupied by people of the same racial or ethnic background or sexual orientation, similar social class, or by families who are in the same stage of the family life cycle. Examples of mutual interests or styles of living might be found in a "university neighborhood," an "Italian neighborhood," or a "singles neighborhood."

Slums, ghettos, and barrios are special types of neighborhood. These terms are often associated with high-poverty neighborhoods in large urban areas. *Slum* implies an area of extreme poverty, with deteriorated and abandoned structures. Although often used interchangeably with slum, the terms *ghetto* and *barrio* refer to neighborhoods with distinct racial or ethnic cultures that often are, but are not necessarily, poor. There are features of strong resident identification and positive social interaction within their boundaries, but few links with the larger community (Fellin, 1995, p. 88).

Issues and Trends

Cities and Suburbs

Although some large cities (e.g., New York, Miami, Los Angeles) continue to gain population due in large part to an influx of immigrants (Thio, 2000), most large cities are declining.

Industrial cities in the "sunbelt" (e.g., Atlanta, Birmingham, and Chattanooga) have been losing population since 1980, just as industrial cities in the "rust belt" (the Northeast and the Midwest) have been losing residents for some time.

Two significant trends of the last half-century that have implications for communities are the decline of central cities and the growth of suburbs. Several factors have contributed to these interrelated trends. These include a period of economic prosperity beginning at the end of World War II, increasing reliance on automobile transportation, government policies that penalize central cities and support suburbs, political fragmentation that prevents effective regional planning, and the loss of blue-collar jobs due to the relocation of industries. These factors are discussed in more detail next.

Between 1945 and 1960, per capita income in America increased by 35 percent (Coontz, 1992). This made it possible for working-class and middle-class people to purchase single-family homes. Eighty-five percent of the new homes were built in the suburbs (Mason, 1982).

When workers bought automobiles, they no longer needed to live close to jobs or public transportation systems. Even though President Eisenhower's new interstate highway system was perceived to serve important military functions, the primary beneficiaries were suburbanites who used it for commuting back and forth to work (Jackson, 1985). Although in the past few years more communities are taking a critical look at the effects of outward growth, by and large suburbs were and continue to be designed and built around the needs of cars (Cieslewicz, 2001). That is unlikely to change as cars now outnumber licensed drivers in the United States (Naughton, 2003).

The government subsidizes suburban commuters by failing to collect in gasoline or other taxes the full cost of road construction and maintenance, patrol and rescue services, and environmental damage. Other subsidies come to the suburbs in municipal outlays for extensions of electric power, water, and sewage lines. Perhaps the greatest impact of government policy results from national tax and economic policies directly related to housing. In the 1950s, almost half of the housing built in suburbia depended on federal financing (Coontz, 1992; Duany, Plater-Zyberk, & Speck, 2000). The federal government provided insurance to lenders, and mortgages to families through the G.I. Bill and Veterans Administration, the Federal Housing Authority (FHA), the Federal National Mortgage Association ("Fannie Mae") and the Government National Mortgage Association ("Ginnie Mae"). In the post World War II period, millions of Americans received mortgage loans with artificially low interest rates (2 to 3 percent) and down payments of as little as 5 to 10 percent (or even just a single dollar when borrowing from the Veterans Administration) (Lee, 1986).

National tax and economic policies continue to favor wealthy suburban dwellers. In 1995, the federal government lost nearly four times as much in tax subsidies to middle- and upper-class home owners as it spent for low-income housing (Howard, 1997; Lazare, 2001). Most of the tax savings from mortgage deductions—44 percent—went to the top five percent of households in terms of income (Zachary, 1995), leading some to call the various federal tax deductions "mansion subsidies" (Lazare, 2001). Urban advocates suggest that government subsidies that go to suburban home owners might be more wisely spent in cities for mass transportation or infrastructure maintenance.

The *political fragmentation* of large metropolitan areas has resulted in lack of regional planning and support for central cities. Although many suburbanites rely on the nearby city for employment, entertainment, air travel hubs, specialized medical care, and various public services, they pay their local property taxes only to suburban governments. Because suburbanites are able to use the resources of the city without contributing to its maintenance costs, they have little motivation to assume any responsibility for solving city problems (Altshuler, Morrill, Wolman, & Mitchell, 1999; Schneider, 1992).

The last factor contributing to the decline of central cities is the decrease in real opportunity brought about by the loss of blue-collar jobs due to deindustrialization and the suburbanization of employment (Wilson, 1987). Heavy industries have moved out of cities to rural areas, or even other countries, where space and labor costs are lower. Light industries and service businesses have moved to edge cities where land is cheaper, and utility rates and property taxes are lower (Kendall, 2001). Although many inner-city residents were able to find jobs in service and retail sectors, their average annual earnings fell by 25 to 30 percent (Wilson, 1996).

Suburban Sprawl and New Urbanism

While there is a general understanding that central cities are often inhospitable environments (Helling, 2002; Lazare, 2001; Wilson, 1987, 1996), suburbs generally don't carry similar negative connotations. Nevertheless, some urban designers describe the character of modern American suburbs as "soulless subdivisions, residential 'communities' utterly lacking in communal life; strip shopping centers, 'big box' chain stores, and artificially festive malls set within barren seas of parking; antiseptic office parks, ghost towns after 6 p.m.; and mile upon mile of clogged collector roads" (Duany, Plater-Zyberk, & Speck, 2000, p. 5). Since each piece of suburbia serves exclusively one type of activity (e.g., residential, commercial, office, recreation, industrial park), residents must spend much of their time getting from one place to another, usually driving alone in a private automobile because walking, bicycling, and public transportation are rarely options. The result of continuous outward growth (called *suburban sprawl*) is the abandonment of existing, more centrally located neighborhoods.

Squires (2001) suggests that suburban sprawl detracts not only from connectedness to place but also from a sense of community. Schneider (1992) asserts that the major attraction of suburbs is privatization: backyard patios or decks instead of front porches, private cars instead of buses, video rentals instead of theaters, and privately owned malls instead of town squares. The increasing segregation and homogeneity of neighborhoods, too much time devoted to commuting and too little time available for civic engagement, and the separation of home and work result in both physical and social fragmentation (Putnam, 2000).

In a relatively recent approach to urban planning, a small group of developers is applying what they've learned about the flaws of modern subdivisions and the relative benefits of traditional neighborhoods to build model communities such as Seaside and Celebration (in Florida), Laguna West (in California), Harbortown (in Tennessee), and Middleton Hills (in Wisconsin). Following the prescriptions of *new urbanism,* these towns offer streets laid out in a grid pattern, front porches instead of large lawns, small shops and offices within walking distance of homes—or even attached to homes—and many small shared green areas (Duany, Plater-Zyberk, & Speck, 2000; Penn, 1998). These efforts at a more logical construction of communities have not been widely copied, although more than 200 local and state laws and initiatives aimed at controlling sprawl have been adopted since 1998. Overall, the trends of the last half-century clearly do not reflect a history of successful community development or maintenance.

The Minority Urban Experience.   As discussed here, structural factors—particularly economic changes—affect all communities. In the "rust belt" of the upper Midwest, African Americans suffered most from the decline of central cities. A logical response to repressive conditions was the migration of middle- and working-class African Americans out of the inner city into areas with more favorable economic conditions. The result was an increased concentration of the very poor in the central city. Wilson (1987, 1996) argued that the social life of these inner-city neighborhoods declined because of the intensification of poverty and the accompanying isolation from mainstream institutions and role models.

While Wilson (1987, 1996) focused on the mass "out-migration" of middle-class blacks from inner-city Chicago, Latino communities have experienced only gradual out-migration of successful residents and at the same time welcomed vast waves of energetic and hopeful new immigrants. A result of this pattern in Latino communities was that well-established Latino families could be found living next door to new immigrants and relationships across social class were developed and maintained (White, 1988; Valdez, 1993). This meant that local institutions, such as churches, might have changed, but they were not abandoned. In the case of Central American immigrants in Los Angeles, new small businesses—stores, markets, restaurants, and street vendors—continually appear, contributing "to the bustling street life and ethnic identity of the neighborhood" (Chinchilla, Hamilton, & Loucky, 1993, p. 55).

Like inner-city African Americans, Latinos suffered from economic restructuring. Since most Latinos lived in areas other than large Midwestern cities, however, their experience of economic change was shaped according to location. Historically, Latino barrios in the Southwest were scattered throughout the metropolitan areas so social isolation was not so much a problem. Latinos live in neighborhoods where houses are both closer to job opportunities and cheaper. One factor contributing to their affordability is the contribution of in-kind assistance. For example, in Albuquerque, not only do many Mexican American carpenters and laborers build their own homes, but they also help in the construction and repair of the homes of their friends and relatives (Gonzales, 1993). In addition, Latinos are unlikely to experience the level of housing discrimination that plagues African Americans (Fellin, 1995). The result is that one-third to one-half of the homes of the Latino poor are owner-occupied (Moore & Pinderhughes, 1993, p. xxxiv). This contributes to neighborhood stability and pride.

Obviously there is great diversity within ethnic groups and their housing arrangements and locations, often determined by a combination of ethnic/racial identity and social class (Fellin, 1995). For example, Cubans are more likely to be found in suburbs and Puerto Ricans in central cities. Filipinos, Koreans, and Indians, because they are more likely to be of a higher social class than other Asian groups, are less likely to live in segregated inner-city areas and more likely to live in suburban neighborhoods. Southeast Asians, who arrived in this country as impoverished refugees, are likely to live in segregated areas. Many Native Americans reside in inner-city neighborhoods, although these neighborhoods usually include other ethnic minorities.

Like the Latino communities, urban Chinatown communities, particularly in San Francisco, Los Angeles, and New York, have been reinvigorated by an influx of new refugees who created new demands for food, goods, services, and entertainment (Gold, 1999; Yung, 1999). Vietnamese and other Indochinese refugees have established enclaves adjacent to Chinatowns, or in new locations, notably in the California cities of Westminster, Long Beach,

San Diego, Santa Ana, Garden Grove, and San Jose (Min, 1995b). Southeast Asian refugees have developed a large number of voluntary associations that serve myriad functions and helped to rebuild organized communities. The development and unification of Southeast Asian communities has been supported by an active media that produces newspapers, magazines, and radio and cable television programs (Gold, 1999, p. 518).

Another minority population that has had a relatively positive urban experience is the gay community. In the 1970s, many lesbians and gay men gravitated to specific neighborhoods in large cities that were known to be accepting. Among the most prominent of these geographically bounded areas are the West Village in New York City, the Castro District in San Francisco, the South End in Boston, the Dupont Circle area in Washington, DC, Newtown in Chicago, and West Hollywood in Los Angeles (Garnets & D'Augelli, 1994). Research studies indicate that there is an association between sizeable gay communities and economically viable cities. Other cities across the country are now looking hard at the contribution gays bring. Detroit, for example, is trying to lure gay residents by offering domestic partner benefits to city employees (Robberston, 2003).

Rural Communities. Beginning in 1991, the Bureau of the Census defined *rural areas* (also called "nonmetropolitan areas") as a county or group of counties without a large central city (having a population of at least 50,000). Three major characteristics of rural communities are small-scale, low-density settlement; distance from large urban centers; and a specialized, nondiverse, rural economy (Deavers, 1992). In contrast to urban communities, rural communities have less adequate public services, such as schools, fire protection, road maintenance, health care, and recreation and entertainment facilities (Ginsberg, 1993; Queralt, 1996). Unemployment rates are also likely to be higher.

The most rural state in the country is Vermont, where more than two-thirds of residents live in rural areas; the most urban state is California, where only 7 percent live in rural areas (Henslin, 2001). Rural areas contain both the most ethnically homogenous and ethnically diverse American communities, depending on the region of the country (Flora, Flora, & Houdek, 1992). For example, half of the 50 counties in the United States with the least diverse populations are in Iowa and Nebraska.

Historically, it was not unusual for rural communities to depend on industries related to natural resources (e.g., agriculture, forestry, fishing, mining) to sustain their economy. Although farming and mining still dominate the local economy of many rural counties, those areas are losing population. In some agricultural areas, family farms have been replaced by large-scale meat and poultry processors (Johnson, 1999). The contemporary economic base of many rural counties is dependent on government funding (payrolls) for military bases, prisons, and state universities (Flora, Flora, & Houdek, 1992; Huling, 2002). In the 1970s, lower wages made it profitable for companies to move production facilities from cities to rural areas, but beginning in the 1980s the trend shifted to moving plants overseas, where labor was even cheaper. In rural areas, many shutdowns hit company towns with long-established ties to a single manufacturer (Geller, 2003).

Although declining population has been a common problem in rural counties in the past, during the decade of the 1970s, more than 80 percent of rural counties gained population (Johnson, 1999). This trend slowed in the 1980s, but returned in the 1990s, when 71 percent of rural counties gained population. New arrivals in rural communities include blue-collar workers (who make up 30 percent of the workforce in rural areas), disenchanted city dwellers, and many older adults. Wealthy retirees are attracted to the forested lake counties of Minnesota, Wisconsin, and Michigan, winter sports areas in California, Nevada, Wyoming, and Utah, coastal areas of California, South Carolina, and Florida, and the foothills of the Ozarks in Arkansas and of the Appalachians in Virginia, Kentucky, North Carolina, and Tennessee (Johnson, 1999). When rich former city dwellers purchase or build vacation or retirement homes in rural areas, they drive up the cost of housing, but they may at the same time produce a demand for workers in construction, retail, service, and other local businesses, providing new employment opportunities.

Indian Reservations.   A special type of rural community is the Native American reservation. According to the Bureau of Indian Affairs, there are 314 reservations (which the federal government recognizes as independent territories) and an additional 240 "trust lands" that are protected by the federal government but are primarily associated with a particular tribe or reservation (Wright, 2002). Fewer than 500,000 Native Americans live inside these federally "identified areas." This is about one-eighth of the people in this country who identify themselves as Native Americans/Alaskan Native or Native American in combination with other races.

Reservations range in size from less than 100 acres to the 16 million acres of the Navajo reservation that covers parts of Arizona, Utah, and New Mexico (Snipp, 1999). Historically, reservations have been marked by severe economic distress. Although the federal government has always encouraged Indians to support themselves through agriculture, less that one percent of all reservation land is highly productive farmland (Snipp, 1999). According to the Southwest Indian Foundation (based on data from the 1990 Census of the Navajo Reservation), more than half of Navajo homes burn wood for heat and lack complete plumbing for exclusive use; more than three-fourths of Navajo homes have no telephone; more than one-third of Navajo persons have less than a ninth grade education; the average per capita income on the Navajo Reservation is $4,106; 57.9 percent of Indian persons on the Navajo Reservation live below the poverty level; and almost 25 percent of the Navajo labor force is unemployed.

Although not suitable for farming, many reservation lands are rich in increasingly rare resources: coal, oil, natural gas, uranium, timber, grasslands, and water, especially in western states (Bordewich, 1996; Fixico, 2002). Leasing of Indian land by energy and lumber companies, ranchers, and other outside interests, including multinational corporations, must be approved by the Interior Department; many Native Americans have criticized the government for failing to adequately protect their interests (Fixico, 2002).

Beginning in the middle 1970s and into the 1980s, reservation Indians took advantage of their legal status as "domestic dependent nations" to open gaming (gambling) halls and casinos. This economic strategy was supported by a 1987 Supreme Court decision that determined that Indian tribes could conduct any gaming activities not specifically prohibited by state law (Fixico, 2002), and by the Indian Gaming Regulatory Act of 1988, which was designed to promote Native American self-sufficiency via gaming as an alternative to the federal dole (Bordewich, 1996). In 2002, 290 Indian casinos were run by some 130 tribes in 37 states (Bartlett & Steele, 2002; Fixico, 2002). Especially for those located near tourist attractions or major population centers, this new economic endeavor provided employment for reservation residents and cash income to support schools, housing, day-care centers, health clinics, community recreation centers, nursing homes, industrial parks, convenience stores, and museums (Bartlett & Steele, 2002; Kehoe, 1999). One should note that some Native Americans oppose gambling (1) on moral grounds and (2) because it is marketed in a form that is incompatible with Native American culture (Schaefer, 2000, p. 190). The exercise of this sovereign power has made a limited number of Native American communities wealthy. The majority, however, remain in poverty and more closely resemble third world rather than U.S. communities (Kehoe, 1999, p. 72).

In a special investigation report, Bartlett and Steele (2002) demonstrate just how lopsided the distribution of revenues from gaming is. Casinos in California, Connecticut, and Florida, where only 3 percent of the Indian population lives, receive 44 percent of all revenue. Five states where nearly half of all Native Americans live (North and South Dakota, Montana, Nevada, and Oklahoma) receive less than 3 percent of all casino proceeds. While the majority of Native Americans continue to live in poverty, profits from casinos are going to many non-Indian investors, including foreigners. Only a quarter of gaming tribes distribute cash directly to their members, and most members receive no more than a few thousand dollars each.

Understanding Communities

Ecosystems Perspective

As noted in Chapter 1, the ecosystems perspective views person and environment as integrated, interdependent systems. Often concerns about *habitat* (meaning the natural home of an organism) are expressed in discussions about the degradation of wetlands or rainforests and the loss of wildlife. To view community as habitat is a useful way to understand the individual in his or her environment. This should lead social workers to consider the physical aspects of the environment such as crowding, noise levels, air pollution, sanitation, and access to transportation. Habitats are especially important for some populations. For example, both very young children and older adults are more dependent on their local environments than other age groups that have more independent mobility.

Mismatch theory is a hypothesis that explains high rates of depression and anxiety in modern life as the result of humans living in habitats quite different from those for which natural selection shaped their hominid ancestors (Wright, 1995). Not only is the physical setting of large buildings and paved streets different from the forests and savannahs of humans' ancestral Africa, but also the resulting social environment is very different. Primitive humans lived in small bands of related individuals who interacted almost continuously. In today's society, social isolation is a result of the physical structure of communities, particularly for stay-at-home suburban mothers. Even in cities, loneliness can occur in a crowd of strangers, where interactions tend to be economic rather than social.

The ecosystems perspective also encourages an examination of the fit between a community and its larger environment. Communities that are unable to obtain needed resources experience entropy. *Entropy,* which means decline or breakdown, occurs whenever a system uses up more energy than it takes in. Thus, when a city spends more on infrastructure (such as maintaining roads or sewers) than it takes in taxes, the community experiences entropy.

People who drive through central cities with boarded-up storefronts and garbage-filled streets have witnessed the results of the process of entropy.

Another ecological term that can be applied to communities is *succession*. In the natural environment, succession occurs when one species is displaced by another, such as when African killer bees drive out local populations of native honeybees. In the community, succession directs us to look at the process of neighborhood change when one population replaces another. One example is when one ethnic group is replaced by another, such as when Mexican Americans replaced the Lithuanians in the Marquette Park area of Chicago in the mid-1980s. Another example of succession is when a low-income population is replaced by young, upper-middle-class individuals through the process of gentrification. *Gentrification* is the renovation or replacement of older homes in desirable areas with upscale residences. Gentrification often results in the removal of poor and elderly residents for whom affordable replacement housing is scarce.

Functionalist Perspective

In Part II, we discussed social institutions and the functions that they perform in society. These functions are usually carried out on the local level. They include production, distribution, and consumption of goods and services; planning and decision making; law enforcement, public safety, and social control; education and socialization; provision of health care and social welfare; and information dissemination. Warren (1978, p. 9) defined community as "that combination of social units and systems that perform the major social functions having locality relevance." Thus communities provide the settings for the local components of major social institutions: businesses, local governments, schools, places of worship, clinics and hospitals, social service agencies, media outlets, and other organizations.

Communities are the interface between individuals or families, and social institutions. Healthy communities provide necessary supports and resources that enhance the functioning of smaller social systems. At an informal level and on a spontaneous basis, communities provide opportunities for social participation and mutual aid and support. An example would be the way that neighbors organize multifamily garage sales or share tasks like transporting children to and from after-school events. Another informal function of communities is provision of a base for political action.

Breakdown in the functioning of one subsystem in a community requires that another subsystem step in. For example, if there is not adequate planning for recreation, bored adolescents are more likely to get into trouble, requiring extra police patrols. Or, if the economic system falters and there are massive layoffs, local food banks may be called on to fill the gap in the provision of nutrition basics.

Conflict Perspective

Conflict theorists argue that community life reflects the inequalities of wealth and power in American society. Community viability is influenced by investment decisions made by the political and economic elite who entertain little input from local residents. The societal oppression of poor people and people of color is readily apparent in American communities. This is seen most clearly in patterns of segregation and environmental injustice, topics that are discussed in depth in the section on how communities obstruct well-being later in this chapter.

Rational/Social Exchange Perspective

An important premise of the rationalist perspective is that individuals act in their own self-interest. "Rational" does not mean that people get together to determine what would bring the greatest good to society as a whole, or even to large numbers of people in the community, but rather to themselves and their immediate family.

This idea of self-interest is particularly evident in the pattern of automobile dependence in our society. Hart and Spivak (1993) explain that Americans do not seek alternatives to use of the private automobile because it is a "free good"; in other words, they pay only a fraction of the actual cost. If motorists were required to absorb the true expense of building highways, paving parking lots, cleaning up pollution, and providing emergency medical care for accident victims, the cost of gasoline would increase by four to ten dollars a gallon (Delucchi, 1996; Hart & Spivak, 1993; Holtzclaw, 1993; Korb, 1996). But because gas taxes are kept artificially low, others must shoulder the costs of suburban sprawl. As confirmed individualists, American prefer to go where they want, when they want, without taking into account the needs of others. Only when mass transit alternatives are readily available and the cost of driving and/or parking is prohibitive, will Americans give up traveling in their own private cars. New York, where the cost of parking is extravagant, is the only American city in which the majority of households don't own one or more automobiles (Seabrook, 2002).

Constructionist Perspective

A constructionist perspective would emphasize the different meanings that people give to the term *community.* Sociologist Ferdinand Tonnies (1963) used the terms *gemeinschaft* and *gesellschaft* to describe the ways that people related to each other in their communities. *Gemeinschaft* is found in communities where residents share traditions, know each other well, and are eager to offer mutual support. *Gesellschaft* describes communities where relationships are impersonal and contractural. Tonnies believed that communities could exhibit both characteristics, but that usually one was predominant. Tonnies suggested that as society became more urban and industrialized, communities would exhibit more features of *gesellschaft* than *gemeinschaft.* Despite his predictions, many Americans would still describe their community experience as *gemeinschaft,* reflecting on their involvement in neighborhood associations, shared interests and responsibilities for local children, participation in holiday or ethnic celebrations, support for school or city sports teams, and socializing in local taverns and restaurants (Fellin, 1995; Oldenburg, 2001).

Preferred Perspectives

Descriptions of communities often focus on deficits, particularly in relation to communities of people of color. Despite obvious challenges in many poor and minority communities, the strengths perspective promotes the assumption that all communities have assets. There are many kinds of community assets: natural beauty, a pleasant climate, strategic location, thriving industries, skilled leaders, and strong social institutions. Distinct from these is the idea of *social capital* (Bourdieu, 1986; Coleman, 1988, 1990, 1993; Putnam, 2000). In this text, we will take social capital to mean the following:

> the set of resources that inhere in relationships of trust and cooperation between people. . . . Social capital is a collective asset, a feature of communities, rather than the property of an individual. As such, individuals both contribute to it and use it, but they cannot own it. (Warren, Thompson, & Saegert, 2001, p. 1)

Stolle and Rochon (2001, pp. 145–146) include in their list of "indicators" of social capital such factors as participation and engagement in "politics generally and in the community specifically," generalized trust that fosters "norms of reciprocity" within the community, trust toward public officials and institutions, individual willingness "to do one's share in collective endeavors," and optimism about the future in relation to social and political relationships.

One type of social capital is bonding within communities. Strong community institutions, such as schools, places of worship, parent/teacher groups, fraternal organizations, and small business associations are essential for creating an environment where social capital can develop (Warren, Thompson, & Saegert, 2001).

Historically and currently, immigrants, refugees, and ethnic enclaves have been constructive forces in many cities. In addition to the economic vitality of immigrant-serving businesses, traditional social controls are revived, networks are strengthened, and old community institutions are changed or new community institutions emerge to meet the needs of new residents (Gold, 1999; Moore & Pinderhughes, 1993; Padilla, 1993; Wysocki, 1991). Mutual aid linked to strong extended family networks is a characteristic of many immigrant groups.

In poor communities, social capital is a critically important factor for survival when other forms of capital (e.g., financial capital) are missing. The use of social capital is often the only factor that allows community residents to cope. Poor communities are more likely to have religious institutions whose missions may include more than just the spiritual life of its members. African Americans develop and maintain some of the strongest forms of social capital, stemming from a tradition of high rates of church membership and participation (Lincoln & Mamiya, 1990). Even the much-maligned "projects" at one time provided a positive home and close-knit community for many inner-city African American residents. In describing her experiences growing up in the Ida B. Wells Homes in Chicago in the 1950s, newspaper columnist Leanita McClain (1986) spoke of

> lives as full of personal cheer as anyone else—birthday parties, graduation celebrations, block club parties. . . . [T]here were dance classes and sewing classes and charm classes, when we weren't roller skating or bicycling. There was a corner soda shop, Doc's, that made the best malts in our limited world. People raised money to pay the rent by selling baked goods or chicken dinners. Every Sunday there was a parade of scrubbed Sunday school children. . . . And there were fathers who were fathers to those without them, and plenty of working people, factory workers and domestics whose rush hour began long before dawn. (pp. 141–142)

Nevertheless, even high levels of social capital cannot withstand the overwhelming negative forces found in oppressive economic and political systems. Wuthnow (2002, p. 101) notes that a significant share of the decline in social capital in the United States over the past two decades has occurred among marginalized groups:

> [P]eople need to feel entitled in order to take part in the political process, and they need to feel that their participation will make a difference. Part of the decline is also due to the fact that people need other resources in order to create social capital, not the least of which are adequate incomes, sufficient safety to venture out of their homes, and such amenities as child care and transportation.

The Impact of Communities on Individuals and Families

How Communities Obstruct Well-Being

Negative Impacts on Childhood.   In his studies of concentrated poverty, Jargowski (1997) notes that where you live clearly affects how you grow up. Some groups of people in particular are affected by neighborhood deficits: these categories include people living in extreme poverty, older adults, and children. They are trapped in the sense that they cannot move and many do not even leave the neighborhood regularly because they lack access to transportation or are too frightened to go out.

When they enter school, children encounter the world beyond family and home. Schools that are prepared to deliver sound educational services to children and their families are critical in communities that are economically deprived (Garbarino, 1992). Unfortunately, it is the poorest communities that are most likely to have schools that are only marginally able to meet the needs of students.

Growing children also need safe areas for play. Heavily trafficked streets, alleys strewn with litter and used drug paraphernalia, playgrounds with broken equipment, and dark stairwells and hallways limit children's access to healthy physical activity.

Childhood safety is also threatened by community violence. A thirteen year old describes his life on the South Side of Chicago:

> If you act like a little kid in this neighborhood, you're not gonna last too long. 'Cause if you play childish games in the ghetto, you're gonna find a childish bullet in your childish brain. If you live in the ghetto, when you're ten you know everything you're not supposed to know. When I was ten I knew where drugs came from. I knew about every different kind of gun. I knew about sex. I was a kid in my age but my mind had the reality of a grown-up, 'cause I seen these things every day! (Jones & Newman, 2000, p. 116)

Researchers have confirmed that the experience of this child is not uncommon. A third of inner-city children have witnessed a homicide by the time they reach age 15 (Bell, 1991).

This child's perspective demonstrates how blighted neighborhoods present not only physical threats, but psychological ones as well. As cognitive powers develop and children are able to make social comparisons, they become aware of the discrepancies between their home neighborhood and more affluent ones. Kozol (1995) records how a 15-year-old Harlem resident views her environment:

> "It's not like being in jail," she says, "It's more like being 'hidden.' It's as if you have been put in a garage where, if they don't have room for something but aren't sure if they should throw it out, they put it there where they don't need to think of it again." (pp. 38–39)

In the last decade of the twentieth century, photographer/ethnographer/author Camilo Jose Vergara (1995) documented the "vacant land, ruins, and fearsome structures" of American ghettos. He quotes a slum resident who notes:

> "Who wants to be told that they live at the very bottom, in one of the worst places in the city, where the police don't police, sanitation don't clean, where there is no health department and people have a 'Wild West attitude'? If you think that of your home, how can you keep your self-respect? What will prevent you from committing suicide?" (p. 7)

Another community factor that detracts from the well-being of children is the lack of social density. *Social density* measures

> the degree to which an environment contains a diversity of roles for children to learn from and for parents to draw upon. . . . The socially undeveloped urban neighborhood may have so little going on that it impoverishes the social experience and knowledge of its children. Even further, what is going on may not enrich their lives. (Garbarino, Galambos, Plantz, & Kostelny, 1992, pp. 208–209)

Children are enriched when they can observe different occupational, kinship, and acquaintance roles. A neighborhood made up exclusively of mother-headed families, with no adult male role models and no consistent male disciplinary presence leaves boys to "learn about manhood on the streets, where the temptation is strong to demonstrate prowess through lawbreaking, violence, and fathering a child" (Schorr, 1989, p. 20). McClain (1986) speaks of a "poverty of the spirit" that differentiates such neighborhoods from "poverty of the pocket." Lack of social density is also apparent in new residential suburbs where children are likely to grow up surrounded by young families in similar middle-class circumstances. The only adult roles these children encounter in their neighborhoods are those of parents, joggers, dog walkers, and the ice cream vendor. They don't have regular interaction with shopkeepers, mechanics, retirees, or even extended family members.

Environmental Racism.   *Environmental racism* is the term used to describe the consistent pattern whereby environmental hazards are located near poor people of color (Bullard, 1990; Hoff & Rogge, 1996; Wolcott & Milligan, 1992). Ethnic minority groups are disproportionately exposed to the dangers associated with environmental degradation. For example, Hoff and Rogge note that just three communities, all of them more than 78 percent minority, hold 40 percent of the landfill capacity of the entire country. Lipsitz (2002, pp. 67–68) summarizes a number of reports documenting the inequitable distribution of risks; among them, in Houston, Texas, African Americans make up 25 percent of the population, but 75 percent of the municipal garbage incinerators and 100 percent of the city-owned garbage dumps are located in black neighborhoods; penalties for violating federal environmental laws regulating air, water, and waste pollution were 46 percent lower in minority communities than in white communities; and across the nation, 60 percent of African Americans and Latinos live in communities with uncontrolled toxic waste sites. The short- and long-term effects of exposure to toxic elements in the environment remain unclear (Rogge, 1993). Nevertheless, for young people, local environmental hazards have been associated with high rates of stunted growth and lead poisoning, and residents of all ages are susceptible to asthma, various types of cancer, and other serious illnesses (Lipsitz, 2002).

Conflict theory suggests that it is more difficult for marginalized populations to keep their communities free of environmental degradation. Poor communities without other choices may accept environmentally hazardous industries and/or commercial waste operations in their neighborhoods in order to create jobs in the local economy (Beasley, 1990; Bullard & Wright, 1986). The relationship between poverty and environmental threats is clear

> in polluted inner city neighborhoods where children of color suffer from high rates of asthma; in crop lands where poor migrant workers carry agricultural pesticides home to their families on their work clothes; in low-income Louisiana parishes along the industrial "Cancer Alley" stretch of the Mississippi; and in the unsanitary, crowded, hastily and poorly constructed *maquiladoras* that house Mexican plant workers along the United States-Mexico border. (National Association of Social Workers, 2000, pp. 103–104)

The pattern exits on the international level as well. The imbalance of power among nations is reflected in the movement of toxic chemicals from industrialized to developing countries (Rogge & Darkwa, 1996).

Violations of indigenous peoples provide the most graphic and poignant illustrations of environmental racism (Hoff & Rogge, 1996, p. 45). For example, the Goshute reservation in Utah is surrounded by a magnesium plant on the north, a stockpile of chemical weapons on the east, an Army testing ground for exposure to nerve gas on the south, and a bombing range and hazardous waste incinerator on the west (Wolfson, 2000). In order to bring donations for a cultural center and desperately needed jobs, the tribal chairman has agreed to let eight power companies from California, New York, Minnesota, Wisconsin, Michigan, Georgia, Pennsylvania, Florida, and Alabama use a part of the reservation as a nuclear waste dump. Corporations and even the federal government "systematically target Native American reservations when looking for locations for hazardous waste incinerators, solid waste landfills, and nuclear waste storage facilities" (LaDuke, 1993; Lipsitz, 2002, p. 68).

Segregation by Race and Class.   In America, a limited number of financial institutions and developers finance and construct most suburban housing and large city projects. Given the dynamics of the capitalist system, their motivation rests not in benefiting the community, but in making a profit. Developers are seldom called on to think about, much less pay for, the impact of their development on surrounding areas in terms of traffic congestion, pollution, excessive demands on infrastructure (schools, utilities, water, and sewers), or destruction of existing neighborhoods. Typically, people of color and the lower social classes pay disproportionately for these developments even though they derive little direct benefit from them (Feagan & Parker, 1990).

Prior to the 1960s, although many neighborhoods were segregated by race and ethnicity, most were integrated by socioeconomic class, both in large cities and small towns (Fellin, 1995). Historically in America, gulfs between classes were not reflected in physical distances; even in cities with terrible slums, the middle class lived with or very near the poor (Coontz, 1988). As whites and middle-class blacks and other minorities moved to the suburbs, center cities became more homogenous by race and class, and poverty and deprivation become increasingly more concentrated (Jargowski, 2002; Powell, 2002; Wilson, 1987). Between 1970 and 1990, the number of poor persons living in high-poverty neighborhoods almost doubled (Jargowsky, 1997). (*High-poverty neighborhoods* are defined as census tracts with poverty rates of 40 percent or higher.) This trend was reversed during the prosperity of the 1990s; however, it is likely that the recent economic downturn will signal a return to the previous pattern (Jargowsky, 2003). The most debilitating effect of the concentrated poverty of those left behind in the central cities is not lack of lawns and shopping malls, but denial of access to educational and employment opportunities. Unemployment rates for African American teenagers in central cities runs about 40 to 45 percent, well above the 25 percent jobless rate for the nation during the Great Depression (Schaefer, 2000).

Seldom are developers interested in building affordable or low-income housing in new suburbs. Instead, they concentrate on upscale, high-profit neighborhoods. Adding insult to injury, many of the most exclusive new neighborhoods are literally walled off from the rest of the community. Duany, Plater-Zyberk, and Speck (2000) note that it is not the walls per se, however, that threaten social unity, but the homogeneity and exclusivity of the people living behind them. The residents of these private, gated communities are uniform in terms of both race and class. They have little regular contact with people at the lower end of the socioeconomic ladder—with the exception of the cleaning women and gardeners who show up to do the tasks that wealthy residents prefer to hire out.

Suburbs are rarely zoned for multifamily dwellings or other forms of affordable housing. Codes that restrict the building of houses in a new development that do not meet minimum cost or square footage requirements are used to separate even the very rich from the very, very rich. For the first time in our history

> we are now experiencing ruthless segregation by minute gradations of income. . . . To prove this point, one need only to attempt to build a $200,000 house on an empty lot in the $350,000 cluster; the homeowners' association will immediately sue. . . . The real estate business caters to this elitism so relentlessly that even some mobile home parks are marketed in this way. (Duany, Plater-Zyberk, & Speck, 2000, pp. 43–44)

Wealthy and powerful community residents use building codes and zoning ordinances not only to insulate themselves from their poorer neighbors, but also to exclude people with disabilities. Persons with mental illness or retardation, for example, who are able to live in a group home in the community are often shut out of upscale neighborhoods by property holders who assert, "I think it's great to have half-way houses for people like that, just not here!" Such *N.I.M.B.Y.* ["not in my backyard"] attitudes often result in necessary important facilities being clustered in older transitional neighborhoods bordering on retail or industrial areas where public transportation is available, houses are relatively large, and political power is small.

While suburban areas focus on segregation by class, center cities struggle with a lack of affordable and structurally sound housing. During the 1950s and 1960s, while the Federal Housing Authority [FHA] provided subsidies for suburban housing, the federal government built large, high-rise housing projects in major cities. Because tenant selection procedures were done without resident input, urban renewal projects had the effect of destroying important social networks that had existed in the poor neighborhoods that were razed, and instead promoted anonymity and social isolation (Goering, Kamely, & Richardson, 1997). Ninety percent of the low-income housing units removed during the urban renewal programs were never replaced (Lipsitz, 2002, p. 65). Even the construction of interstate highways was detrimental to those living in the central city. Overpasses destroyed or devalued urban neighborhoods and limited access roads were used as physical barriers between neighborhoods, separating different racial and ethnic communities. For example, the Dan Ryan Expressway in Chicago established a barrier between African American neighborhoods to the east of it and white ethnic neighborhoods to the west of it. Many stable racial minority communities were destroyed; more than 60 percent of those displaced by urban renewal projects were people of color (Jackson, 1985; Zarembka, 1990).

Although housing segregation by class is a new and growing concern, segregation by race has a long history in this country. It was and is fostered by different mechanisms. As Southern blacks migrated to northern industrial centers, and especially after desegregation laws made it harder to avoid contact with African Americans, whites moved to outlying areas. (This pattern is called *white flight*). Although it might appear at first that patterns of residential segregation can be attributed solely to the personal choices of individual white homeowners, Powell (2002) explains how the government was significantly involved in the segregation of people of color into less desirable neighborhoods. Beginning in the 1920s and extending through the post–World War II period, government housing authorities instituted policies that were specifically designed to discriminate against minorities in mortgage loans and insurance. These government agencies assessed neighborhoods in which people of color lived in the lowest-value category, without consideration of the actual worth of the housing stock. On FHA maps, these neighborhoods were marked by red ink. The term *redlining* thus came to refer to the practice of identifying minority neighborhoods to be excluded from consideration for granting mortgage funding. While these federal programs denied home ownership to minorities, the same policies encouraged investment in white-only suburbs. A third mechanism of racial discrimination against minority individuals is mortgage lending: African Americans and Latinos who meet the same financial standards as whites are 60 percent more likely to be rejected (Passell, 1996; Thomas, 1992). A final mechanism is *steering*. This occurs when real estate agents take people of color to see houses in some neighborhoods and direct white people to others (Feagan & Sikes, 1994).

The most racially segregated cities in America are found in the North: Gary-Hammond-East Chicago, Chicago, Detroit, Cleveland, Milwaukee, Newark, New York, and Buffalo (Massey & Denton, 1993). In Chicago, an individual has only a 1 in 25 chance of encountering a person of a different race within his or her home neighborhood (Garbarino, Galambos, Plantz, & Kostelny, 1992, p. 203).

How Communities Promote Well-Being

Communities promote well-being at three levels: formal service organizations, small businesses that meet a service need, and families and individuals acting as neighbors. Various formal local organizations provide services to community residents. These include neighborhood centers, Boys and Girls Clubs, schools, places of worship, VFW halls, and lodges. Some of the services that are offered include day care and preschool, recreation opportunities for children and older adults, disaster shelters, food pantries, health services (e.g., flu shots, blood pressure screening), and space for organizations ranging from Scouts to Alcoholics Anonymous and Weight Watchers. Such activities are not limited to white, middle-class communities. Solomon (1976, p. 220) reports that, contrary to common perceptions, voluntary associations "abound" in black communities. These include church-related organizations; lodges; veterans' groups; political clubs; professional, business, and service groups; sports and athletic clubs; civil rights or social action groups; and social clubs. In Latino communities, Catholic churches and protestant evangelical churches may provide a range of social services (Chinchilla, Hamilton, & Loucky,1993; Moore & Vigil, 1993). Concrete services might include help finding an apartment or getting food and furniture; providing literacy training and English-as-a-Second-Language classes; assistance in locating jobs; and legal assistance regarding immigration and filling out forms for permanent resident visas. Services might also include advocacy on the behalf of neighborhood residents for a supermarket chain to improve the quality of its products, for an insurance company to lower exorbitant rates, for politicians to improve transportation services, or for a corporate office park to provide jobs. Some churches have also declared themselves sanctuaries for families from Central America seeking political refuge (Chinchilla, Hamilton, & Loucky, 1993).

Particularly in minority communities, small businesses may fulfill both commercial and social service roles. For example, African American barbershops and beauty parlors are not only a forum for the exchange of ideas (McCormick, 1998), but also sources of information on how to prevent death from breast and prostrate cancer (Halebar, 2002). Studies of Latino/a-owned businesses have documented their provision of social services (Delgado, 1998). They also provide financial services (check cashing or loans), assistance made necessary by the absence of banks and automatic tellers in many Latino neighborhoods (Levitt, 1995). Latina business owners report that they have both an obligation and a God-given "gift" to be of help to their communities (Delgado, 1998; Lazzari, Ford, & Haughey, 1996). Many small businesses (e.g., bookstores, theaters, and restaurants) in lesbian and gay neighborhoods foster a powerful psychological sense of community and encourage information exchanges among different social networks (Garnets & D'Augelli, 1994). During the 1980s, urban gay communities in New York, San Francisco, and Los Angeles responded to the challenge of the HIV/AIDS crisis by constructing entire caring systems (Garnets & D'Augelli, 1994).

In addition to formal helping organizations and local businesses, families and individuals in communities also offer services to each other. These may involve a network of neighbors, such as those in Neighborhood Watch Associations or babysitting exchange groups. On an individual level, neighbors take in mail while others go on vacation; share tools; help look for lost pets; swap plant cuttings; mow yards or shovel walks for neighbors who are elderly or sick; and provide food when there is a death in the family. "Neighboring" also can include "watching out" for each other, such as checking on older adults when the weather is extreme. These forms of mutual aid improve the quality of residents' lives.

Social Workers and Communities

The lives of the most vulnerable populations are inextricably linked to the condition of the communities within which they reside. Because communities both promote and obstruct the well-being of clients, social workers who are engaged in "direct practice" with individuals and families view the community as both a resource for clients and as a possible source of client problems.

The client system for other social workers is the community per se. These macro social workers engage in community planning and development, working in partnership with community members and groups to create a more positive social environment (Bruggemann, 1996). Macro social work practitioners should be prepared to view the community as possessing assets and solutions to problems, and to see partnership with community members and groups as a way to create a more positive social environment.

In small or rural communities, social workers are more likely to have a broad range of responsibilities and engage in practice at several system levels. They may use their generalist skills not only as direct service workers, but also as administrators, organizers, planners, and consultants (Ginsberg, 2001).

Looking Ahead

In the next chapter, we examine the role of organizations in communities and society. We also examine the influence of organizations on the lives of those who work there or receive services.

Key Points

- The profession of social work has its roots in community practice.

- The three essential elements of locational community are geographical area, social interaction, and common ties.

- Communities are the interface between individuals or families and social institutions.

- Two significant trends of the last half-century that have implications for communities are the decline of central cities and the growth of suburbs. National tax and economic policies continue to favor wealthy suburban dwellers.

- Rural communities are likely to have less adequate public services and higher unemployment rates than urban areas.

- The societal oppression of poor people and people of color is readily apparent in American communities. Although housing segregation by class is a new and growing concern, segregation by race has a long history in this country. In the past, government policies were specifically designed to discriminate against minorities.

- Poor ethnic minority groups are disproportionately exposed to environmental hazards.

- In poor communities, social capital is a critically important factor for survival.

Questions to Think about and Discuss

1. Ask your parents or grandparents about the neighborhood where they grew up. How was it different from where you grew up?

2. What factors do you take into consideration in your choice to use or not use public transportation?

3. Do you think that the current pattern of residential segregation will be changed or is it inevitable that neighborhoods in American communities will continue to be separated by race and class?

4. What is your image of an ideal community? How has that been shaped by your own experience of community?

5. How do you think environmental policies would change if toxic waste were distributed equally across all communities?

6. What do you consider important community supports for older adults?

7. What settings, events, and opportunities in your neighborhood contribute to a sense of community?

Recommended Readings

Duany, A., Plater-Zyberk, E., & Speck, J. (2000). *Suburban nation: The rise of sprawl and the decline of the American dream*. New York: North Point Press.

Garreau, J. (1991). *Edge city: Life on the new frontier*. New York: Anchor Books.

Hoff, M. D., & Rogge, M. E. (1996). Everything that rises must converge: Developing a social work response to environmental injustice. *Journal of Progressive Human Services, 7,* 41–57.

Kotlowitz, A. (1991). *There are no children here*. New York: Doubleday.

Kuletz, V. L. (1998). *The tainted desert: Environmental and social ruin in the American West*. New York: Routledge.

Perry, M. (2002). *Population, 485: Meeting your neighbors one siren at a time*. New York: Harper Collins.

Rainwater, L. (1970). *Behind ghetto walls: Black families in a federal slum*. Chicago: Aldine.

Schneider, W. (1992, July). The suburban century begins. *The Atlantic Monthly*, pp. 33–44.

Vergara, C. J. (1995). *The new American ghetto*. New Brunswick, NJ: Rutgers University Press.

Internet Search Terms

Community development	Housing and urban development	Urban development
Community organization	Neighborhood	Urban fringe
Gemeinschaft and gesellschaft	Rural urban issues	

9

Organizations

A large part of our daily lives, and the lives of our clients, occurs within the context of organizations: day-care centers, schools, and businesses. Social work students also must be concerned with organizations as providers of social services and as employers of social workers. Organizations act in ways that affect, not only individuals and families, but also other organizations, communities, and even entire societies. Some sociologists argue that large organizations are the key phenomenon of our time (see Perrow, 1991).

Defining Organizations

A *formal organization* is a social system that is deliberately established for the purpose of achieving specific goals. Most organizations have both official goals and operative goals (Perrow, 1961). *Official goals* are goals the organization acknowledges in its charter, mission statement, annual reports, and other public documents. *Operative goals,* on the other hand, reflect what the organization actually does from day to day, regardless of what the official goals are. These may or may not reflect similar purposes. For example, some for-profit psychiatric facilities may advertise their organizational mission as helping people suffering from mental illnesses while their operative goal is to admit patients who have good insurance coverage.

Goals in organizations change over time. There are two types of changes: goal displacement and goal succession (Etzioni, 1964). "*Goal displacement* often occurs when the means to a goal becomes the goal itself" (Holland & Petchers, 1987, p. 208). An example of this would be in a health care setting when filling out charts takes priority over patient care. The process, rather than successful consumer outcomes, then becomes the organization's product.

When an agency's mission is achieved, it doesn't go out of business. Instead it shifts its attention to new goals. *Goal succession* involves the replacement of an accomplished goal with a new one. A classic and often cited example is the March of Dimes, which began as an organization dedicated to raising money to fund research to eradicate polio. The disease ceased to be a major health problem when an effective vaccine was developed, and the March of Dimes turned to raising money to combat birth defects instead.

Pfeffer (1997) suggests that defining organizations in terms of goal pursuit is problematic in that many employees either do not know the organization's goals or do not support them (p. 7). On the other hand, he notes that there is one goal that appears to be common to all organizations. Whether acknowledged or not, it is the organization's own survival. Organizations are more likely than other social systems to hold this goal of self-perpetuation (Pfeffer, 1997, p. 9). An example is the Interstate Commerce Commission, a federal agency that survived for almost 15 years after virtually all of its functions were removed (Sanger, 1996).

Types of Organizations

For social work purposes, organizations can be divided into three basic types: (1) public/government, (2) private nonprofit/voluntary, and (3) private for-profit. Examples of public/government organizations include public universities, welfare offices, and police departments. Examples of private nonprofit/voluntary organizations are United Way agencies, the NAACP, and privately funded foundations, such as the Children's Defense Fund. Many social workers and their clients are employed by or otherwise affected by public and private/nonprofit organizations.

Some for-profit organizations are owned by individuals or families; others are owned by stockholders who are paid dividends based on the profits the company earns. Examples of well-known private for-profit organizations are General Motors, Time-Warner, Wendy's, and The Limited. Today, large numbers of health provider organizations (hospitals, nursing homes, psychiatric in-patient units) are part of large, for-profit corporations. Many nonprofit organizations have chosen to pursue for-profit activities, blurring the distinction between them and the for-profits. Both of these trends have led to concerns about who will serve the most needy (Karger & Stoesz, 2002; Salamon, 1993).

Issues and Trends

Technology

Technology, and especially "commuting electronically," has made working at home a possibility for many people. Tasks that once required an office setting can now be done at home if the worker has a fax machine, computer, and access to the Internet.

Some people who work at home, however, may miss the opportunities to socialize that face-to-face contact with coworkers offers. The potential for, or reality of, friendships in the work setting is clearly an important factor in the decision to be committed to a particular job.

Another problem for those who work outside of the home as well as those who are paid for work they do at home is that the line between work and home life is becoming more permeable. Even more so than the telephone, computer-mediated communication strengthens the expectation that workers will be available 24 hours a day, seven days a week. People have to use additional technology at home, such as answering machines, to shield themselves from work-related interruptions.

Accountability

Another trend is that human service agencies, like other organizations, are being asked to be accountable to their stockholders and funding sources. Rather than just reporting activities or outputs (volume of work accomplished—such as how many clients were seen), they must measure and report on program outcomes (United Way, 1996). *Outcomes* are the actual benefits or changes experienced by individuals or client populations during or after participating in program activities; these might include new knowledge, increased skills, changed attitudes, modified behaviors, and improved conditions or altered statuses (United Way, 1996, pp. 2–3).

Criticism of Affirmative Action

Title IV of the Civil Rights Act of 1964 prohibits discrimination. *Affirmative action* goes beyond nondiscrimination to encourage special efforts to reach out to particular groups. It evolved over time from executive orders and court decisions. In practice, it is the explicit and intentional consideration of a person's group identity (race, ethnicity, or gender) as a criterion in making selection decisions; among candidates who are qualified on other criteria, members of underrepresented groups are selected in preference to those from overrepresented groups (Cox, 1993, p. 250). Thus affirmative action addresses two goals: equal opportunity to redress the results of past discrimination and promotion of diversity within the organization.

There are three common misconceptions about affirmative action that contribute to its negative image: that it requires the use of rigid quotas, that it results in the selection of unqualified individuals, and that it is essentially "reverse discrimination." Although broad goals and timetables may be used anywhere, specific quotas apply only in cases where a court has found evidence of past discrimination within an organization. Affirmative action requires that gender, race, or ethnic background be counted only in reviewing the files of *qualified* candidates; those who don't meet minimum requirements need not be considered, regardless of their group identity. Lastly, if the use of affirmative action "is viewed in the context of overall employment opportunity and the history of opportunity (both within the organization and within the society), then characterizing it as reverse discrimination seems inaccurate" (Cox, 1993, p. 249). In the opinion of many, American society has yet to establish the "level playing field" that would make affirmative action programs obsolete.

Nevertheless, critics of affirmative action argue that it promotes diversity at a special cost to some (white males) who cannot logically be held responsible for patterns of past discrimination. But many of those who protest most vocally are themselves the beneficiaries of another kind of insidious advantage—the *legacy privilege* that is accorded the relatives and friends of the rich, powerful, and well-connected (Kinsley, 2003).

Corporate Crime

Since the 1980s, corporate crime has emerged as topic of concern with the general public. Corporate crimes are "illegal acts committed by corporate employees on behalf of the corporation and with its support" (Kendall, 2001, pp. 214–215). Examples include price fixing, tax evasion, copyright infringements, antitrust violations, false advertising, knowingly selling faulty or dangerous products, or deliberately polluting the environment, where the purpose is to increase profits at the expense of consumers, competitors, and the general public (Benson & Cullen, 1998; Friedrichs, 1996). A study of the largest 25 Fortune 500 companies found that all of them were found guilty of either criminal behavior or civil violations at some time (Donahue, 1996). The savings and loan scandal of the 1980s and early 1990s typified the lax nature with which corporate crime is prosecuted and punished within the criminal justice system (Simon, 2002). The judicial response to the deception, dishonesty, and cunning of the Enron corporate executives will let us know if times have changed (Huffington, 2003).

The most egregious examples of corporate crime involve sacrificing worker safety for company profits. It is estimated that more than 100,000 American workers die each year as the result of some executive's decision to cut corners on safety in order to enhance the bottom line (Reiman, 1998). This represents a total that is five times the number of victims of street crime (Simon & Eitzen, 1993). Generally, reports of corporate crime do not appear on the evening news and those who commit it are not brought before criminal courts. Instead these perpetrators appear before regulatory agencies that have no power to imprison (Henslin, 2001).

Understanding Organizations

Throughout most of human history, most people lived and worked within small groups of family, friends, and neighbors. Only a few categories of organizations existed prior to industrialization; these included armies and religious hierarchies. With industrialization, formal organizations became common, and they are now a central feature of contemporary society.

Ecosystems Perspective

The environmental context in which an organization exists is critically important to the organization's ability to survive. Scientists who study *organizational ecology* (using what is called the *population-ecology model*) have applied Darwinian principles to organizational analysis (see Aldrich, 1979; Freeman & Hannan, 1989; and Hannan & Freeman, 1977). The population-ecology model emphasizes resource scarcity and competition.

As Darwin and other evolutionists pointed out, the evolution of natural species occurs through change in individuals. Population ecologists argue, on the other hand, that evolutionary dynamics must be studied at the level of the population. Thus analysis moves from ex plaining how individual organizations adapt to their environment to understanding how different "species" (types of organizations) or whole industries rise and fall (Morgan, 1986, p. 67).

In a series of studies, population ecologists Hannan and Carroll (1992) found a common pattern across many kinds of organizations. The first appearance of a new type of organization (such as life insurance companies or beer breweries) is followed by a gradual and then dramatic increase in numbers. Just as natural environments can support only so many individual organisms, the business environment can support only so many organizations of the same type. The organizations must compete with each other and only those that are most "fit" survive. Eventually the density falls to a level that can be supported by the environment, and there is relative stability in numbers. Within these numbers, however, individual organizations come and go as some are better able to adapt to changing environmental resources and demands.

From an ecosystems perspective, it is important for an organization to establish a good fit between itself and its environment. Important aspects of the environment include economic and political trends, population patterns, and other organizations (Macionis, 2001). Local demographics, for example, will determine the available workforce and the market for an organization's products or services.

Human service agencies depend on outside sources of funding; those that receive income from a variety of sources are in a better position to make independent decisions regarding their future. Human service organizations also compete for clients. They have learned from the business world how to "market" themselves, both through public relations efforts and through making their services more appealing and "user friendly"—offering evening and weekend appointments, for example.

Rapid changes in society mean that organizations must remain flexible. For example, an agency that has received government funding in an era of relative prosperity must be ready to seek alternative revenue sources when there are budget cutbacks. An agency that has provided counseling to a middle-class clientele may find that as lower-income people move into the surrounding neighborhood, client demands change from psychotherapy to concrete services, such as provision of day care or a food pantry.

Functionalist Perspective

For functionalists, members of organizations come together to cooperate in achieving a common goal efficiently (Thio, 1998). Their focus is on technical competence and task completion rather than in fostering positive ongoing personal relationships. Whereas a family might be able to operate a small restaurant, retail store, or repair shop, economy of scale and the need for uniformity and technical competence often favors large organizations.

Organizations are functional for society in that they epitomize productive efficiency. Large corporations are an important source of employment for people around the world. They tend to pay employees better than smaller firms can, and they usually have more formalized and objective hiring procedures, thus equalizing individual opportunities (Stockard, 2000).

A number of systems terms can be explained in the context of organizations. All social systems perform a variety of types of functions; these categories of functions occur in families, groups, and communities, as well as in organizations. In a human service organization, *goal-directed functions* are those activities that directly address the purpose of the organization. Examples might include counseling clients or licensing foster homes. *Integrative functions* are those activities that are directed at maintaining peace and harmony among members of the system; in a human service organization, this might mean holding regular staff meetings. *Maintenance functions* are those activities that meet the needs of the organization; these might include staff training or strategic planning. (Effective organizations attend to their own needs as well as consumer needs.) The *adaptation function* refers to those activities involved in responding to changes in the environment; in an organization, these might include developing new services to accommodate changing client demographics.

As organizations grow and change, they become more complex and the units within them become more *specialized*. In other words, there is a division of labor. For example, in a small agency, the director might handle staff recruitment and hiring, public relations, fundraising, and budget preparation. A large agency not only has more personnel, but each person is likely to have a more specialized role. In fact, there may be whole departments with special functions, such as personnel or accounting. Small isolated human service agencies are more likely to need generalist practitioners, while large multifunction agencies are more able to hire practitioners with expertise in one or two areas.

Conflict Perspective

In the view of conflict theorists, the history of organizations is a history of asymmetrical power relations that result in the majority working to support the interests of the few. Whether the organization had as its goal the building of pyramids, the establishment of trade routes, the conquest of neighboring states, or the manufacturing of personal computers, the "pursuit of the goals of the few through the work and labor of the many continues. Organization, in this view, is best understood as a process of domination" (Morgan, 1986, p. 275).

Individuals' interests may be abused, not only by the forces of societal oppression, but also by the normal functioning of impersonal organizations (Scott, 1981). The many ways in which workers in organizations may suffer is detailed later in this chapter in the section on how organizations obstruct well-being.

Sources of power in organizations include (among others) formal authority, control of scarce resources, control of information, and interpersonal alliances (Morgan, 1986, p. 159). Formal authority is related to one's position. Power is also associated with the resources that an individual or unit can bring and whether those resources are available through other means. Thus, a social worker who sees sliding-scale clients may have less power in a counseling agency than a psychiatrist who sees third-party-payer clients. The effectiveness of a strike by unionized workers (and hence their relative power) depends on the availability of other workers ("scabs") who might be hired to fill their positions. Some individuals can favor their own interests by withholding information or slowing its dissemination. Through various kinds of interlocking networks, some people in organizations are able to access mentors and other friends in high places. Politically astute workers build and cultivate informal alliances and coalitions, trading current support for the potential of future assistance in a ritual of mutually beneficial exchange.

Robert Michels (1949) suggested that eventually all formal organizations, as they get bigger, replace the goals of meeting the needs of their customers or clients and the needs of the organization with serving the interests of a small number of individuals who have gained power within the organization. This theory is called the *iron law of oligarchy*. Although Michels studied political parties and labor unions, an excellent recent business example that supports his hypothesis would be the 2002 corporate scandals in which top executives made themselves rich through unethical practices while their companies suffered, investors lost millions of dollars, and employees lost their pension funds and/or their jobs. In the nonprofit sector, the William Aramany scandal at the United Way continues to impede the ability of the charity to raise funds. In 1995 this CEO was sentenced to jail after he misappropriated $1.2 million in United Way funds for perks, such as trips to Europe on the Concorde and a New York penthouse apartment. In the early 1990s, one-fourth of the 117 largest nonprofit agencies paid their CEOs a salary of more than $200,000 (Simross, 1992).

Rational/Social Exchange Perspective

The rationalist perspective in organizations emphasizes efficiency. Programs are evaluated on the basis of the ratio of costs to benefits (Holland, 1995). The rationalist perspective is also used to explain the relationship between management and employees. Using this perspective, managers act on the assumption that employees will put their own interests before those of the company (Hodge, Anthony, & Gailes, 1996). *Equity theory* suggests that if employees think they invest more in their work than they get back in wages and benefits, they will act to reduce the imbalance, perhaps by working less or taking company resources for personal use (Adams, 1963). An example would be using the company phone to make personal long-distance calls. Organizations respond by setting up systems to monitor employees' time and use of resources.

Controlling employee behavior through close supervision of workers is one of several themes of *scientific management theory,* whose focus is maximum productivity (Taylor, 1911). Frederick Taylor was particularly interested in increasing the efficiency of factory workers. One way he did this was to conduct "time and motion" studies to determine the most efficient way of designing each job or task.

In common usage, bureaucracy has come to be associated with inefficiency and "red tape," particularly in public administration (Pugh, Hickson, & Hinings, 1985). Max Weber (1922/1978), however, originally assigned the term *bureaucracy* to organizations that employ strictly rational methods to maximize efficiency. In addition to a *hierarchy of authority* that ensures that each worker is closely supervised, Weber listed several other characteristics of an ideal bureaucracy: specialization, rules and regulations, written communications and records, qualification-based employment, and impersonality. *Specialization* means that each employee is responsible for a specific and limited number of tasks. Formal (usually written) and standardized *rules and regulations* guide the day-to-day operation of the organization. *Written communication* (e.g., memos) and *records* are used to track what is said and done. *Qualification-based employment* means that people are hired and retained based on their ability to perform the functions of their job, rather than on personal relationships or other factors not directly related to job performance. *Impersonality* means treating everyone the same, regardless of any special circumstances that fall outside of procedural guidelines.

Bounded rationality is a term coined by March and Simon (1958) to describe the limits on logical decision making in organizations imposed by incomplete information and the inability (due to limited resources, including time) to identify and explore all of the possible alternatives available. The result is an outcome called *satisficing* (March & Simon, 1958), or settling for a satisfactory solution rather than seeking an ideal one. An example would be sending only supervisors to receive training in a new clinical technique rather than sending front-line staff. Another quasi-rational approach to decision making in organizations is *incrementalism* (Hickson, 1987), or making shifts in small steps to avoid conflict and limit irreversible commitment to a major change. In a school, this might mean using temporary portable classrooms rather than building a permanent addition.

Organizational rationality in the early twenty-first century represents a continuation of the scientific management approaches of Frederick Taylor. According to Ritzer (1996), the methods used by McDonald's restaurants have become the current model of rationality. *McDonaldization* is "the process by which the principles of the fast-food industry are coming to dominate more and more sectors of American society as well as the rest of the world" (p. 1). Organizations everywhere of every type (e.g., beauty parlors, hospitals and clinics, retail stores, universities, travel agencies, and car maintenance shops) are adopting the principles of McDonaldization: efficiency, calculability, predictability, and increased control though automation. For example, customers may experience *efficiency* as getting an entire breakfast by simple going through the McDonald's drive-thru and ordering an Egg McMuffin. Efficiency is also enhanced by having restaurant customers themselves place their orders, pick up their food, refill their drinks, and bus their tables. Ritzer explains *calculability* as an emphasis on the quantitative aspects of products (e.g., the Quarter Pounder) and the time it takes to deliver them ("ready in three minutes or it's free"). *Predictability* is the result of a highly rational approach that prescribes every ingredient and every step of the process. Predictability ensures that a Big Mac purchased in Los Angeles next year will be identical to one purchased in New York last year. At McDonald's, employees are trained to do a limited number of tasks in precisely the way they are told to do them. Managers make sure the workers follow the prescribed routine. But because human beings are not always predictable or controllable, the restaurant replaces them with machines, such as drink dispensers that shut off automatically when the cup is full or French fry machines that lift the basket out of the oil when the fries are crisp.

Constructionist Perspective

The constructionist perspective is implicit in the study of organizational culture. *Organizational culture* is "the constellation of values, beliefs, assumptions and expectations" that shape the behavior of members of an organization (Holland, 1995, p. 1789). "Shared meaning, shared understanding, and shared sense making" are different ways of describing organizational culture (Morgan, 1986, p. 128). Organizational cultures reflect larger, national cultures as well as regional cultures in a country as large and diverse as the United States. A U.S. automobile manufacturing plant would have different expectations than a plant in Germany, and one in Michigan may have a different culture than one in Alabama or South Carolina.

Within a given workplace, organizational culture is the product of a stable social unit with a significant shared history—that means there may be several [sub]cultures operating, including a managerial culture, various occupationally based cultures, and group cultures based on locational proximity (Schein, 1985). For example, in a hospital, one might encounter nursing, social work, and accounting subcultures, as well as subcultures related to the intensive care unit, the emergency room, the pediatric wing, and outpatient services. In analyzing an organization's culture, we acknowledge the process of reality construction. Like other types of culture, organizational culture operates largely outside the conscious awareness of group members.

If an organization has only a weak culture, employees with different perspectives, norms, and values are freer to act on their individual inclinations. In a human service agency, a weak culture can result in inconsistencies in the provision of client services. When norms and values are clearly laid out and enforced, an organization is said to possess a strong culture (Mischel, 1977). In such organizations, the culture provides a behavioral standard to which everyone subscribes. Organizations with strong cultures may also have more informal penalties for nonconformity. For example, in an agency that has a cultural norm that prescribes that workers remain in the building at lunchtime so that they can be available for clients, a new worker who goes out to eat may be greeted by sarcastic comments from peers when he returns.

Edgar Schein (1985, p. 2) suggests "the only thing of real importance that [organizational] leaders do is to create and manage culture and that the unique talent of leaders is their ability to work with culture." Among the ways the leaders can reinforce organizational culture are through what they pay attention to, measure, and control; reactions to critical incidents; criteria for the allocation of rewards and status; criteria for recruitment, selection, promotion, and "excommunication" of employees; and deliberate role modeling, teaching, and coaching (Schein, 1985, pp. 224–225). For example, a manager who values group process can support that kind of organizational culture not only by creating many different committees and advisory groups, but also by attending their meetings.

The physical design of an organization also reflects its cultural values. The number, location, size, and furnishings of private offices; the presence of conference rooms and break rooms; and the ambience of waiting areas (including the provision of comfortable seating, current magazines, a television, fish tank, or toys) speak volumes about the organization's regard for employees and clients. For example, "welfare clients in a drab, unattractive waiting room, sitting on hard benches, are being given an unequivocal message of their inferior status in the welfare system, if not in society" (Seabury, 1971, pp. 47–48).

In addition to organizational culture, the constructionist perspective also frames theories about management styles and employee motivation. Three names often associated with these topics are Douglas McGregor, Frederick Herzberg, and Elton Mayo.

Noting the importance of subjective assumptions, McGregor (1960) identified two management styles that he labeled "Theory X" and "Theory Y." Theory X managers view workers as motivated only by rewards or by threats of punishment; these managers respond by providing much structure and close supervision. Theory Y managers view employees as wanting to grow and develop, and being motivated by internal rewards; they respond by giving their workers new challenges and responsibilities.

Theory Y is consistent with Herzberg's classic theory of employee motivation. Herzberg (1986) identified *hygiene factors*—such as pay, benefits, status, job security, and working conditions—that keep employees from being dissatisfied but do not motivate them. Truly *motivating factors* include opportunities for challenge, responsibility, advancement, recognition, or achievement.

Mayo conducted research at the Hawthorne Plant of the Western Electric Company between 1927 and 1932 (Homans, 1986). Although his goal was to investigate the effects of physical conditions such as lighting, humidity, equipment, and worker fatigue on performance, he discovered that productivity increased regardless of changes in the physical environment or working hours. He concluded that psychological and social factors were as important as other work conditions. The attention given the workers in the experiment and their interpretation of this attention was a crucial factor in their increased productivity. This reaction has been dubbed the "Hawthorne effect." The implication of this finding is that workers should be invited to participate in decisions that affect their work. In this and other experiments, Mayo also found that informal work group norms have a significant effect on worker output; production rates above or below the informal norms resulted in social pressure to conform. This emphasis on understanding and using psychological and social variables is part of the *human relations model* of organizational administration (Mayo, 1933). Interest in the human relations model led to further research on small groups and the development or refinement of concepts such as group norms, roles, leadership, and decision making. An understanding of organizational life is often dependent on an appreciation of the small groups that function within organizations.

Preferred Perspectives

Among the alternatives to traditional, bureaucratic organizations are *consensus organizations* (Iannello, 1992). In consensus organizations, rules are kept to a minimum and decisions are reached by mutual agreement. Often leadership positions are rotated and there is no special financial reward for leaders. Authority rests with the members rather than with a select few individuals at the top of the organization. Examples of consensus organizations, especially popular in the 1970s, include alternative schools, free medical clinics, legal collectives, food cooperatives, communes, and, most common, craft cooperatives (Morgen, 1994). Consensus is most easily achieved in organizations that have a homogenous workforce and a strong, shared ideology and culture.

Collectives are consensus organizations that are owned and managed by the members. They tend to be quite small (averaging 6.5 member-employees) and to operate in special niches of the economy that exempt them from competing directly with conventional companies (Rothschild & Russell, 1986; Rothschild & Whitt, 1986). While workers are generally more satisfied and invest greater energy in collectives, stress and burnout may result (Rothschild & Russell, 1986). Rothschild and Whitt suggest that collectivist organizations represent a "countertrend" to the increasing concentration in both economic and government institutions of power and control in fewer and fewer units. They say that what collectivist organizations all have in common is the "simple, but profound, desire for self-initiated, self-paced, self-controlled work . . . [and] the desire for meaningful group life" (p. 183).

Evidence indicates that without small size, nonbureacratic forms of organization are difficult to establish and maintain (Rothschild & Russell, 1986). Nevertheless, in an effort to reap some of the benefits of nonhierarchical organizations, some corporations have made efforts to broaden worker participation in decision making. For example, they may encourage the development of work teams and other intermediate bodies that promise to help decentralize their structures and empower workers.

Specific management approaches that facilitate worker empowerment include Theory Z, total quality management (TQM), and feminist styles. In the 1980s, when the U.S. manufacturing sector was growing weaker, management specialists suggested that the Japanese system of management might be a preferred alternative. This new approach was labeled *Theory Z* by William Ouichi (1981). Unlike the highly specialized career paths of American workers, Japanese workers and managers acquired a wide base of technical knowledge by moving to different assignments around the company. Consistent with Japanese culture, there was a strong emphasis on the importance of the work group. *Quality circles,* made up of five to fifteen individuals, met regularly with their managers to resolve problems related to working conditions or group performance (Ishikawa, 1984). The differential between executive salaries and worker wages was (and is) much smaller in Japan than in the United States. All of these factors were assumed to encourage employee loyalty and high productivity. Organizations that have adapted elements of Theory Z management include divisions of AT&T, Eastman Chemical (Kodak), General Electric, Lexmark International (a former division of IBM), Motorola, and Xerox (Byrne, 1993). An American derivative of these Japanese management principles is called *total quality management* or TQM (Ginsberg, 1995).

Another alternative to more traditional management styles is one often manifested by female managers (although not all women use it and some men do) (Cox, 1993). One characteristic of this style is a manner of communication that values sharing and willingness to ask questions in order to gain a fuller understanding of the situation (Helgesen, 1990; Tannen, 1994). This is in contrast to a "male" style of communication that is task focused and concerned about how asking questions will affect questioner's image (Tannen, 1994). A second characteristic of women's management style is their relationship with subordinates. Women are less hierarchical and tend to offer greater autonomy to their subordinates (Helgesen, 1990; Rosener, 1990). This more egalitarian style of management is often misunderstood as a weakness (Tannen, 1994). It is likely that these differences in style are the result of the cultural socialization of females that leads them to recognize the

> value of supporting and nurturing others, of protecting long-term . . . relationships, of seeking solutions in which everyone wins, and wherever possible, of forging a mutuality of interests. As a result of women's intensive socialization for their likely role in the family, they have often been taught to be responsive to others' needs, to seek mutually acceptable and equitable solutions, to support others, and to share information. (Rothschild & Davies, 1994, p. 588)

The literature suggests that the full participation of members of different backgrounds in an organization promotes creativity, flexibility, and problem solving (Cox, 1993). Lack of diversity and the resulting omission of minority points of view may encourage *groupthink* (see Chapter 11). An example of this is the sex abuse scandal in the Catholic Church that was exposed in 2002. Primarily celibate older white men made decisions to protect the organization at the expense of vulnerable children. Critics of the Church have argued that if a more diverse group had shared leadership roles, the abusive practices would not have been tolerated.

On the other hand, if diversity is not well managed, communication problems may increase and morale may suffer. Given the changing demographics of the workforce, workplace diversity is inevitable in most sectors. Social workers need to draw upon their values and skills to help make workplace diversity a positive feature of organizational life.

The Impact of Organizations on Individuals and Families

How Organizations Obstruct Well-Being

Labor history and literature suggest that organizational settings are sources of oppression and health hazards for many people. This section documents the ongoing negative effects of organizations on today's workforce.

Discrimination. When a particular category of people (such as affluent white males) dominates the hierarchy of most organizations, the result is barriers against people in other categories, such as women and people of color. Even though discrimination based on race and sex has been against the law for some time, many examples of unfair treatment still exist, as evidenced in the limited number of women and minorities in high-level positions, restricted access to authority even when they are in managerial jobs, and lower salaries for women and people of color when compared to white males with similar credentials and experience (Reskin & Padavic, 1994).

The nature of racial discrimination in organizations has changed. Although there are still instances of overt discrimination (Reskin & Padavic, 1994), usually the oppression of racial minorities is not so apparent (Kendall & Feagin, 1983). Today blatant racism may affect profitability, so "companies must promote diversity—or at least pretend to" (Henslin, 2001, p. 188). The presence of people of color in the organization satisfies Equal Opportunity requirements and Affirmative Action goals. Sometimes people of color are hired or promoted in mostly white organizations to be used as *tokens,* or high-profile representatives of their race. Tokenism results in *surplus visibility* (Patai, 1991), or focused attention on the token individual whose achievements or mistakes are then viewed as a reflection on his or her whole race. The presence of a small handful of minorities also enhances *contrast effects,* or an exaggeration of the differences between groups and the similarities within groups. Even if they are a significant part of a company's workforce, people of color are routinely channeled to support positions or departments where they are limited to dealing with other people of color who are customers or employees: their job assignments are comprised of affirmative action, community relations, and minority affairs (Collins, 1989; Collins, 1993; Cose, 1993; Reskin & Padavic, 1994). Despite important-sounding titles, these positions are unlikely to prepare the employee for advancement to more powerful positions in the organization. Sometimes lateral moves to areas from which executives are promoted are blocked; the resulting barriers are called *glass walls* (Schaefer, 2000).

Scholars have identified certain factors that account for the concentration of people of color in entry-level or peripheral positions. Berheide (1992) called this phenomenon the *sticky floor.* These factors include lack of mentors and role models, exclusion from informal communication networks, limited access to training, and early "tracking" into less challenging assignments (Cose, 1993; Feagin, 1991; Irons & Moore, 1985; Kanter, 1993; Simon & Akabas, 1993).

Many of the same factors are cited to explain why women appear to perform more poorly than men in organizations. Surplus visibility, contrast effects, negative stereotypes, exclusion from informal networks, lack of mentors, limited training opportunities, and in addition, ill-fitting clothing or equipment designed for male bodies, inadequate bathroom facilities, and a climate of sexual harassment make some work environments more hostile for women (Simon & Akabas, 1993). Because women continue to carry major responsibilities for meeting family needs, they may be forced to take jobs that have short or flexible hours so that they can accommodate the schedules of their husbands and children. *Mommy track* is the term used to describe work affording flexible or shorter hours. Although the Family and Medical Leave Act of 1993 protects some women who need to take time off work to care for a newborn or other dependent family member, the United States remains one of only six industrialized countries that have no requirement for paid maternity leave (DiNitto, 2000). Women who take extended breaks from employment to deal with family needs may be penalized by missing opportunities for promotion or simply gaining seniority.

In 2002, women constituted 46.6 percent of the U.S. labor force and 15.7 percent (up from 8.7 percent in 1995) of corporate officers in the largest 500 firms according to Catalyst, a New York-based women's advocacy group that collects the data biannually (Gomez, 2002). There were six women CEOs (compared to just one in 1995). According to the same survey, 71 of the Fortune 500 companies had no women corporate officers.

There is a form of gender discrimination labeled the *glass ceiling*. This is a mostly invisible barrier that keeps women from being promoted to the highest levels of an organization. In contrast, men who are employed in traditionally female occupations, such as social work, nursing, and elementary education encounter not a glass ceiling, but a *glass escalator* that provides an express ride to the top. Compared to their female coworkers, they are promoted to higher-level positions, given more desirable work assignments, and paid higher salaries (Williams, 1995).

Workplace Hazards and Other Forms of Exploitation of Employees.   Social work students may have learned about the 1911 Triangle Shirt Waist factory fire in New York that created the impetus for federal involvement in setting and enforcing worker safety standards. In spite of government regulations that should protect them, over 11,000 workers die from on-the-job injuries every year and 50,000 die from occupationally related diseases; in addition, there are 1.8 million job injuries and 60,000 of these involve permanent disability (Parenti, 1995). Parenti notes that this "is mostly due to inadequate safety standards and lax enforcement of codes" (p. 109). As recently as 1991, a fire at the Imperial chicken plant in Hamlet, North Carolina, killed 25 people and injured 49. Emergency exits had been chained shut. Company executives had ordered the doors locked "to keep employees from going outside for coffee breaks, or stealing chickens" (Wright, Cullen, & Blankenship, 1995). Most of those killed were African American women. In addition to occupations that have obvious dangers, such as law enforcement, meat packing, or mining, occupations that expose workers to various hazardous materials include pest control, paper, wood, chemical, drug, and paint industries, as well as beauty shops and drycleaners (Draper, 1993).

Perhaps less alarming but more commonplace are the chronic physical and mental illnesses that result from psychological pressures in the workplace. These include cardiovascular diseases (high blood pressure, heart attacks, and strokes), anxiety, and depression (Ironson, 1992). Moody (cited in Ehrenreich, 2001, p. 35) argues that there is a new system of "'management by stress' in which workers in a variety of industries are being squeezed to extract maximum productivity to the detriment of their health." McNeely (1992, p. 235) reports that the satisfaction of female human service workers was affected much more than that of their male coworkers by perceptions of excessive on-the-job pressure and of job performance expectations—perhaps because they were at the same time experiencing work-family conflict.

A term used to describe one type of reaction to job stress is *burnout.* Burnout has been defined as "psychological withdrawal from work in response to excessive stress or dissatisfaction" (Cherniss, 1980, p. 16). Craig (1999) notes that individuals in the helping professions—social workers, police officers, nurses, therapists, teachers, and others who often work in tension-filled situations—are especially at risk. She says that those "who suffer job burnout are idealistic, highly motivated, extremely competent workers who finally realize they cannot make the difference they once thought they could" (pp. 336–337). An example of burnout in a human service agency might involve a social worker who does the bare minimum in terms of job requirements, complains of psychosomatic illnesses and is frequently absent as she or he "counts down" the months to retirement. Craig suggests that to avoid burnout, workers should be realistic in their goals, not take work troubles home with them, and develop interests outside their jobs. Smaller caseloads, better pay, and other improvements in working conditions also would help alleviate burnout in human service workers.

In addition to threats to life and health, employees at the bottom of the organization are also subjected to exploitation in other forms. For example, companies can avoid paying overtime by labeling certain low-level employees "managers" who then become "exempt" from wage and hour regulations (and thus ineligible for overtime pay), or by hiring people for less than full-time positions so that they don't have to provide benefits such as health insurance or paid time off. Allowing bathroom breaks for employees was not legally required until 1998 (Linder & Nygaard, 1998).

Worker Responses. Although workplace conditions and family-related policies may be addressed by government or company directives, any hope for change has to take into account the unequal status of employee and employer; overall, working people have limited power to change the workplace to better accommodate their needs (Draper, 1993; Piotrkowski & Hughes, 1993). This is especially true for people from lower-socioeconomic classes who have limited finances and limited alternatives. Employees are not passive victims of their work environments, however. Workers may respond to problematic situations by resistance, slowdowns, or strikes, and collective bargaining. Labor unions have contributed significantly to the 40-hour workweek standard, health and retirement benefits, and workplace safety, and union workers typically earn higher wages than do nonunion workers in comparable jobs. In the past 40 years, the proportion of unionized workers in the United States has declined, although the number of unionized workers has increased largely as a result of the growth of public employee unions (Kendall, 2001, p. 420).

Effects on Consumers. In addition to the ways organizations obstruct the well-being of their employees, they may use their considerable power to inhibit the well-being of others who come into contact with them. An example that many people encounter is *red tape,* or a bureaucratic preoccupation with rules and procedures that get in the way of meeting the needs of customers and clients. Other frustrations occur when a company or agency puts its own needs ahead of those of consumers. Nearly everyone has experienced the frustration of dealing with an organization's ineffective phone answering system that was purportedly designed to "serve you better" but instead only replaces direct telephone contact with the organization's staff with a series of tape recorded messages.

On a more significant level, some organizations have chosen to put profits before the health and safety needs of consumers. A well-known recent example of this was the decision by the Ford Motor Company to resist a recall of their Explorer SUV model even when they were aware that there were serious flaws that put motorists at risk and resulted in a number of deaths. Another example is the ongoing promotion of cigarettes, which contribute to the illness and deaths of many consumers, despite a 1997 court ruling that regulated the sale of tobacco. This industry targets adolescents, women in their early twenties, blue-collar men, and African Americans and Latinos.

How Organizations Promote Well-Being

Even traditional organizations can contribute to the well-being of employees through a variety of measures. In addition to the obvious advantages of salaries, benefits, and job satisfaction, these may include flextime and on-site day care to help with family responsibilities, employee assistance organizations [EAPs] to help with personal problems, on-site gyms to keep employees healthy, and employee stock ownership plans.

Every October *Working Mothers* magazine identifies the "ten best places to work" based on support for employees and their families. Some of the more unusual benefits noted were on-site auto maintenance for employees, take-home dinners, on-site hairstyling, and a gradual "phase back" program to reintegrate new moms and dads into the workplace after taking family leave. While these companies are notable, the reality is that they represent but a small portion of American employers.

Corporations have led the way in promoting equal treatment of gay men and lesbians. Among the Fortune 500 companies, 318 have rules barring discrimination against gay employees, and 197 provide domestic partners with medical coverage (Kershaw, 2003).

Many corporations also make substantial contributions to charities and foundations. It should be understood, however, that this generosity allows these corporations to place their resources with nonprofits that benefit their employees and their communities at the same time that they enhance their public image and save on taxes (Odendahl, 1990).

Organizations as Providers of Social Services and as Employers of Social Workers

Social workers are employed in a variety of organizations. In many, social workers are directly involved in meeting the primary goals of the organization. Examples would include agencies that provide child protection services, mental health or family counseling, and battered women's shelters. In others, called *host organizations,* social workers provide ancillary services. Examples of host organizations are schools, hospitals, and prisons. It is not uncommon for social workers in host settings to be called upon to work with clients' families, and to locate and arrange for services or funding from other agencies. These social workers also may be called upon to present, explain, and defend social work values and to advocate for clients.

In addition to providing social services per se, many social workers in various organizations supervise support staff, paraprofessionals, and volunteers.

Social service agencies and host organizations are subject to the same economic trends as other companies. In difficult economic times, staff are likely to be asked to do more with less, to live with threats of being "downsized," or to focus services on clients who can pay full fees themselves or have adequate insurance coverage. These situations present barriers to optimal services as well as ethical dilemmas.

Looking Ahead

In Chapter 10, we address a special kind of organization, residential institutions. These are not the social institutions we discussed in Part II, but rather the settings and facilities that house individuals who pose a threat to society or have very special needs that cannot be met in the community.

Key Points

- A formal organization is a social system that is deliberately established for the purpose of achieving specific goals.

- Many nonprofit agencies have chosen to pursue for-profit activities, blurring the distinction between themselves and for-profits organizations.

- Affirmative action has become a controversial issue in organizations, although legacy privilege is seldom acknowledged or challenged.

- Deaths caused by company violations of safety regulations outnumber homicide deaths by a ratio of five to one.

- Sources of power in organizations include formal authority, control of scarce resources, control of information, and interpersonal alliances.

- Organizations everywhere of every type are adopting the principles of McDonaldization: efficiency, calculability, predictability, and increased control though automation.

- When norms and values are clearly laid out and enforced, an organization is said to possess a strong culture.

- In consensus organizations, rules are kept to a minimum and decisions are reached by mutual agreement.

- Lack of diversity and the resulting omission of minority points of view may encourage a negative process called *groupthink*.

- Even though discrimination based on race and sex has been against the law for some time, many examples of unfair treatment still exist.

- In the past 40 years, the proportion of unionized workers in the United States has declined, although the number of unionized workers has increased.

Questions to Think about and Discuss

1. Everyone is aware of the negative aspects of bureaucracy. Provide some examples from your college or employment experience.

2. Although many people think they would like to work at a consensus organization, such as a free clinic, can you think of any aspects of this type of employment that might be difficult?

3. Have your experiences in organizations made you a believer in the "Iron Law of Oligarchy" or not? What examples can you give to support your position?

4. Can you think of examples of how the principles of McDonaldization have been applied to settings other than fast-food restaurants?

5. Choose two different organizational settings in your community. Describe the organizational culture of each.

6. Do you believe that your field placement agency values diversity? What steps has it taken to promote diversity within its staff?

Recommended Readings

Korten, D. C. (1995). *When corporations rule the world*. West Hartford, CT: Kumarian Press.
Linder, M., & Nygaard, I. (1997). *Void where prohibited: Rest breaks and the right to urinate on company time*. Ithaca, NY: Cornell University Press.
Simon, D. R. (2002). *Elite deviance* (7th ed.). Boston: Allyn & Bacon.

Internet Search Terms

Affirmative action   McDonaldization   Organizational culture
Bureaucracy   Nonprofit organizations   Total Quality Management
Burnout

10

Residential Institutions

The lives of many social work clients are affected by institutions. In the *Social Work Almanac,* Ginsberg (1995) estimates that 27 percent of social workers in the year 2005 will be employed in prisons, hospitals, nursing and personal care facilities, and other forms of residential care. The role of institutions in America has changed dramatically in the past two centuries. For example, "jails and prisons have increasingly become America's social agency of first resort for coping with the deepening problems of a society in perennial crisis" (Currie, 1998, p. 34).

Defining Institutions

Institutions are organizational settings where residents exercise little or no choice about their participation, have virtually no input into how they are treated, and cannot leave without being officially released or discharged. Moore and Starkes (1992) identified three kinds of institutional settings: those that are medically oriented, those that are residential and service oriented, and those that are custodial and/or correctional. "All provide some mix of custody and treatment," they note, and the total milieu is considered to be part of the service delivery process. This total milieu idea was emphasized in a book about residential child care centers, *The Other 23 Hours* (Trieschman, Whittaker, & Brentro, 1969), which pointed out that what happens in the hours outside the therapy session may have more of an impact than what happens in it, and that the cook or the groundskeeper, not to mention the recreation therapist and the child care staff, may play as important a role in a youth's treatment as his or her therapist.

    Erving Goffman (1961) perceived the defining characteristic of an institution to be the inability of residents to leave at will. Wolf Wolfensberger (1972), on the other hand, believed that it was the features of *deindividuation* that make institutions different from other organizations and residences. These features include numbers of residents distinctly larger than might be found in a large family, a high level of regimentation, a physical or social environment that aims at a low common denominator, and a place in which all or most of the transactions of daily life are carried out under one roof or on one "campus" (pp. 28–29). For example, a traditional children's residential treatment center might have dozens or even hundreds of residents; it certainly would not be mistaken for a typical single family home even if it were located in a residential neighborhood. Residents all eat breakfast at 7 a.m. and dinner at 5:30 p.m. whether they are hungry or not; there are craft activities on Wednesday evenings and videos on Fridays; group therapy is offered on Tuesdays and Thursdays. If the neediest resident can't manage an outing to the mall, then no one can go to the mall. Most residents sleep, eat, socialize, attend classes, study, play, exercise, watch TV, and receive counseling on the same campus, if not in the same buildings, day after day.

At a less coercive level on the continuum are institutional settings where people live for extended periods of time, but are not so isolated from society. These include assisted living centers, half-way houses, group homes, and other *community-based facilities*. Residents living in these facilities often participate in the same activities, at the same locations, as other community members. For example, children living in a community-based group home are likely to attend a public school and swim at the local Y. At the other end of the continuum are *total institutions* (Goffman, 1961), those organizations that isolate residents (sometimes called *inmates* in these settings) from the rest of society and put them under the control of the officials who run the institution. Usually total institutions attempt to resocialize the residents to become more compliant and accepting of institutional and societal norms. Rewards (or more commonly punishments) are used to encourage conformity. The success of total institutions in rehabilitating and preparing their clients for reintegration into society has been strongly and widely challenged (Kendall, 2001).

A Brief History of Institutions

In the mid-nineteenth century, there appeared a well-intentioned effort to provide a new kind of help for at least some at-risk populations. Originally conceived as sanctuaries, *asylums* were established in the countryside with the intention of resocializing and rehabilitating inmates (including not only prisoners, but also people with mental illness, mental retardation, and dependent children) in a wholesome environment far from the chaos, temptations, and exploitations of the city (Rothman, 1971). Physical separation of the asylum from the community was consistently practiced.

At the turn of the century, what began as efforts toward reform had been transformed into a system of custodial and/or punitive care. By the 1950s, public attention was brought to bear on the deplorable conditions that existed in asylums. Exposes such as Goffman's *Asylums* (1961) pointed out the deleterious effects of institutions on the lives of inmates who were given minimal custodial care without treatment (a process called *warehousing*). At the same time, the growing costs of institutional care, advances in pharmacology, and changes in public assistance policies supported a drive for deinstitutionalization. The term *deinstitutionalization* refers to preventing inappropriate admissions to institutions and developing appropriate alternatives in the community.

The civil rights movement in this country provided fertile ground for legal action on behalf of institutionalized persons. Reflecting the "due process clause" of the Fourteenth Amendment to the Constitution, several court cases that were heard during the 1970s and early 1980s, augmented by federal and state statutes, public licensing, and private accreditation standards, affirmed the basic rights of institutionalized people. These included the rights to be housed in the least restrictive setting; to receive minimally adequate, reasonable, appropriate, and humane treatment, rehabilitation, or training in the least restrictive manner (e.g., without the unnecessary or excessive use of physical restraints or isolation); to refuse treatment; to refuse to participate in involuntary or uncompensated work for nontherapeutic reasons; to be assured of confidentiality of records and privacy in treatment; to have personal property (within reason) and to wear one's own clothes; and to live without supervision in the community if the individuals pose no threat to themselves or others (Saltzman & Proch, 1990). Unnecessary restraints and excessive use of seclusion in prisons have also been ruled unconstitutional.

Unfortunately, the implementation of desinstitutionalization policies often resulted in the precipitous discharge of residents without concurrent development of family support and community resources (DiNitto, 2000). Thus, many patients with chronic mental illnesses became homeless "street people," while others ended up in places smaller but no less "institutional" than their previous setting, or worse yet, in local jails. This pattern of moving from one institution to another is called *transinstitutionalization* (Segal, 1995).

Issues and Trends

Privatization

A recent trend in institutional care is the privatization of facilities. Large private, for-profit corporations have developed nursing homes, psychiatric treatment centers, and especially prisons (Bohm & Haley, 1997; Karger & Stoesz, 2002). The trend toward privatization in prisons is discussed in more detail in Chapter 3.

"Revolving Door" Care

The term *revolving door* refers to a pattern of care that involves repeated admissions and discharges. This has been particularly clear in the case of people with chronic mental illnesses. Although the push for deinstitutionalization has prevented unnecessary, long-term custodial care, it also has encouraged premature discharges and repeated readmissions (Segal, 1995). In general, patterns of mental health admission to institutions now are periodic, temporary, frequent, and short-term (Moore & Starkes, 1992, p. 173). The term can also be applied to other institutionalized populations. For example, among state prisoners, 62 percent are rearrested within three years of their release and 41 percent are reincarcerated (Slevin, 2000). (The percentage of convicts who are rearrested is called the *recidivism rate*.)

Moore and Starkes (1992, p. 173) also note that concern now seems to have turned away from the location of care to issues of continuity-of-care. The *continuity-of-care* perspective views institutionalization as only one aspect of treatment and assumes that professionals will develop and implement a plan for working with significant others in clients' lives and for appropriate aftercare and follow-up after discharge.

Other trends in institutional care in America vary by population. Some of these patterns have been well publicized, while others are less well known. They are discussed below.

Criminal Justice

There has been extensive press coverage of the explosion in the prison population in this country, thanks in part to data collected by the nonprofit watchdog group "The Sentencing Project" (www.sentencingproject.org). Between 1970 and 1997, the prison population in American grew by 635 percent while the general population increased by only 31 percent (*Statistical Abstract,* 1995/1999). In the last 20 years, the percentage of drug offenders in federal prisons increased from 25 percent to almost 60 percent (Maguire & Pastore, 2001). The number of youth under the age of 18 incarcerated in adult institutions doubled between 1985 and 1997 (Talbot, 2000).

Because of new "get tough" on crime policies and problems created by massive prison overcrowding, the federal courts began to retreat from their active engagement in prison reform in the 1980s (Saltzman & Proch, 1990, p. 372). Negative conditions in federal and state prisons remain an ongoing concern for advocates of social justice.

Although prison overcrowding is an ongoing concern, *jails* currently represent one of the most problematic aspects of institutional care. Jails serve a "catchall function," holding convicted offenders serving short-term sentences, convicted offenders awaiting transfer to prison, probation and parole violators, vagrants, drunks, people who are mentally ill and/or homeless, and increasingly, juveniles. In addition to being overcrowded, many are old, unsanitary, and inadequately staffed. Problems result from the limited and unstable nature of local taxes, a general lack of public support for jail reform, rapid rates of inmate turnover that make it difficult to develop and coordinate programs, and the immense diversity of risks and needs found among inmates (Bohm & Haley, 1997, p. 339). Jails are a prime example of the effects of deinstitutionalization. With 3,000 inmates receiving psychiatric services, the Los Angeles County jail system is now said to be the largest mental institution in the United States, and also, the largest homeless shelter (Izumi, Schiller, & Hayward, 1996).

Older Adults

Older adults who were confined to public mental hospitals were the principal beneficiaries of policies of deinstitutionalization, but in the last decade there has been a steady growth in the institutionalization of older adults (Segal, 1995, p. 710). At any one time, about 4.5 percent of the population over 65, and 50 percent of those over 95, can be found in a nursing home (National Center for Health Statistics, 1999). Estimates of an older person's chance of spending time in a nursing home are 30 percent for men and 50 percent for women (Hooyman & Kiyak, 2002). The average length of stay dropped from 89 days in 1985 to 45 days in 1997 (Sahyoun, Pratt, Lentzner, Dey, & Robinson, 2001). In both 1985 and 1997, the main reasons for admission were cognitive impairment, incontinence (difficulty controlling bowel or bladder functions), and other types of functional decline, although cardiovascular diseases were the most common malady (Sahyoun et al., 2001). Because there are more impaired older adults living in the community than in nursing homes, one might safely conclude that institutionalization often results from lack of a care provider or support services rather than disabilities of old age per se.

According to a study ordered by Congress (Fleck, 2002), more than 90 percent of the nation's nursing homes are inadequately staffed, putting residents at risk for bedsores, bloodborne infections, dehydration, malnutrition, and pneumonia. The nursing home industry blames low rates of reimbursement under federal Medicaid and Medicare programs. Critics counter that government rates more than doubled between 1992 and 1998, and nursing homes chose to use the money to boost profits or to finance takeovers rather than to increase staffing (Fleck, 2002, p. 16).

People with Mental Illness

After deinstitutionalization led to the closing of most wards in state mental hospitals without the adequate development of community-based alternatives, care of the mentally ill population shifted to detention centers, jails, and prisons. More than 35 percent of correction facility inmates may have serious mental health problems (Severson, 1994). Of the 10 million adults booked into local jails each year, approximately 700,000 have active symptoms of mental illness (The Sentencing Project, 2002). The number of seriously mentally ill inmates in the jails and prisons may be twice that in state mental hospitals on any given day (Torrey, 1995). Most mentally ill offenders are arrested for minor offenses such as trespassing, vagrancy, urinating in public, or shoplifting at the corner convenience store. Many of them also have substance abuse problems, but cannot get into drug- and alcohol-treatment programs because of their mental illnesses. Due to budget cuts and lack of space in state mental health hospitals, some mentally ill individuals may remain in jail for up to two years—even with court intervention—before being admitted to a more appropriate facility (Bell, 2002).

People with Developmental Disabilities

Before deinstitutionalization, many people with developmental disabilities (e.g., mental retardation) lived in the same institutions as people with mental illnesses. The service system for people with developmental disabilities has moved away from institutionalization and segregation. Current practice emphasizes habilitation and rehabilitation training, and consumer-driven, highly individualized supports (Freedman, 1995). Now most people with disabilities live with their families or reside in community-based facilities, including intermediate-care facilities, foster homes, group homes, boarding homes, and supervised apartments (Segal, 1995).

Children and Youth

The rate of institutionalization of children has remained relatively stable for the past two decades, although the names or purposes of the facilities have changed (e.g., from "children's homes" caring for dependent children to "residential treatment centers" rehabilitating those with emotional problems) (Segal, 1995). Armstrong (1993) suggested that another trend was parents placing their children in private psychiatric facilities, possibly reacting to the aggressive marketing campaigns of those corporations as they responded to the willingness of third-party insurers to cover the costs of inpatient treatment, but not the costs for outpatient interventions. On the other hand, a 1999 survey conducted by the National Alliance for the Mentally Ill found that nearly half of those parents responding said that their child was denied services by a managed care plan and 36 percent of the parents said that because needed mental health services were not available, their child was placed in the juvenile justice system (Families Managed Advocacy Project, 2001).

Understanding Institutions

Ecosystems Perspective

Because they cannot voluntarily leave, institutional residents are more affected by the physical characteristics of their environment than people who can come and go at will. Historically, most institutions were immense buildings with high ceilings, long corridors, and large sleeping wards. The recognition of the importance of architectural design in promoting healthier social functioning created an impetus for new institutional facilities. In psychiatric hospitals, there was a shift from large wards to smaller rooms and more home-like, personalized spaces. Research suggests that violence in prisons would be reduced if facilities had carpeted floors, conventional upholstered furniture, and rooms with outside windows (Wener, Frazier, & Farbstein, 1985). Similarly, more home-like designs, privacy, and personal control in settings for persons with profound retardation would decrease social withdrawal and dependency (Friedman, 1976). An example of another innovation in institutional design is the use of enclosed outdoor patio pathways that allow patients with dementia to "go for walks" without getting lost or wandering away from the facility.

Unfortunately, for many residents in institutions, negative reactions to the setting are viewed as examples of individual pathology rather than as normal responses to a hostile environment (see, for example, Rosenhan, 1973). An example is the common reaction by residential group care facilities to children who "act out" upon returning from a weekend "home visit"; the staff decide to limit family contact rather than to explore aspects of the facility or program that make it a negative place to be (Bush, 1980; Milham, Bullock, Hosie, & Haak, 1986).

The general concept of person-environment fit was discussed in Chapter 1. Lawton (1982) and others (see Cavanaugh & Blanchard-Fields, 2002; Lawton & Nahemow, 1973; Murray, 1938) have suggested that one way of examining the person-environment fit is to look at the individual's level of *competence* (his or her capacity to function across several dimensions) and *environmental press* (the demands of the environment). If competence and press are in balance, there is *adaptation*. If there are too many demands and too little competence, the result is maladaptive behavior and negative affect. And if there are too few demands and excess competence, the result is still maladaptive behavior and negative affect. This latter condition is applicable to many institutional settings where there is little in the daily routine that might offer a challenge or opportunity for growth to residents. For example, many nursing home staff members assume a lower level of functioning for residents than they are capable of and make decisions for them, causing residents to appear to be even more dependent than they are (Baltes, 1994, Wahl, 1991; Zarit, Dolan, & Leitsch, 1999). When researchers introduced decision-making options for residents, residents not only demonstrated higher activity levels and greater well-being, but also lower mortality rates (Langer & Rodin, 1976; Rodin & Langer, 1977; Schulz & Hanusa, 1979).

Functionalist Perspective

Functionalists recognize several societal benefits of institutions. Some inmates are in institutions because they represent an immediate threat to society. In removing "deviants" from the community, institutions help to reinforce a greater commitment on the part of the conforming majority to conventional norms and behaviors (Ward & Stone, 1996).

A latent function of institutions is providing employment. An example would be a new prison built in a rural area that lacks other kinds of industries. Functionalists would hold that the employment opportunities and economic growth that result are a positive contribution to the well-being of an area that extends beyond the manifest functions of the institution itself. Studies have shown, however, that the actual outcomes are less encouraging (see Huling, 2002). For example, job turnover rates in for-profit prisons are very high due to poor training and low wages, a majority of prison jobs go to people living outside the community anyway, and prisons fail to foster local retail development because they are likely to attract large chain stores and franchises (Wal-Mart, McDonald's) whose profits will go elsewhere.

Rational/Social Exchange Perspective

Institutions are a special type of organization, called *coercive organizations* by many sociologists because, for the most part, residents are there against their will. As organizations, institutions are designed using a bureaucratic model (see Chapter 9). That means that they have a hierarchical structure, a complex division of labor, and many rules and regulations that apply to staff as well as residents. One of the major complaints that is made about many nursing homes, for example, is that their programs serve to meet the needs of the institution rather than the needs of residents. Regimented scheduling is valued by such facilities despite arguments by gerontologists that such routines are detrimental to residents' well-being (Langer & Rodin, 1976).

On an individual level, the rationalist perspective underlies the deterrence theory of imprisonment (see Chapter 3). *Deterrence theory* suggests that people who are rational will refrain from committing crimes if they believe that the "costs" of the punishment (e.g., incarceration) outweigh the "benefits" of the crime.

On a societal level, a cost-benefit analysis of institutional care suggests that really not much rational thought has gone into planning. The same amount of money invested in preventive programs and community-based care would improve the lives not only of those who end up in institutions but others as well.

Conflict Perspective

From a conflict perspective, institutions satisfy the need to remove from society those who are unable to comply with the demands of the capitalist system (Ward & Stone, 1996). These would include those who are too old or too young to work, those who are chronically ill, or those who are a danger to themselves or others. Spitzer (1980) states it more strongly, saying that institutions are an instrument of social control, used to warehouse the surplus labor population that fails to contribute to capital accumulation.

In institutions, differences in power are everywhere. For residents, freedom of movement is restricted, contact with staff and outsiders is limited, and personal privacy is minimal. Although they are monitored almost continuously, residents have so little power that they may be treated as if they are invisible. Rosenhan (1973, p. 256), for example, reported incidents of ward attendants abusing mental patients in front of other patients, and of a nurse who "unbuttoned her uniform to adjust her brassiere in the presence of an entire ward of viewing men" as if they weren't there. Although in the past few decades laws and regulations have been put in place to protect the basic rights of many institutionalized adults, the reality is that they are still among the most oppressed of our society's citizens.

Given the current political climate, the mistreatment of prisoners is often ignored or even condoned. There is a societal attitude that convicted and incarcerated felons have forfeited their rights to be treated as human beings (Stringfellow, 1990/1991); thus the potential for human rights abuses at both large "supermax" facilities and at smaller, overcrowded facilities is great.

Constructionist Perspective

According to labeling theory, labels such as *patient* or *criminal* may result in institutional residents accepting and internalizing the attributes of those roles (Goffman, 1961). The impact of labeling is not limited to the label recipient but extends to those with whom she or he interacts. For example, once a person is labeled a psychiatric patient, staff may interpret even normal behaviors as symptoms of mental illness (Rosenhan, 1973).

Preferred Perspectives

Along with deinstitutionalization came a movement for institutional reform called *normalization.* In simple terms, normalization means making available to institutionalized people living arrangements that closely resemble those enjoyed by other citizens (Nirje, 1976; Wolfensberger, 1972). This approach suggests that facilities should be small (i.e., designed for no more than six to eight residents). They should resemble valued homes in the community—there should be no signs in front (or on the program vehicle) that identify the residents inside as different from other citizens. Facilities should be integrated into the community so residents can walk, or have available public transportation to the library, shopping centers, movie theaters, bowling alleys, and so forth. Residents should work or receive services away from the facility. There should be a continuum of options available, but residents should not have to move simply because their needs change; instead, services should be adapted so that residents can experience a sense of permanence and security in their living arrangement.

A more recent effort to reform institutions is called the *Eden Alternative*™. This approach was a response to the sterile, pathology-based, treatment orientation of nursing homes that results in loneliness, helplessness, and boredom. Eden Alternative™ founder William Thomas enumerates three fundamental principles of this new kind of care: acknowledging each resident's capacity for growth, focusing on the needs of the residents rather the needs of the institution, and emphasizing quality long-term nurturing care while providing short-term treatment as needed (Thomas, 1994). This new philosophy of care involves

> aesthetically transforming the physical environment of facilities with the addition of pets, plants, and children, creating a "human habitat"; placing maximum possible decision-making authority in the hands of residents and those who care for them; de-emphasizing program activities by encouraging resident involvement in the "human habitat"; and de-emphasizing the use of prescription drugs. (Long-Term Care Paradise, 1999, p. 3)

At the nursing home where Thomas first implemented his program, there was a 50 percent decrease in infection rates, a 71 percent drop in daily drug costs, and a 26 percent decrease in nursing aide turnover (Bruck, 1997). Eden Alternative™ nursing homes in Texas reported a 33 percent reduction in the use of PRN (as needed) medications for anxiety and depression and a 44 percent drop in staff absenteesim (Ransom, 1998).

In contrast to the usual hierarchical, bureaucratic, department-based organizational design of most nursing homes, in the Eden Alternative™ facilities, staff members form multidisciplinary work-teams that assume responsibility for an area and make their own schedules and work assignments. Thus a cooperative work environment is cultivated and staff feel empowered.

The Impact of Institutions on Individuals and Families

How Institutions Obstruct Well-Being

Erving Goffman was a well-known early critic of psychiatric hospitals and other "total institutions," such as prisons and concentration camps. In his groundbreaking ethnographic work, *Asylums: Essays on the Social Situation of Mental Patients and Other Inmates*, Goffman argued that institutionalization was a traumatic and "mortifying" experience brought on by isolation, invasion of privacy, regimentation, and labeling (1961, pp. 13–14). Deegan (1993) echoes this sentiment in describing psychiatric hospitalization as the "radically dehumanizing and devaluing transformation from being a person to being an illness" (p. 7).

Most people dread living in an institutional setting because of the expected loss of freedom and privacy. The powerlessness and deindividuation associated with most institutions makes members of many vulnerable populations, such as the aged and those with chronic physical or mental illnesses, choose marginally adequate living arrangements or even homelessness over inpatient status.

The regimentation of most institutions results in residents becoming *institutionalized*. *Institutionalism* is a syndrome characterized by apathy, withdrawal, submissiveness, and a reluctance to leave the institutional setting (Wirt, 1999). In other words, residents are resocialized to become compliant and dependent. In learning to adapt to the institutional environment, they lose the skills and attitudes—such as self-care and independent decision making, assertiveness, and self-confidence—they need to reenter and function successfully in the outside community. Wirt suggests "the restrictive environment of institutional settings coupled with oppressive staff [are] capable of producing institutionalism in almost any person regardless of diagnosis, predispositions, or personality" (p. 260). Prolonged confinement in isolation in prisons can even provoke symptoms usually associated with psychosis or other severe disorders, such as panic attacks (www.hrw.org/reports/1999/redonion/Rospfin-03.htm).

In some institutional settings, particularly those designed for offenders, a *deviant subculture* develops and imposes its values and patterns on the residents, regardless of what goes on in the rest of the institution (Polsky, 1962; Dyer, 2000). Sometimes called the *convict code* or *deprivation model* in corrections settings, this theory suggests that an environment of shared deprivation give inmates a basis for solidarity (Bohm & Haley, 1997). The subculture represents a functional, collective adaptation of inmates to their environment. Norms of the convict code include not informing the staff about the illicit activities of other prisoners, skills in "conning" and manipulation of staff, and an ability to show strength, courage, and toughness. Rather than trying to combat the subculture, staff members learn to accommodate it. Thus, one result of incarceration may be that inmates learn to be more successful in their criminal activities.

One might ask whether the money spent on institutional care might be put to better use in prevention or community-based services. "The money spent on prisons is money taken from the parts of the public sector that educate, train, socialize, treat, nurture and house the population—particularly the children of the poor" (Currie, 1998, p. 35). For the cost of a year's imprisonment in California ($21,000), a state resident could pay for tuition, fees, books, and room and board for a year of undergraduate study at UC-Berkeley ($14,576 as of spring 2003) with enough left over to buy a good used car.

How Institutions Promote Well-Being

For small numbers of individuals, institutional placement is the most appropriate alternative both for them and for the rest of society. Some people are clearly a danger to themselves or others and need a protective, structured environment. Institutions do have a place in a modern, democratic society. Problems occur when they are overcrowded, underfunded and understaffed, poorly designed, and used by default rather than by plan.

Social Workers in Institutions

Ginsberg (2001) summarizes the many tasks that social workers perform in institutional settings. In hospitals, they work on discharge planning and help patients arrange for financing. They not only provide social services in long-term care facilities for older adults, but also provide consultation around licensing issues. In prisons and penitentiaries, they may be called on to provide individual counseling and group therapy sessions and to help inmates stay in contact with their families.

Because most clients in institutional settings are involuntary, social workers have a special ethical responsibility to them. Often "it is social workers who must inform those who have been institutionalized or who face institutionalization of their rights or interpret their rights for them. Many times only social workers are available to act as advocates for those who are institutionalized, insuring that their rights are recognized and respected" (Saltzman & Proch, 1990, p. 360). In a corrections context in particular, but also in other institutional settings, social workers must be prepared to advocate "for safe, humane, and equitable treatment of all individuals" (NASW, 2000, p. 57).

Looking Ahead

Institutional and other congregate care settings offer the possibility of the productive and positive use of intervention groups to improve the lives of residents. In Chapter 11, we discuss various kinds of intervention groups, as well as other types of formed groups. Some of these include social action groups, which are building blocks for the formation of social movements. We end the text discussing the significance of social movements, suggesting how society can be changed for the better through the use of collective action.

Key Points

- Institutions are organizational settings where residents have few freedoms.

- Community-based facilities are settings where residents live for extended periods of time but are not isolated from society.

- In total institutions, inmates are isolated from society.

- Institutionalism is the result of the process of resocializing residents to make them compliant and dependent.

- The rights of institutional residents are legally protected by the Fourteenth Amendment of the Constitution.

- The ideal of deinstitutionalization is to prevent inappropriate admissions and to develop alternatives in the community. The reality is a pattern called transinstitutionalization—simply moving individuals from one institutional setting to another.

- Normalization means making institutional facilities more like other homes in the community.

- The convict code is an example of a deviant subculture that encourages antisocial behaviors.

Questions to Think about and Discuss

1. Do you think that wilderness camps and other outdoor alternatives are less "institutional" than traditional children's residential treatment centers? Why or why not?

2. Think of other quasi-institutional settings, such as college dormitories, hospitals, and family, women's, or youth shelters. Would you include them in the category of institutions? Why or why not?

3. Many social workers are reluctant to work in corrections settings. How would you reconcile social work values with the authoritarian and involuntary nature of a prison?

4. In the Eden Alternative™, animals are introduced into nursing homes but the responsibility for caring for them remains with the staff. There are some prisons in this country where inmates can volunteer for an in-house program to provide basic obedience training for puppies selected for service animal programs (e.g., guide dogs for the blind) or for dogs rescued by

local humane shelters so that they can be adopted by families rather than being destroyed. What do you think the advantages of such programs might be? Can you think of any disadvantages?

5. Imagine a time when you will be choosing a long-term care facility for your parent(s) or grandparent(s). What factors would contribute to your selection of one facility over another?

6. A small number of child welfare advocates have suggested that a high quality, stable, long-term, group care environment is a better alternative for dependent children who cannot live at home than is the "revolving door" of multiple foster home placements and failed family reunifications. The middle-aged and older adults who grew up in traditional children's homes note that the majority of their cohort have had productive careers and satisfying family lives. Do you think there is a place for congregate care for children in the twenty-first century? If so, what restrictions would you place on such facilities?

Recommended Readings

Armstrong, L. (1993). *And they call it help: The psychiatric policing of America's children*. Reading, MA: Addison-Wesley.

Gould, J. (2000). *Tales from Rhapsody Home: Or what they don't tell you about senior living*. Chapel Hill, NC: Algonquin Books.

Lerner, J. A. (2002). *You got nothing coming: Notes from a prison fish*. New York: Doubleday Broadway.

Rosenhan, D. L. (1973). On being sane in insane places. *Science, 179,* 250–258.

Smith, J. D. (1995). *Pieces of purgatory: Mental retardation in and out of institutions*. Pacific Grove, CA: Brooks/Cole.

Thomas, W. H. (1999). *Learning from Hannah: Secrets for a life worth living*. Acton, MA: VanderWyk & Burnham.

Internet Search Terms

Community treatment	Juvenile justice policy	Social control
Group home	Norms (group)	Social integration

11

Other Social Settings

Groups and Social Movements

Groups and Social Movements as Contexts for Change

People are social animals, they have a need to belong (Maslow, 1954). Outside of the family and intimate dyads, small groups are the major means through which important social relationships are experienced. Groups provide the formal and informal frameworks that support organizations, communities, and societies.

Group work has a long, but not always respected, history in social work.

> Group workers were different, often were thought of as unprofessional by the caseworkers. They worked at night, even venturing into the "bad" neighborhoods, were out of the office more than behind the desk, and went camping with their group members. They were women who didn't wear hats and men in plaid shirts without suitcoats and neckties. . . . They were workers whose work may have appeared chaotic and not so controlled, who encouraged the community to vote and become active in political and community affairs, for they were concerned with action and social issues. (Middleman, 1992, p. 26)

Group work as a method appeared at the beginning of the twentieth century. It was practiced in such places as settlement houses, YMCAs, and Jewish community centers. Group work clients were considered to be "normal." The group work method was employed to build character, socialize immigrants to American ways, and promote social change (Kurland & Salmon, 1998, p. 14). It wasn't until the middle of the century that schools of social work began to teach group work. Kurland and Salmon (1998) argue that group work is still a neglected area of social work education.

Just as groups are a powerful medium for individual change, social movements can be a medium for economic, social, and cultural change. Social workers have supported but seldom led social movements. Ignoring the power of collective action leaves practitioners to focus on helping individuals adjust to social injustice rather than challenging the status quo.

As noted in the introduction to Part IV, social systems can be studied not only as contexts for examining individual behavior, but also as entities in their own right. Scientists who have analyzed groups and social movements have identified common patterns of development in these social systems. We will discuss these theories under an added heading, *stage perspective,* as they contribute to our understanding.

Groups

Defining Groups

A group is not just a collection of people who happen to be in the same place at the same time. Groups are made up of two or more individuals who identify and interact with each other. They perceive themselves as belonging to the group and are reciprocally influenced by the group's norms (Norlin, Chess, Dale, & Smith, 2003; Johnson & Johnson, 2000; Kurland & Salmon, 1998; Toseland & Rivas, 2001).

Types of Groups

Groups are categorized as primary or secondary depending on the level of caring and intimacy. Actually, rather than being a dichotomy, primary and secondary groups lie at opposite ends of a continuum; some real-life groups have characteristics of both.

Members of *primary groups* demonstrate enduring, close relationships. Families, circles of close friends, gangs, some employee groups, and children's playgroups are examples of primary groups. Primary groups spend a lot of time together, engage in a variety of activities, and know each other well.

Members of *secondary groups* pursue a specific goal or activity. They may have weaker ties to each other and less of a sense of shared identity as a group when compared to primary groups. The secondary group is often larger than a primary group and likely to be short-lived. A good example of a secondary group is a set of students who attend a class together for a semester. Secondary groups fail to meet people's need for intimacy; consequently, secondary groups tend to break down into primary groups. So, for example, within a class of students, smaller, longer lasting friendship groups may develop.

Another way to define groups is to categorize them as natural or formed. "*Natural groups* come together spontaneously on the basis of naturally occurring events, interpersonal attraction, or the mutually perceived needs of members" (Toseland & Rivas, 2001, p. 14). Most primary groups are natural groups. *Formed groups* are consciously constructed through an outside influence or intervention to perform a task or to achieve a goal. Most secondary groups are formed groups. Examples of formed groups are committees, therapy groups, educational groups, sports teams, task forces, and advisory boards.

In writing for social work students, Toseland and Rivas (2001, p. 15) further divide formed groups into treatment [intervention] groups and task groups. In *treatment groups,* the purpose is to address members' social and emotional needs. For example, a highly cohesive therapy group might serve not only as an audience for self-disclosure and venting of emotions, but also provides members with a sense of belonging and acceptance (Yalom, 1995). Treatment or intervention groups that a social worker might lead or be involved with include therapy, psychoeducational, self-help, and mutual aid groups.

A *therapy group* (or psychotherapy group) treats individuals with emotional and behavioral problems using specialized group treatment techniques. Therapy groups are typically small (six or fewer members). They are led by a trained professional and are usually time-limited and *closed* (i.e., no new members are allowed to join after the group begins).

A social worker's involvement in a *psychoeducational group* does not involve treatment so much as "expertise for direction in the form of lectures, seminars, and study groups" (Reid, 1997, p. 10). Psychoeducational groups are usually larger than therapy groups. They may meet for only one or for several sessions. Examples of psychoeducational groups are groups that teach parenting skills, coping with loss and grief, avoiding caregiver burnout, dealing with divorce, managing anger, or learning to live with a chronic illness.

Self-help groups were developed as a response to the deficiencies of professional service providers (Powell, 1995, p. 2118). Social workers and other professionals often serve as consultants and referral sources; however, leadership is shared among group members. Self-help processes are based on shared experience rather than professional expertise (Powell, 1995, p. 2117). Self-help groups can offer much that is provided in professionally run groups, but from a different perspective; these functions include information dissemination, support, and advocacy. Examples of self-help groups are those affiliated with such organizations as Alcoholics Anonymous, Parents of Murdered Children, Adult Survivors of Incest, Parents and Friends of Lesbians and Gays [PFLAG], the Alliance for the Mentally Ill, and Parents Without Partners. Self-help groups are usually ongoing and *open* (i.e., admitting new members at any time).

Mutual aid groups differ from self-help groups in that they usually have a trained or professional leader. Groups for battered women, adolescents in a residential setting, parents of children with cancer, and older adults living in institutions are examples of mutual aid groups. Members of mutual aid groups who initially come together for support may add social action to their group's agenda (Gitterman & Shulman, 1994).

In contrast to different types of treatment groups, in a *task group* the purpose is not to change the group members but to accomplish a task or create a product that will benefit a broader constituency (often the organization). For example, a social worker may serve on an agency committee to review intake policies; although she may experience indirect benefits as a practitioner, the focus of the committee is client and agency needs. Other examples of task groups that social workers might encounter include treatment teams, planning committees, management groups, boards of directors, and delegate councils.

Another type of group identified by sociologists is the *voluntary association,* a group made up of volunteers who organize based on some mutual interest (Henslin, 2001, p. 184). Examples of voluntary associations include the Boys and Girls Clubs, Kiwanis, Lions, Alpha Kappa Alpha, Knights of Columbus, the League of Women Voters, Neighborhood Watch, the Chamber of Commerce, Junior League, the American Legion, Veterans of Foreign Wars

[VFW], and time-limited groups that organize to address a particular cause, such as putting on a Martin Luther King Day parade, preserving a historic building, or raising money for an animal shelter. Often these groups have a mission of service to the community, in addition to meeting members' perceived needs. Many are affiliated with national organizations that have paid employees, but at the local level they rely on unpaid leaders and staff.

A new type of group, born of modern technology, is the *virtual community*. A virtual community is a group "that emerge[s] from the net when enough people carry on those public discussions long enough, with sufficient human feeling, to form webs of personal relationships in cyberspace" (Lapachet, cited in Schriver, 2001, p. 523). Menon (2000) documents the development of a virtual community from an on-line discussion forum. Mental health consumers, parents, and professionals originally came together on-line simply to share information on schizophrenia. The participants became a virtual community in response to the incarceration of a woman with mental illness who was arrested for failing to pay for a cup of coffee. A sense of mutual support, cohesiveness, and achievement developed among the group members as a result of their on-line communications. Their advocacy efforts eventually led to television coverage that served to educate members of law enforcement and the general public about issues related to mental illness.

Issues and Trends

While group work holds an important place in social work practice, the changing practice environment has encouraged the choice of group interventions to save time and money rather than to take advantage of the unique potential of group process (Kurland & Salmon, 1998). "New market realities," reflecting "bottom line" orientation, dictate the use of group interventions based on the needs of third-party funders rather than on the therapeutic and social needs of clients (Strom & Gingerich, 1993).

According to Robert Putnam, who wrote *Bowling Alone* (2000), involvement in voluntary associations—such as parent-teacher organizations, labor unions, veterans' groups, card-playing and garden clubs, and bowling leagues—dropped dramatically in the last three decades of the twentieth century. Even group sporting activities have fallen off, replaced with solitary workouts at the gym, use of in-home exercise equipment, and being a sports spectator. This trend has been documented by a variety of sources: organizational records, surveys, time diaries, and accounts of consumer expenditures on dues. The overall slump appears not to reflect changes in individual patterns but generational ones—each successive generation allocates less time to community life. Possible causes of this trend are changing family demographics (dual-earner and single-parent families), geographic mobility, time spent watching television, and time spent on the Internet.

Exceptions to this pattern of decreasing group participation are membership in religious organizations, "mailing list membership" groups, and self-help and mutual support groups. Mailing list membership groups are those whose "members" send a check a few times a year but never actually meet or establish personal ties (e.g., the Sierra Club, the National Abortion and Reproductive Rights Action League, Common Cause, the National Rifle Association). Putnam (2000) notes that self-help and support groups are not nearly so closely associated with regular community involvement as traditional civic associations related to voting, volunteering, working on community projects, or talking with neighbors (p. 151).

Understanding Formed Groups

Ecosystems Perspective.   Like other social systems, groups are dependent on their environment for a variety of resources and inputs. These include members, space to meet, information exchange, and often, financial support. The environments of groups reflect the political, economic, and social constraints of society. For example, political and social considerations may dictate where groups convene. The board of directors for a corporation might meet at a private club, a PTA committee might meet in a school library, a book club might meet in a coffee house, and an Alcoholics Anonymous meeting might be held in a church basement.

Functionalist Perspective.   Groups are a midlevel system located between individuals and their communities. The small group is both the product of culture and one of the major transmitters of culture. Formed groups can be an effective societal force in promoting the interests and meeting the needs of different people. In addition to social institutions, both natural groups and formed groups act as agents of socialization, with the latter becoming more significant as individuals move outside their families and peer groups into the world.

Some of the systems terms that can be understood by applying them to group socialization processes are *norms, positive and negative feedback,* and *roles. Norms* are shared expectations about appropriate ways to behave in a particular cultural setting. *Prescriptive norms* identify behaviors that are appropriate and acceptable in a society. *Proscriptive norms* identify behaviors that are inappropriate or unacceptable. An example of a prescriptive norm taught by a formed group would be respect for persons in positions of authority. An example of a proscriptive norm would be poor sportsmanship.

Norms are important in shaping group behaviors. Often norms emerge as the group develops. The majority of group norms are not explicitly stated, as are by-laws or posted rules, but rather evolve informally through the interaction of group members. Individuals who behave in some ways receive *positive feedback,* or indications that their actions are appropriate and acceptable to others. Individuals who behave in other ways receive *negative feedback,* or indications that their actions are inappropriate and not acceptable. For example, a committee member who volunteers to take minutes will be praised. If a group member consistently arrives late for meetings, the remarks and body language of other members will reflect social disapproval.

Roles are related to norms. While norms are shared expectations that extend to everyone, *roles* are shared expectations that apply only to individuals in particular positions (Toseland & Rivas, 2001, p. 84). Bormann (1990) notes, "when the other members know what part a person will play and that person knows what part they expect of her or him, that person has assumed a role" (p. 161).

Roles are important to groups because they allow for *specialization* and ensure that important functions will be carried out (Toseland & Rivas, 2001, p. 84). Often specialization begins with the recognition of a group leader. Some leaders, such as committee chairs, are appointed or elected. Leadership in other groups may be determined more informally, and reflect the relative knowledge, skill, power, or charisma of an individual.

Many social scientists divide group role functions into two categories: *task-oriented* and *socioemotional-oriented* (Benne & Sheats, 1948). Socioemotional-oriented activities are also sometimes called *group maintenance roles,* as these are functions that serve to maintain the group itself, rather than being goal-focused (Johnson & Johnson, 2000). Group members and leaders who facilitate communication, mediate conflict, praise others, or develop compromises, are filling socioemotional-oriented roles. Group members and leaders who seek or provide information, keep track of assignments, refocus discussion on goals, or make recommendations, are filling task-oriented roles. Many individuals tend to stick with a preferred role, or one that is most compatible with their personal style, either focusing on tasks or socioemotional concerns of the group. Skillful leaders are able to switch roles according to the needs of the group and the situation.

Some task and maintenance roles are listed in Table 11.1. Although they may be performed by any member, they are particularly important for social work group leaders. In contrast, some member roles include negative, destructive, or process-hindering behaviors (Kurland & Salmon, 1998; Salazar, 1996). Some of the common negative roles in groups are clown, monopolizer, scapegoat, martyr, troublemaker, clock-watcher, whiner, flirt, and help-rejecting complainer. Initially, even negative roles may appear to be beneficial to group process (Kurland & Salmon, 1998). For example, in the beginning stage of a group, members who keep things light (the clown role) or talk a lot (the monopolizer role) may be appreciated by others. In the middle stage of group development, these same roles may hinder group progress.

TABLE 11.1   *Positive Roles in Groups*

Task Roles	*Definitions*
Information seeker	Asks for facts, ideas, and opinions
Information giver	Provides facts and data for making decisions
Comprehension checker	Asks others to summarize discussion to make sure they understand
Direction and role definer	Calls attention to tasks that need to be done and assigns responsibilities
Summarizer	Pulls together related ideas or suggestions and restates them
Evaluator-critic	Compares group's progress in relation to goals
Maintenance Roles	*Definitions*
Encourager	Lets members know their contributions are valued, demonstrates acceptance, and openness to ideas of others. Acknowledges members' strengths
Communication helper	Asks for clarification. Encourages group members to express themselves clearly and to listen respectfully to others
Process observer	Uses observations of group dynamics to suggest how the group process can be improved. Encourages others to offer feedback that will enhance group functioning
Interpersonal problem solver	Helps people understand how they affect each other. Encourages resolution of differences through open discussion and involving the group in decision making

Note: Content adapted from Brown (1991), Johnson & Johnson (2000), and Benne & Sheats (1948).

People come to groups with roles that they have exercised in other social environments. They bring established patterns of behaviors to the group and other group members tend to expect these patterns to continue, thus causing the member to get "locked into" a role (Kurland & Salmon, 1998). When group roles become inflexible, they detract from both task and maintenance functions. In a successful group, the leader or peers help other members to play more differentiated roles in order to further group progress.

Conflict Perspective.   Using a theory called *social identity,* social psychologists suggest that an important part of our self-concept is derived from our group memberships (Myers, 1999). Due to *in-group bias* we automatically assume that our group is better than other groups, known as *out-groups.* "Ingroup and outgroup distinctions may encourage social cohesion among members, but they also may promote classism, racism, sexism, heterosexism, and ageism" (Kendall, 2001, p. 168).

Numerous experiments have demonstrated that clustering people into groups using even random, nonsensical approaches, such as coin flips or the last digit of a social security number will result in feelings of group identity and in-group bias (Myers, 1999). This suggests that humans are genetically programmed to think in "we" versus "them" terms and provides empirical support for use of the conflict perspective in explaining social relationships among groups of people.

Rational/Social Exchange Perspective.   Social exchange theory suggests that people join groups and stay in them if they believe that they are getting back as much as they contribute. Particularly in today's society, when people have limited time and resources, individuals exercise an informal, ongoing cost-benefit analysis of whether group membership is worth their while. As noted in the section on Issues and Trends, Putnam (2000) reports that memberships in groups ranging from bowling leagues to Parent Teacher Associations have declined dramatically in the past half-century.

Constructionist Perspective.   A *reference* group is a group that an individual uses to evaluate his or her appearance, behavior, values, goals, and so on. It may be a group of which the individual is already a member or it may be a group that the individual aspires to join in the future. For example, a college student who hopes to become a member of a particular sorority will notice the way the current members dress and the ways in which they socialize, and judge herself accordingly. A *negative reference group* is a group that exemplifies those characteristics or traits that an individual hopes to avoid. For example, a college student may observe the behavior patterns of a group of students who are jeopardizing their GPAs by excessive partying and choose to avoid such practices. Reference groups and negative reference groups help explain why someone's behaviors and attitudes may differ from those of his or her membership group (Kendall, 2001).

Powell (1995) points to the *referent power* of self-help groups in boosting morale through support and shared understanding of experiences. Help-seeking clients are empowered as they adopt a new perception of themselves as help-givers.

Stage Perspective.   There are many ways of understanding group change over time. There are two general categories of theories, the recurring-phase or cyclical models and sequential stage theories. Recurring-phase models suggest that certain group processes occur over and over again. For example, Bales (1965) believed that groups struggle to establish a balance between task-oriented work and dealing with socioemotional concerns. According to Bales, groups move back and forth between these two processes. Other theorists describe recurring shifts that involve reactions to the leader, control issues, and group cohesion (Bion, 1961; Schultz, 1958). The recurring-phase model suggests that the basic themes that are important in group dynamics are never fully resolved but come up repeatedly during the course of the group.

Many research studies support the perspective that group development occurs in a series of sequential stages (Wheelan, 1994)—even though certain themes may reoccur at different stages. Although the exact type and number of stages may vary by setting, group goals, leader characteristics, and member characteristics, group work authors generally agree on the basic concepts inherent in a group's progression (Kurland & Salmon, 1998, p. 35).

Looking at models proposed by different writers, most seem to contain the stages of beginning, middle, and end. The beginning stage is characterized by uncertainty, anxiety, and testing as norms for interaction, power, and authority are established. Members hope to belong to the group while at the same time maintaining a sense of autonomy. Garland, Jones, and Kolodny (1976) identify this ambivalence as "approach-avoidance conflict."

During the middle stage, conflicts over group norms and roles are resolved and give way to established patterns of interaction (Toseland & Rivas, 2001, p. 91). The middle stage is characterized by intimacy, bonding, negotiation, problem solving, and performing. There is development of strong group feeling. During this stage, the work of the group gets done.

The end stage is characterized by termination and separation. Tasks are completed. Group cohesion begins to weaken as members find other satisfying relationships outside the group. Most members view termination with ambivalence (Kurland & Salmon, 1998).

Preferred Perspectives.

Strengths. Human service professionals have been aware of the power of formed groups for over a century. Groups "have several unique advantages over solitary contemplation and dyadic discussion for those who want to grow, develop, and change" (Johnson & Johnson, 2000, p. 519). Group members provide a variety of sources of social feedback so that individuals can try out new behaviors and gain a new understanding of their problems. Individuals can practice and master new social skills that can then be integrated into the rest of their lives.

Groups offer many opportunities for "mutual give and take," particularly for those who seldom have the opportunity to "give." Support groups, for example, normalize what is often a traumatic and isolating life experience. Members can interact with others who share their problem. Members of a cancer support group, a group of adoptive parents, or a group of school children dealing with the effects of divorce often have insights that a service provider may lack. Because support groups are characterized by shared experiences, there is often a high level of personal disclosure and emotional bonding. Benefits of support groups include companionship, access to special information, empowerment, stress reduction, increased social functioning, and improved problem solving (Powell, 1995).

Diversity. Much of the research on small-group composition is dated and was conducted using college students. Findings indicate that the gender, class, and race/ethnicity of group leaders and members have a major impact on group behavior and process (Brown & Mistry,

1994). *Status characteristics theory* states that "external status differences among members of a task group determine the distribution of power and prestige within the group" (Berger, Cohen, & Zelditch, 1966. p. 43). For example, Garvin and Reed (1983) suggest that in mixed groups the needs of women tend to get subordinated to those of the men, reflecting the unequal status and prestige of the genders in the larger society.

The research on mixed- and same-gender groups is limited, as well as dated, and findings are complex. Results may vary according to the size of the group, the gender composition, the setting, and the purpose of the group. In general, the size of the group has been linked to gender preference. Both males and females prefer mixed-gender groups if the group is large. If the group is small, women prefer same sex-groups. Some evidence suggests that women do better in same-sex groups (Butler & Wintram, 1991; Davis & Proctor, 1989; Garvin & Reed, 1983; Home, 1991). The literature also suggests that people with a masculine, or dominant, orientation are more task-focused and those with a feminine, or friendly and warm, orientation are more concerned with socioemotional issues and group harmony (Davies, 1994; Siebert & Gruenfeld, 1992); thus, it may be more important to consider personality characteristics rather than gender per se in creating groups.

There is little research on the influence of socioeconomic status in small groups. What exists suggests that task groups are more able to tolerate class differences than groups requiring more intimacy and sharing (Davis & Proctor, 1989). Personal growth groups require some familiarity with the backgrounds of other group members in a way that task groups do not.

The little research that is available on the topic of groups made up of members of different racial or ethnic backgrounds (see McLeod, Lobel, & Cox, 1996) suggests that interactions are complicated. In study of group member preferences, Davis (1979) found that black and white participants favored different group compositions. When asked to compose a group, African Americans chose roughly equal numbers of black and white group members. White students, on the other hand, composed groups that contained a clear white majority. Often a racially homogenous group is both preferred by members and more productive, especially when issues of racial identify, racism, and culture are part of the task (Brown & Mistry, 1994, p. 9).

Clearly there are advantages to having a variety of perspectives in accomplishing tasks, particularly those that require knowledge of different cultures. On the other hand, it may be more difficult for group members to develop cohesion because of differences in the cultural values that members bring to the group. (See Chapter 6.)

Group composition often is not under the control of either group leaders or group members. Even when a social work group leader has control over group membership, to exclude someone on the basis of race or gender when no alternative group experience is available is discriminatory and may be unethical (Brown & Mistry, 1994).

The Impact of Formed Groups on Individuals and Families

How Formed Groups Obstruct Well-Being.
Groups sometimes foster negative behaviors. One example is *social loafing,* or the tendency of people to put forth less effort when they are part of a group because they believe that their individual performance is not being noted or evaluated (Karau & Williams, 1993; Latané, Williams, & Harkins, 1979). People in collectivist cultures, such as Asian countries, exhibit less social loafing than do people in individualist cultures, and women do less social loafing than men (Karau & Williams, 1993).

The normal desire to be accepted or admired by others in one's group can lead to negative consequences. A negative example of group conformity is *groupthink* (Janis, 1972; Janis, 1982; Miranda, 1994; Whyte, 1991). A tendency to suppress dissent in the interest of harmony may cause group members to avoid full exploration of alternative plans of action or the possible negative consequences of a proposed choice. Disastrous policy decisions—such as those leading to the Bay of Pigs invasion, the Vietnam War, and the Challenger explosion—have been attributed to groupthink. While groupthink does not necessarily lead to disasters, it often results in errors in decision making and such errors result in poorer outcomes. According to Janis (1982), five factors contribute to groupthink: a high level of group cohesiveness, group members who have weak ties with or awareness of external groups, directive leaders, groups composed of persons of similar backgrounds and ideologies, and groups addressing a crisis situation.

How Formed Groups Promote Well-Being.   For many individuals without a natural support network, groups can provide a sense of community and acceptance that is not tied to social status or achievements. Putnam (2000) suggests that "in some respects support groups substitute for other intimate ties that have been weakened in our fragmented society, serving people who are disconnected from more conventional social networks" (p. 151).

Some groups also come to pursue broader social goals as they develop into social action groups. A *social action group* is developed to pursue goals through collective action, usually to make changes in the social or physical environment of group members. What draws members to the group is a shared perception of inequity and a need for change (Toseland & Rivas, 2001). Although the needs of individual members may be satisfied by the group's work, effects may benefit people outside the group as well. Examples of social action groups include a neighborhood group seeking better street lighting, a tenants' group threatening a rent strike to get needed repairs, or a group of senior citizens advocating for improved bus service. "Primary associations and face-to-face contacts provide solidarity for collective action among people who know and trust one another" (Tarrow, 1994, p. 60). These everyday ties among people also may form the basis of developing social movements. People who have conducted research on social movements—such as the civil rights movement, the feminist movement, and the disability movement—have noted that "social bonds . . . i.e., friendship networks, drew many people to become active participants" (Wilson & Orum, 1976, p. 198).

Social Movements

It is important for social work students to appreciate the power of social movements in creating and shaping social change. The benefits of social movements are often easier to appreciate in retrospect (Tarrow, 1994). Many of the social benefits that we take for granted in today's society—such as voting rights for women and minorities, child labor laws, the right to form a labor union, and the end of legal segregation—are the result of social movements that involved many people who were motivated to take action to change society. The efforts of workers, consumers, women, people of color, gay men and lesbians and their families and friends, animal and nature lovers, all have changed our society for the better.

In today's world, many social issues and public concerns give rise to social movements. Some social movements arise in support of an issue and bring about social change; others arise in opposition to it and inhibit social change.

Defining Social Movements

Social movements are organized and concerted efforts by large numbers of people over an extended period of time to promote or resist social change through collective action. Central to social movement ideology is a sense of social injustice (Klandermans, 1997).

Social movements are not the same as *social movement organizations* (Della Porta & Diani, 1999). Many social movement networks include social movement organizations and are closely identified with them, but the two terms are not synonymous and shouldn't be used that way. Examples of social movement organizations are the National Organization for Women [NOW], National Association for the Advancement of Colored People [NAACP], the American Indian Movement [AIM], the Sierra Club, the United Farm Workers, People for the Ethical Treatment of Animals [PETA], the Moral Majority, the National Rifle Association [NRA], and the Ku Klux Klan [KKK]. The fluidity of the boundaries of social movement networks distinguish them from the more structured pattern of organizations. Social movement organizations have identifiable *members* who hold offices and/or pay dues and whose names are found on an organizational chart or a mailing list. In contrast, social movements have *participants,* some of whom might exhibit long-term commitment and activism, while others might simply show up for one event or write one letter to the editor.

Academics from different theoretical perspectives identify several characteristic aspects of social movements (Della Porta & Diani, 1999, pp. 14–16). First, a social movement is an informal network of individuals, groups, and organizations. In some social movements, this network may be very loose, while in other it is tight. These networks are conduits for the flow of information, expertise, and material resources. They create the preconditions necessary for mobilization. Second, social movements rely on the development of a collective identity as well as a shared value system. These two factors exist even in the absence of activities (such as protests and marches). A final characteristic of social movements is the willingness of participants to use unconventional forms of protest.

These characteristics are illustrated by the civil rights movement in the United States. Some of the organizations involved were the NAACP, CORE [Congress of Racial Equality], and the SCLC [Southern Christian Leadership Conference]. They were supported, in turn, by African American churches and black colleges (Morris, 1984). The rash of student sit-in protests that began in 1957 reflected not only organizational ties among these groups but the use of personal networks as well (Morris, 1993). Churches provided leadership and opportunities for recruitment of new participants, and added the fervor and conviction of the faith community. The collective identity of the African American community, born of centuries of oppression, was melded with the ideals of social justice—values that invited solidarity with whites and non-Christians alike. Arguments centered around the proper nature of society: whether there was a "natural social order" dependent on a racial hierarchy and separation or whether the demands of a democratic society dictated a sharing of power, access, and opportunity. Because they were denied conventional access to political power through the vote, black participants in the civil rights movement were forced to rely on unconventional means, such as protests.

Protest is a political resource of the powerless. Protests are

> engaged in by relatively powerless groups; and they depend[ed] for success not upon direct utilization of power, but upon activating other groups to enter the political arena. Because protest is successful to the extent that other parties are activated to political involvement, it is one of the few strategies in which even politically impoverished groups can aspire to engage. (Lipsky, 1965, p. 1)

Protests can take many forms, including rallies, marches, boycotts, sit-ins, rent strikes, work stoppages or slow-downs, and other acts of insubordination.

Civil disobedience is nonviolent action carried out by protesters who seek to change an unjust policy or law by refusing to comply with it (Kendall, 2001). Della Porta and Diani (1999) categorize civil disobedience as forms of protest that they define as *bearing witness*. Actions of this kind tend to reinforce the moral message being promoted by the movement because activists are willing to assume considerable personal risk, including significant monetary losses, imprisonment, or even loss of life, to demonstrate the strength of their convictions.

Types and Examples of Social Movements

Some sociologists (Blumer, 1974) classify social movements according to the target and extent of change desired. Those movements that advocate radical change in individuals are called *redemptive* conversions, such as fundamentalist Christianity or the Hare Krishnas. Those movements that advocate partial or limited change in individuals are called *alternative social movements;* examples include the "new age" movements that emphasize spirituality and connections to the natural world and the vegetarian movement that denounces the eating of meat and the wearing of animal skins and fur. A social movement that advocates substantive or total change in society is called a *transformative* or *revolutionary social movement;* examples include the abolitionist movement against slavery, the communist revolution in Cuba, utopian groups, and militia groups that encourage isolationism and defiance of government authority. Social movements that advocate partial changes in society are called *reformative social movements;* examples include consumer movements, the environmental movement, and disability rights activism.

The four types of social movements described above advocate change. *Resistive* (or *reactive*) *social movements,* on the other hand, work to maintain the status quo, to prevent or undo change, returning society to more traditional values and practices. Resistive social movements often arise to combat the efforts of reformative or revolutionary movements. Examples include the pro-life/anti-abortion movement and various antitax movements.

Understanding Social Movements

Functionalist Perspective.   Structural functionalists believe that the smooth functioning of society is disrupted by sudden and widespread social changes. Role expectations and traditional values are subjected to new kinds of pressures. Sociologist Neil Smelser (1962) suggested, in part, that social movements arise in response to the effects of rapid, large-scale social transformation, which he called *structural strain*. When the balance of society is disrupted, citizens have an expectation that people in authority will correct the problem. When this doesn't happen, collective behavior is likely to occur.

We believe that this perspective is most useful in explaining resistive social movements. An example would be the massive efforts of religious conservatives to promote "traditional" family values in response to demands by gay men and lesbians for equal rights.

Conflict Perspective.   In contrast to the functionalist perspective, which assumes that society is based on shared social values, the conflict perspective assumes that groups hold values that are in conflict with other groups. Conflict theorists say that social movements arise when groups with relatively less power seek social change. Most theorists who espouse the conflict perspective believe that progressive social change occurs only as a result of collective action.

Environmentalists believe that preserving natural resources and protecting the quality of air and water should take priority over short-term profits. Their views and values are in conflict with corporations that see competitiveness and growth, not to mention return on investment, as paramount. When the government sides with corporate interests, individual efforts are inadequate to protect the environment; coordinated efforts are much more likely to be successful.

Rational/Social Exchange Perspective.   Several theorists define collective social movements as rational, purposeful, and organized actions, derived from an assessment of costs and benefits (Oberschall, 1973; Tilly, 1978; Zald & McCarthy, 1987). The tactical choices made by movements are determined by the type and nature of the resources available, hence the name *resource mobilization theory*. One common way of minimizing costs is to use preexisting networks and structures, such as those found among college student organizations or churches (McAdam, McCarthy, & Zald, 1996). This was seen in the civil rights movement and its roots in black churches and historically black colleges, and in various peace movements found on campuses all over the world. Currently it is seen in the ties of the contemporary pro-life/anti-abortion movement to Catholic and conservative Protestant churches.

Constructionist Perspective.   Erving Goffman, in his seminal work, *Frame Analysis* (1974), argued that people's interpretation of events is dependent on their perspective, or the framework they apply in making sense of social structures. Building on this insight, other sociologists (Snow, Rochford, Worden, & Benford, 1986) focused on the role of shared meanings in the development of social movements. *Framing* is defined as the "conscious, strategic efforts by groups of people to fashion shared understandings of the world and of themselves that legitimate and motivate collective action" (McAdam, McCarthy, & Zald, 1996, p. 6). The appeal of framing a movement's goals in terms of moral imperatives was exemplified in the civil rights movement, when white people participated in voter registration, Freedom Rides, and protest marches based on their ideological commitment to the principles of social and political justice, rather than any expectation of personal gain.

Relative deprivation theory suggests that social movements arise when people perceive that they have been deprived of their "fair share" in comparison to others who are similarly situated and what they believe they deserve (Orum & Orum, 1968; Rose, 1982). Movements are most likely to occur when social conditions are improving, creating rising expectations, and then conditions decline, so that there is a growing gap between expectations and actual conditions (Davies, 1962). For example, if workers anticipate that their lives are going to continue to improve based on a growing economy, and then there is a sudden recession and they are asked to agree to wage concessions or a cut in benefits, they more likely to organize a protest than if their positive expectations were never encouraged to begin with.

Stages of Development.   As with groups, researchers have identified several stages of development within social movements (Blumer, 1969; Lang & Lang, 1961; Mauss, 1975; Spector & Kitsuse, 1977; Tilly, 1978). During the first stage, there is some recognition of social discontent. Unless this feeling is widespread, the movement may fail at this stage. At stage two, discontent must be transformed into a message that attracts public attention, mobilizes resources, and leads to the formation of alliances among organizations that share similar views. At this stage, there is the first appearance of collective action, such as rallies. In stage three, the movement takes on organizational attributes; there is a greater focus on routine tasks as the movement becomes more institutionalized. Excitement wanes and the radical edge of the movement may be lost. In the final stage, especially if leaders care more about running a bureaucracy, or worse yet, worry only about their own positions, rather than the goals of the movement, there may be a period of decline. Another source of decline is that the movement becomes mainstream—that is, it becomes a part of "the system." Critics of the contemporary labor movement, for example, suggest that it has become so mainstream that it has more in common with business leaders than with the workers it represents (Macionis, 2001, p. 619).

Preferred Perspectives.   Although arguably men have played, and continue to play, a prominent role in most social movements, some movements have been characterized by the leadership of women. Beyond those that focus(ed) specifically on women's issues—the feminist movement, women's suffrage, women's health, pro-choice, and anti–domestic violence movements—women have played disproportionately important roles in the abolitionist, temperance, consumer rights, and environmental justice movements (Girdner & Smith, 2002; Macionis, 2001). Readers might be surprised to learn that Jane Addams was one of the founders of the NAACP (Pollard, 1995). Nevertheless, men continue to outnumber female participants in social movements and often dominate leadership roles; "male dominance has been the norm even in social movements that otherwise oppose the status quo" (Macionis, 2001, p. 616).

People of color have taken a commanding leadership role in many social movements. A major source of inspiration for modern social movements was Mahatma Gandhi; the Hindu leader was committed to the de-colonization of India and the social development of his people. He practiced nonviolent civil disobedience and was one of many social movement leaders who paid with his life for his principles. Dr. Martin Luther King, Jr. was strongly influenced by the life and writings of Gandhi, as well as by his study of Christian theology. He advanced the philosophy and practice of nonviolent protest and resistance in this country. Other social movements that benefited from the momentum and strategies used by African Americans and their supporters in the civil rights movement include the migrant worker movement, the disability rights movement, and the gay rights movement (Gamble & Weil, 1995).

The Impact of Social Movements on Individuals, Families, and Communities

How Social Movements Obstruct Well-Being.   "There are plenty of bad as well as good protest movements" (Jasper, 1997, p. 369). Some social movements, particularly those that represent a backlash against social progress, can victimize individuals who are perceived as behaving in ways that are inconsistent with established social hierarchies. For example, the white supremacy movement, represented by such organizations as the Ku Klux Klan and the Aryan Nation, promotes intolerance, hatred, or even violence toward minority groups that have only relatively recently gained legal recognition of their civil rights.

How Social Movements Promote Well-Being.   Many leaders of social movements have paid a high price for their actions, including giving up the time and attention [needed] for traditional marriage and family roles; they marry later, postpone the birth of a first child, have fewer children, and experience a higher divorce rate than their nonparticipant peers (Whalen & Flacks, 1989). On a more positive note, many continue their political commitments and active involvement, and choose work in the public sector as teachers, researchers, social workers, journalists, or independent professionals—careers that accommodate their political beliefs (Fendrich, Tarleau, & Lovoy, 1988). In addition to directing career choice, social movements provide their participants with opportunities to express their vision of an ideal society and a path to defining their identity (Jasper, 1997).

Beyond the benefits to individual participants and their particular causes and collective goals, social movements benefit society as a whole as well. The successful functioning of a democracy requires an ongoing dialogue among competing interests and ideas. Social movements articulate alternative perspectives. "Social movements work at the edge of a society's understanding of itself . . . formulating and elaborating [visions] so that they can be debated" (Jasper, 1997, p. 375).

Social Movements in the Twenty-First Century

A distinctive feature of recent social movements is their international character. As technology connects people all over the world, social movements have the opportunity to become global in form. Examples include the environmental movement, the human rights movement (e.g., movements to protect the rights of women, indigenous peoples, and political prisoners), and the contemporary peace movement.

In looking ahead to the new century, Buechler (2000, pp. 213–214) notes that we need "not just recognition but cultivation of the promise of social movements." We believe that within the constraints of social structure, economics, politics, culture, and history, people can act collectively to change their circumstances (Warren, Thompson, & Saegert, 2001, p. 2). The profession of social work boasts a strong reform tradition of advocating for policy change (Jansson, 1999). If social workers are going to be a part of progress toward social and economic justice, they need to be in the ranks, if not in leadership roles, of social movements.

This text could lead students to be pessimistic about their potential to facilitate social change. The testimony of social movements is that individuals, in connection with other like-minded souls, have the capacity within them to make change occur. When we say we are powerless, we give power away. When we believe we can make a difference, the strengths perspective is realized within ourselves, our colleagues, and those whom we seek to support. As Margaret Mead said, "Never doubt that a small group of thoughtful, committed individuals can change the world: indeed it is the only thing that ever has."

Key Points

- *Groups* are made up of two or more individuals who identify and interact with each other. Members perceive themselves as belonging to the group and are reciprocally influenced by the group's norms.

- Outside of the family and intimate dyads, small groups are the major means through which important social relationships are experienced. Groups provide the formal and informal frameworks that support organizations, communities, and societies.

- *Formed groups* are consciously constructed through an outside influence or intervention to perform a task or to achieve a goal.

- The changing practice environment has encouraged the choice of group interventions to save time and money rather than to take advantage of the unique potential of group process.

- Groups can be an effective societal force in promoting the interests and meeting the needs of different people.

- Due to *in-group bias,* we automatically assume that our group is better than other groups.

- *Groupthink,* a tendency to suppress dissent in the interest of group harmony, may result in poor decisions.

- A *social action group* is developed to pursue goals through collective action, usually to make changes in the social or physical environment of group members.

- *Social movements* are organized and concerted efforts by large numbers of people over an extended period of time to promote or resist social change through collective action.

- Protest is a political resource of the powerless.

- Social movements are classified according to the target and extent of change desired.

- Conflict theorists believe that significant positive social change occurs only as a result of collective action.

- Examples of social movements that brought about major changes in American society are the civil rights movement and the labor movement.

Questions to Think about and Discuss

1. Compare your time investment in voluntary associations and other community groups to that of your parents or grandparents. Do the patterns agree with the trend identified by Putnam in *Bowling Alone?*

2. Identify the leadership style observed in a formed group of which you are a member.

3. Have you observed social loafing in a student group project? Did the "loafer" get away with it? What was the reaction of other group members?

4. What social movements are represented by organizations on your campus?

5. Do you believe that collective action is a prerequisite for structural social change?

6. Do you believe professional social workers should "work outside the system" more often to promote change?

7. What do you think should be the role of social workers in social movements in the twenty-first century?

Recommended Readings _____

Breton, M. J. (1999). *Women pioneers for the environment*. Boston: Northeastern University Press.

Feinstein, J. (1989). *Forever's team*. New York: Simon and Schuster.

Gabriel, Y., & Lang, T. (1995). The consumer as activist. In Y. Gabriel & T. Lang, *The unmanageable consumer: Contemporary consumption and its fragmentation* (pp. 152–201). Thousand Oaks, CA: Sage.

Iannello, K. P. (1992). The feminist peace group. In K. P. Iannello, *Decisions without hierarchy: Feminist interventions in organization theory and practice* (pp. 53–77). New York: Routledge.

Janis, I. L. (1982). *Groupthink* (2nd ed.). Boston: Houghton Mifflin.

Johnson, D. W., & Johnson, F. P. (2000). *Joining together: Group theory and group skills*. Boston: Allyn & Bacon.

King, M. L., Jr. (1964). *Why we can't wait*. New York: New American Library.

McAdam, D. (1988). *Freedom summer: The idealists revisited*. New York: Oxford University Press.

Internet Search Terms _____

Collective action	Groupthink	Resource mobilization theory
Collective behavior	Group work	Social action group
Group composition	In-group bias	Social justice
Group dynamics	Leadership	Social loafing
Group membership	Mobilization	Social movements
Group norms	Political movements	Social participation
Group process	Protest movements	Social reform
Group roles	Relative deprivation theory	Support groups

References

Abramovitz, M. (1988). *Regulating the lives of women: Social welfare policy from colonial times to the present.* Boston: South End Press.

Abramovitz, M. (2001). Everyone is still on welfare: The role of redistribution in social policy. *Social Work, 46,* 297–308.

Achenbaum, W. A. (1983). *Shades of grey.* Boston: Little, Brown.

ACLU. (2001). *Fact sheet on domestic violence.* [on-line]. Available: http://www.aclu.org/Womensrights/

Adams, J. S. (1963). Toward an understanding of inequity. *Journal of Abnormal and Social Psychology, 67,* 422–436.

Aguirre, A., & Baker, D. V. (1994). Racial prejudice and the death penalty: A research note. *Social Justice, 20,* 150–155.

Ahmad, M. (2002). Home insecurities: Racial violence the day after September 11. *Social Text 72, 20,* (3), 101–115.

Albrecht, G. L. (1992). *The disability business: Rehabilitation in America.* Newbury Park, CA: Thousand Oaks.

Aldrich, H. (1979). *Organizations and environments.* Englewood Cliffs, NJ: Prentice Hall.

Alter, J. (1999, September 20). Bridging the digital divide. *Newsweek,* p. 55.

Alter, J. (2003, September 15). Packaging patriotism. *Newsweek,* pp. 52–54.

Altshuler, A., Morrill, W., Wolman, H., & Mitchell, F. (Eds.) (1999). *Governance and opportunity in metropolitan America.* Washington, DC: National Academic Press.

American Medical Association. (2000). [on-line]. Available: http://www.ama-assn.org

Ames, K. (1990, December 17). Our bodies, their selves. *Newsweek,* p. 60.

Anderson, R. E., Carter, I., & Lowe, G. R. (1999). *Human behavior in the social environment: A social systems approach* (5th ed.). Hawthorne, NY: Aldine de Gruyter.

Anh, H. N. (1994). Cultural diversity and the definition of child abuse. In R. Barth, J. Berrick, and N. Gilbert (Eds.), *Child welfare research review* (pp. 28–55). New York: Columbia University Press.

Armas, G. C. (2003, January 22). Hispanics outnumber Blacks in U.S. *The State* [Columbia, SC], p. A4.

Armas, G. C. (2003, September 9). Study finds poor hammered by rising cost of rent. *The State* [Columbia, SC], p. B1.

Armstrong, L. (1993). *And they call it help: The psychiatric policing of America's children.* Reading, MA: Addison-Wesley.

Asch, A., & Mudrick, N. R. (1995). Disability. In R. L. Edwards et al. *Encyclopedia of social work* (19th ed., Vol. 1, pp. 752–761). Washington, DC: NASW Press.

Atkinson, D. R., Morten, G., & Sue, D. W. (1998). *Counseling American minorities* (5th ed.). Boston: McGraw-Hill.

Bagdikian, B. H. (2000). *The media monopoly* (6th ed.). Boston: Beacon.

Baker, R. (1997, September/October). The squeeze. *The Columbia Journalism Review,* pp. 30–36.

Bales, R. (1965). The equilibrium problem in small groups. In A. Hare, E. Borgatta, & R. Bales (Eds.), *Small groups: Studies in social interaction* (pp. 444–476). New York: Alfred A. Knopf.

Baltes, M. M. (1994). Aging well and institutional living: A paradox? In R. P. Abeles, H. C. Gift, & M. G. Ory (Eds.), *Aging and quality of life* (pp. 185–201). New York: Springer.

Banks, J. A. (1997). Arab Americans: concepts and materials. In J. A. Banks, *Teaching strategies for ethnic studies* (6th ed., pp. 489–510). Boston: Allyn & Bacon.

Barker, R. L. (1995). *The social work dictionary.* Washington, DC: NASW Press.

Barnett, W. S. (1995, Winter). Long-term effects of early childhood programs on cognitive and school outcomes. *The Future of Children,* pp. 25–50.

Barry, P. (2002, June). Drug profits vs. research. *AARP Bulletin,* pp. 8–9, 10.

Bartlett, D. L., & Steele, J. B. (1998, November 16). Fantasy islands and other perfectly legal ways that big companies manage to avoid billions in federal taxes. *Time,* pp. 78–93.

Bartlett, D. L., & Steele, J. B. (1998, November 23). Paying a price for polluters. *Time,* pp. 72–80.

Bartlett, D. L., & Steele, J. B. (2002, December 16). Indian casinos: Wheel of misfortune. *Time,* pp. 44–58.

Beasley, C., Jr. (1990). Of pollution and poverty, part 3:

Deadly threat on native lands. *Buzzworm, 2* (5), 39–45.

Begley, S. (1995, February 13). Three is not enough: Surprising new lessons from the controversial science of race. *Newsweek*, pp. 67–69.

Bell, C. (1991). Traumatic stress and children in danger. *Journal of Health Care for the Poor and Underserved, 2,* 175–188.

Bell, N. M. (2002, October 31). Mentally ill inmate will move to hospital. *The State* [Columbia, SC], p. B3.

Bellah, R. N. (1967). Civil religion. *Daedalus, 96,* 1–21.

Benne, K. D., & Sheats, P. (1948). Functional roles of group members. *Journal of Social Issues, 4,* 41–49.

Benson, M. L., & Cullen, F. T. (1998). *Combating corporate crime.* Boston: Northeastern University Press.

Berberoglu, B. (1994). *Class structure and social transformation.* Westport, CT: Praeger.

Berger, J., Cohen, B. P., & Zelditch, M. (1966). Status characteristics and expectation states. In J. Berger, M. Zelditch, & B. Anderson (Eds.), *Sociological theories and progress* (Vol. 1) (pp. 29–46). Boston: Houghton Mifflin.

Berger, M. (1977). *Working with people called patients.* New York: Brunner-Routledge.

Berheide, C. W. (1992, fall). Women still "stuck" in low level jobs. *Women in Public Services: A Bulletin for the Center for Women in Government, 3.*

Bernard, J. (1973). *The sociology of community.* Glenview, IL: Scott Foresman.

Best, J. (1989) Extending the constructionist perspective: A conclusion and introduction. In J. Best (Ed.), *Images of issues typifying contemporary social problems* (pp. 243–252). New York: Aldine de Gruyter.

Billingsley, C. A. (1992). *Climbing Jacob's ladder: The enduring legacy of African-American families.* New York: Simon & Schuster.

Bion, W. (1961). *Experiences in groups.* New York: Basic Books.

Blumer, H. G. (1969). Collective behavior. In A. M. Lee (Ed.), *Principles of sociology* (3rd ed., 65–121). New York: Barnes & Noble.

Blumer, H. G. (1974). Social movements. In R. S. Denisoff (Ed.), *The sociology of dissent* (pp. 74–90). New York: Harcourt.

Bohm, R. M., & Haley, K. N. (1997). *Introduction to criminal justice.* New York: Glencoe/McGraw-Hill.

Bok, D. (2003). *Universities in the market place: The commercialization of higher education.* Princeton, NJ: Princeton University Press.

Bollinger, L. C. (2003, January 27). Diversity is essential. . . . *Newsweek*, p. 32.

Bonacich, E. (1972). A theory of ethic antagonism: The split labor market. *The American Sociological Review, 37,* 547–549.

Bordewich, F. M. (1996). *Killing the white man's Indian: Reinventing Native Americans at the end of the twentieth century.* New York: Doubleday.

Bormann, E. G. (1990). *Communicating in small groups: Theory and practice* (5th ed.). New York: Harper & Row.

Bourdieu, P. (1986). The forms of capital. In J. Richardson (Ed.), *Handbook of theory and research for the sociology of education* (pp. 241–258). New York: Greenwood Press.

Brewer, D. J., Gates, S. M., & Goldman, C. A. (2002). *In pursuit of prestige: Strategy and competition in U.S. higher education.* New Brunswick, NJ: Transaction Publishers.

Bridges, G. S., & Steen, S. (1998). Racial disparities in official assessments of juvenile offenders: Attributional stereotypes as mediating mechanisms. *American Sociological Review, 63,* 554–570.

Brinson, C. S. (2003, December 6). Public colleges' future grows more uncertain as state funding slides. *The State* [Columbia, SC], p. A7.

Broder, D. (2002, November 5). The election year of avoidance. *The State* [Columbia, SC], p. A9.

Brody, D. (1980). *Workers in industrial America: Essays on the twentieth-century struggle.* New York: Oxford University Press.

Brown, A., & Mystry, T. (1994). Groupwork with mixed membership groups. *Social Work with Groups, 17,* 5–21.

Brown, L. N. (1991). *Groups for growth and change.* New York: Longman.

Brown, P. L. (2002, July 27). Sex-charged TV steams up airwaves. *Herald-Leader* [Lexington, KY], p. A3.

Bruchac, J. (1991, October). Otstungo. *National Geographic*, pp. 68–83.

Bruck, L. (1997). Welcome to Eden. *Nursing Homes, 46* (1), 28–33.

Bruggemann, W. G. (1996). *The practice of macro social work.* Chicago: Nelson-Hall.

Buckholdt, D. R., & Gubrium, J. F. (1980). The underlife of behavior modification. *American Journal of Orthopsychiatry, 50,* 279–290.

Buechler, S. M. (2000). *Social movements in advanced capitalism. The political economy and cultural construction of social action.* New York: Oxford University Press.

Bullard, R. D. (1990). *Dumping in Dixie: Race, class, and environmental quality.* Boulder, CO: Westview Press.

Bullard, R. D., & Wright, B. H. (1986). The politics of pollution: Implications for the black community. *Phylon, 68,* (1), 71–78.

Burbules, N. C. (2000). Universities in transition: The promise and the challenge of new technologies. *Teachers College Record, 102,* 271–294.

Bush, M. (1980). Institutions for dependent and neglected children: Therapeutic option or choice of last resort? *American Journal of Orthopsychiatry, 50,* 239–255.

Bush-Baskette, S. R. (1998). The war on drugs as a war against black women. In S. L. Miller (Ed.), *Crime control and women: Feminist implications of criminal justice policies* (pp. 113–129). Thousand Oaks, CA: Sage.

Butler, P. (1998, April 26). Appetite for success. *The State* [Columbia, SC], pp. G1–G3.

Butler, S., & Wintram, C. (1991). *Feminist groupwork.* London: Sage.

Byrne, J. A. (1993, December 20). The horizontal corporation: It's about managing across, not up and down. *Business Week,* 76–81.

Calder, L. G. (1999). *Financing the American Dream: A cultural history of consumer credit.* Princeton, NJ: Princeton University Press.

Carlson, M. (1998, October 26). Laws of last resort. *Time,* p. 40.

Carmichael, M. (2003, May 12). Help from far away. *Newsweek,* p. E16.

Carothers, S. C. (1990). Catching sense: Learning from our mothers to be black and female. In F. Ginsberg & A. Lowenhaupt Tsing (Eds.), *Uncertain terms: Negotiating gender in American culture* (pp. 232–247). Boston: Beacon Press.

Cartwright, D., & Zander, A. (Eds.) (1968). Group dynamics: Research and theory (3rd ed.). New York: Harper & Row.

Castex, G. M. (1994). Providing services to Hispanic/Latino populations: Profiles in diversity. *Social Work, 39,* 288–297.

Cavanaugh, J. C., & Blanchard-Fields, F. (2002). *Adult development and aging* (4th ed.). Belmont, CA: Wadsworth/Thompson.

CBSNEWS.com. (2003, June 18). *Bush orders racial profiling ban.* Retrieved July 4, 2003 from http://www.cbsnews.com/stories/2003/06/26/politics/printable560668.shtml

Center for American Women and Politics. (2002). *Women in elective office.* Center for American Women and Politics, Eagleton Institute of Politics, Rutgers. [On-line]. Available: www.cawp.rutgers.edu

Center for Media and Public Affairs [CMPA]. (1996, September 11). *Study finds rise in TV guns and violence; Executive summary.* [On-line]. Retrieved September 14, 2001 from http://www.cmpa.com/archive/viol95.html

Center for Responsive Politics. (2002). [On-line]. *Industry profiles.* Retrieved January 15, 2003 from http://www.opensecrets.org

Center sues to remove monument. (2002, April). *SPLC [Southern Poverty Law Center] Report, 32,* 1, p. 4.

Centers for Disease Control and Prevention. (2001). [On-line]. Available: www.cdc.gov

Centers for Disease Control and Prevention. (2003). *Women, injection drug use, and the criminal justice system.* Retrieved June 30, 2003 from http://www.thebody.com/cdc/women_idu.html

Centers for Medicare and Medicaid Services. (2003). [On-line]. Available: www.cms.hhs.gov/statics/lyol/

Chao, C. M. (1992). The inner heart: Therapy with Southeast Asian families. In L. A. Vargas & J. D. Koss-Chioino (Eds.), *Working with culture: Psychotherapeutic interventions with ethnic minority children and adolescents* (pp. 157–181). San Francisco: Jossey-Bass.

Chavez, R. (1996). The Mexican American. In P. M. Lester (Ed.), *Images that injure: Pictorial stereotypes in the media* (pp. 27–34). Westport, CT: Praeger.

Cherniss, C. (1980). *Staff burnout: Job stress in the human services.* Beverly Hills, CA: Sage.

Chesney-Lind, M. (1986). Women and crime: The female offender. *Signs, 12,* 78–96.

Chesney-Lind, M. (2002). Imprisoning women: The unintended victims of mass imprisonment. In M. Mauer & M. Chesney-Lind (Eds.), *Invisible punishment: The collateral consequences of mass imprisonment* (pp. 79–94). New York: The New Press.

Chess, W. A., & Norlin, J. M. (1991). *Human behavior and the social environment: A social systems model* (2nd ed.). Boston: Allyn & Bacon.

Children's Defense Fund. (2001). *The state of America's children yearbook 2001.* Washington, DC: Children's Defense Fund. Available from Children's Defense Fund Web site: http://www.childrensdefense.org

Chinchilla, N., Hamilton, N., & Loucky, J. (1993). Central Americans in Los Angeles: An immigrant community in transition. In J. Moore & R. Pinderhughes (Eds.), *In the barrios: Latinos and the underclass debate* (pp. 51–78). New York: Russell Sage Foundation.

Churchill, W. (1994). *Indians are us? Culture and genocide in Native North America.* Monroe, ME: Common Courage.

Cieslewicz, D. J. (2001). The environmental impacts of sprawl. In G. D. Squires (Ed.), *Urban sprawl: Causes, consequences & policy responses* (pp. 23–38). Washington, DC: The Urban Institute.

Clawson, R. A., & Trice, R. (2000). Poverty as we know it: Media portrayals of the poor. *Public Opinion Quarterly, 64,* 53–64.

Clemetson, L. (2000, March 27). A ticket to private school. *Newsweek,* pp. 30, 32.

Close, E. (2000, September 18). What's white anyway? *Newsweek,* pp. 64–65.

Cloward, R. A., & Ohlin, L. E. (1960). *Delinquency and opportunity: A theory of delinquent gangs.* New York: Free Press.

Cohen, L. (2003). *A consumers' republic: The politics of mass consumption in postwar America.* New York: Alfred A. Knopf.

Coleman, J. S. (1988). Social capital in the creation of human capital. *American Journal of Sociology* (supplement) *94,* S95–S120.

Coleman, J. S. (1990). *Foundations of social theory.* Cambridge, MA: Harvard University Press.

Coleman, J. S. (1993). The rational reconstruction of society. *American Sociological Review, 58*, 1–15.

Collins, R. (1979). *The credentialed society: An historical sociology of education and stratification.* New York: Academic Press.

Collins, S. (1989). The marginalization of black executives. *Social Problems, 36*, 317–331.

Collins, S. (1993). Blacks on the bubble: The vulnerability of black executives in white corporations. *Sociological Quarterly, 34*, 429–448.

Coltrane, S. (2000). Research on household labor: Modeling and measuring the social embeddedness of routine family work. *Journal of Marriage and the Family, 62,* 1208–1233.

Common Cause. (2000, November 14). *98 Percent of House incumbents win reelection in 2000.* Retrieved January 13, 2001 from http://www.commoncause. org/publications/nov00/111400wl.htm

Cooley, C. H. (1909/1962). *Social organization: A study of the larger mind.* New York: Schocken.

Coontz, S. (1988). *The social origins of private life: A history of American families 1600–1900.* New York: Verso.

Coontz, S. (1992). *The way we never were: American families and the nostalgia trap. The myth of the traditional family.* New York: Basic Books.

Cose, E. (1993). *The rage of a privileged class.* New York: HarperCollins.

Cose, E. (2000, November 13). Prison paradox. *Newsweek,* pp. 42–49.

Costello, C. (1985). WEA're worth it! Work culture and conflict at the Wisconsin Education Association Insurance Trust. *Feminist Studies, 11,* 497–518.

Coulton, C. (1996). Effects of neighborhoods on families and children: Implications for services. In A. Kahn & S. Kamerman (Eds.), *Children and their families in big cities: Strategies for service reform* (pp. 87–120). New York: Columbia University Press, Cross-National Studies Research Program.

Council on Social Work Education. (2001). *Educational policy and accreditation standards.* Alexandria, VA: Author.

Cox, T. H. (1993). *Cultural diversity in organizations: Theory, research, and practice.* San Francisco: Berrett-Koehler.

Craig, G. J. (1999). *Human development* (8th ed.). Upper Saddle River, NJ: Prentice Hall.

Creamer, W., & Haas, J. (1991, October). Pueblo. *National Geographic,* pp. 84–99.

Cripe, C. A. (1997). *Legal aspects of correctional management.* Gaitherburg, MD: Aspen Publishers.

Croteau, D., & Hoynes, W. (2003). *Media society: Industries, images, and audiences* (3rd ed.).Thousand Oaks, CA: Pine Forge Press.

Cruikshank, M. (1992). *The gay and lesbian liberation movement.* New York: Routledge.

Crumbo, C. (2003, May 25). Military attracts blue-collar recruits. *The State* [Columbia, SC], pp. A1, A10.

Curran, J. (1992). Mass media and democracy. In J. Curran & M. Gurevitch (Eds.), *Mass media and society* (pp. 82–117). London: Edward Arnold.

Currie, E. (1985). *Confronting crime: An American challenge.* New York: Pantheon Books.

Currie, E. (1998). *Crime and punishment in America.* New York: Metropolitan Books.

Dalaker, J., & Proctor, B. D. U.S. Census Bureau, Current Population Reports, Series P60-210. (2000). *Poverty in the United States: 1999.* Washington, DC: U.S. Government Printing Office.

Dale, J. G., Andreatta, S., & Freeman, E. (2001). Language and the migrant worker experience in rural North Carolina Communities. In A. D. Murphy, C. Blanchard, & J. A. Hill (Eds.), *Latino workers in the contemporary south* (pp. 93–104). Athens, GA: University of Georgia Press.

Davies, J. C. (1962). Toward a theory of revolution. *American Sociological Review, 27,* (1), 5–19.

Davies, M. F. (1994). Personality and social characteristics. In A. P. Hare, H. H. Blumberg, M. F. Davies, & M. V. Kent (Eds.), *Small group research: A handbook* (pp. 41–78). Norwood, NJ: Ablex Publishing.

Davis, K., & Moore, W. (1945). Some principles of stratification. *The American Sociological Review, 10,* 242–249.

Davis, L. (1979). Racial composition of groups. *Social Work, 24,* 208–213.

Davis, L. E., & Proctor, E. K. (1989). Gender and group treatment. In L. E. Davis and E. K. Proctor. *Race, gender, & class: Guidelines for practice with individuals, families, and groups* (pp. 221–250). Englewood Cliffs, NJ: Prentice Hall.

Davis, N. J., & Robinson, R. V. (1996). Are the rumors of war exaggerated? Religious orthodoxy and moral progressivism in America. *American Journal of Sociology, 102,* 756–785.

Day, P. J. (1996). *A new history of social welfare* (2nd ed.). Englewood Cliffs, NJ: Prentice Hall.

Death Penalty Information Center (2003). *Total number of death row inmates as of April 1, 2003.* [On-line]. Retrieved June 14, 2003 from www.deathpenalty. info.org/DEATHROWUSArecent.pdf

Deavers, K. (1992). What is rural? *Policies Studies Journal, 20,* 183–189.

Deegan, P. E. (1993). Recovering our sense of value after being labeled mentally ill. *Journal of Psychosocial Nursing, 15,* 3–19.

Delgado, M. (1998) Latina-owned businesses: Community resources for the prevention field. *Journal of Primary Prevention,* 447–460.

Della Porta, D., & Diani, M. (1999). *Social movements: An introduction.* Oxford, UK: Blackwell Publishers.

Delpit, L. (1995). *Other people's children: Cultural conflict in the classroom.* New York: New Press.

Delucchi, M. A. (1996, Spring). The total cost of motor vehicle use. *Access, 8.*

Devine, P. G. (1995). Prejudice and outgroup perception.

In A. Tesser (Ed.), *Advanced social psychology*. New York: McGraw-Hill.

DiNitto, D. M. (2000). *Social welfare: Politics and public policy* (5th ed.). Boston: Allyn & Bacon.

Donahue, J. (1996, December). The missing corporate rap sheet: Missing government records of corporate abuses. *Multinational Monitor, 14–16.*

Donaton, S. (1993, September 20). Mercedes in full retreat on ad placement order. *Advertising Age*, p. B8.

Donziger, S. (1996, March 17). The prison-industrial complex. *Washington Post*, p. C3.

Drake, J. C. (2003, July 27). Other states' suits hint at likely outcome. *The State* [Columbia, SC], p. A10.

Draper, E. (1993). Fetal exclusion policies and gendered constructions of suitable work. *Social Problems, 40,* 90–107.

Duany, A., Plater-Zyberk, E. & Speck, J. (2000). *Suburban nation: The rise of sprawl and the decline of the American dream*. New York: North Point Press.

Duignan, P. J., & Gann, L. H. (1998). *The Spanish speakers in the United States: A history*. Lanham, MD: University Press of America.

Dunbar, R. (1996). *Grooming, gossip, and the evolution of language*. Cambridge, MA: Harvard University Press.

Duncan, G. J., Yeung, W. J., Brooks-Gunn, J., & Smith, J. R. (1998). How much does childhood poverty affect the life chances of children? *American Sociological Review, 63,* pp. 406–423.

Durkeim, E. (1965/1912). *The elementary forms of the religious life*. New York: Free Press. (Originally published in 1912.)

Dye, T. R. (1998). *Understanding public policy* (9th ed.). Upper Saddle River, NJ: Prentice Hall.

Dye, T. R., & Zeigler, H. (1993). *The irony of democracy: An uncommon introduction to American politics* (9th ed.). Belmont, CA: Wadsworth.

Dyer, J. (2000). *The perpetual prisoner machine: How America profits from crime*. Boulder, CO: Westview Press.

Economic Policy Institute. (2002a). *Pulling apart: A state by state analysis of income trends*. Available from the Economic Policy Institute Web site: http://www.epinet.org

Economic Policy Institute. (2002b). *The state of working America 2000–2001*. Pulling apart: A state by state analysis of income trends. Available from the Economic Policy Institute Website: http://www.epinet.org

Edwards, B., & Foley, M. W. (2001). Civil society and social capital: A primer. In B. Edwards, M. W. Foley, & M. Diani (Eds.), *Beyond Tocqueville: Civil society and the social capital debate in comparative perspective* (pp. 1–14). Hanover, NH: University Press of New England.

Ehrenreich, B. (2001). *Nickel and dimed: On (not) getting by in America*. New York: Metropolitan Books.

Engels, F. (1884/1902). *The origin of the family*. Chicago: Charles H. Kerr. (Originally published in 1884).

Engstrom, J. D. (2001). Industry and immigration in Dalton, Georgia. In A. D. Murphy, C. Blanchard, & J. A. Hill (Eds.), *Latino workers in the contemporary South* (pp. 44–56). Athens, GA: University of Georgia Press.

Ennis, B. J. (1971). The rights of mental patients. In N. Dorsen (Ed.), *The rights of Americans: What they are—what they should be* (pp. 484–498). New York: Pantheon.

Epstein, H. (2003, October 12). Enough to make you sick? *New York Times*. Retrieved October 12, 2003 from www.nytimes.com/2003/10/12/magazine/12HEALTH.html

Escott, P. D., & Goldfield, D. R. (1991). *The South for new southerners*. Chapel Hill: University of North Carolina Press.

Etzioni, A. (1964). *Modern organizations*. Englewood cliffs, NJ: Prentice Hall.

Etzioni, A. (1975). *A comparative analysis of complex organizations: On power, involvement, and their correlates* (rev. ed.). New York: Free Press.

Ewalt, P., & Mokuau, N. (1996). Self-determination from a Pacific perspective. In P. L. Ewalt, M. Freeman, S. A. Kirk, & D. L. Poole (Eds.), *Multicultural issues in social work* (pp. 255–268). Washington, DC: NASW Press.

Falicov, C. J. (1998). *Latino families in therapy: A guide to multicultural practice*. New York: Guilford Press.

Families Managed Advocacy Project. (2001, summer). Arrest my kid. *MAP Report, 2* (2), p. 1. (Available from ABC for Health, Inc., 152 W. Johnson St., Ste 206, Madison, WI 53703-2213.)

Feagin, J. R. (1991). The continuing significance of race: Antiblack discrimination in public places. *American Sociological Review, 56,* 101–116.

Feagin, J. R., & Feagin, C. B. (1997). *Social problems: A critical power-conflict perspective* (5th ed.). Englewood Cliffs, NJ: Prentice Hall.

Feagin J. R., & Feagin, C. B. (1999). *Racial and ethnic relations* (6th ed.). Englewood Cliffs, NJ: Prentice Hall.

Feagin, J. R., & Parker, R. (1990). *Building American cities: The urban real estate game* (2nd ed.). Englewood Cliffs, NJ: Prentice Hall.

Feagin, J. R., & Sikes, M. P. (1994). *Living with racism: The black middle class experience*. Boston: Beacon.

Federal Register. (2002, February 14). *Poverty guidelines for the 48 contiguous states and the District of Columbia*. (Vol. 67, No. 31). [On-line]. Retrieved April 16, 2002 from http://frwebgate5.access.gpo.gov/

Feeley, M., & Simon, J. (1992). The new penology. *Criminology, 30,* 449–474.

Fellin, P. (1995). *The community and the social worker* (2nd ed.). Itasca, IL: F. E. Peacock.

Fendrich, J. M., Tarleau, A. T., & Lovoy, K. L. (1988). Back to the future: Adult political behavior of former political activists. *American Sociological Review, 53,* 780–784.

Fine, L. (2002, January 23). Report offers solution to special education disparities. *Education Week.* [On-line]. Retrieved June 4, 2002 from http://www.edweek.org

Fineman, H., & Lipper, T. (2003, January 27). Spinning race. *Newsweek,* pp. 26–29.

Fixico, D. L. (2002). The reservation conflict continues. In T. O'Neill (Ed.), *The Indian reservation system* (pp. 113–125). San Diego, CA: Greenhaven Press.

Flanagan, W. G. (1999). *Urban sociology: Images and structure* (3rd ed.). Boston: Allyn & Bacon.

Fleck, C. (2002, April). Nursing home care is found wanting. *AARP Bulletin, 43* (4), pp. 3, 16–17.

Flora, J. L., Flora, C. B., & Houdek, E. (1992). *Rural communities: Legacy and change.* (Study guide). Boulder, CO: Westview Press.

Foley, M. W., McCarthy, J. D., & Chaves, M. (2001). Social capital, religious institutions, and poor communities. In S. Saegert, J. P. Thompson, & M. R. Warren (Eds.), *Social capital and poor communities* (pp. 215–245). New York: Russell Sage Foundation.

Forsyth, D. (1990). *Group dynamics* (2nd ed.). Belmont, CA: Wadsworth.

Foucault, M. (1990). *The history of sexuality: An introduction.* (R. Hurley, Trans.). New York: Vintage.

Frank, T. (2000). *One market under God: Extreme capitalism, market populism, and the end of economic democracy.* New York: Doubleday.

Frankenberg, R. (1993). *White women, race matters: The social construction of whiteness.* Minneapolis: University of Minnesota Press.

Freedman, R. I. (1995). Developmental disabilities: Direct practice. In R. L. Edwards et al., (Eds.), *Encyclopedia of Social Work* (19th ed., Vol. 1, pp. 721–729). Washington, DC: NASW Press.

Freeman, J., & Hannan, M. T. (1989). Setting the record straight on organizational ecology. *American Journal of Sociology, 95,* 425–439.

Friedman, A. (1976, September). On politics and design. *Contract,* pp. 6, 10, 12.

Friedman, T. L. (2002, May 14). "Satellites, Internet spread hate, not understanding." *The State* [Columbia, SC], p. A9.

Friedrich, L. K., & Stein, A. H. (1975). Prosocial television and young children: The effects of verbal labeling and roleplaying on learning and behavior. *Child Development, 46,* 27–38.

Friedrichs, D. O. (1996). *Trusted criminals: White collar crime in contemporary society.* Belmont, CA: Wadsworth.

Fuller-Thompson, E. E., Minkler, M., & Driver, D. (1997). A profile of grandparents raising grandchildren in the United States. *The Gerontologist, 37,* 406–415.

Gabriel, Y., & Lang, T. (1995). *The unmanageable consumer: Contemporary consumption and its fragmentation.* London: Sage.

Gagné, P., Tewksbury, R., & McGaughey, D. (1997). Coming out and crossing over: Identity formation and proclamation in a transgender community. *Gender and Society, 11,* 478–508.

Gallimore, R., Boggs, J. W., & Jordan, C. (1974). Culture, behavior and education: A study of Hawaiian-Americans. *Sage Library of Social Research.* Beverly Hills, CA: Sage.

Gambino, R. (1975). *Blood of my blood.* New York: Doubleday/Anchor.

Gamble, D. N., & Weil, M. O. (1995). Citizen participation. In R. L. Edwards et al., (Eds.), *Encyclopedia of social work* (19th ed., Vol. 1, pp. 484–494). Washington, DC: NASW Press.

Ganje, L. A. (1996). Native American stereotypes. In P. M. Lester (Ed.), *Images that injure: Pictorial stereotypes in the media* (pp. 341–353). Westport, CT: Praeger.

Garbarino, J. (1992). *Children and families in the social environment* (2nd ed.). New York: Aldine de Gruyter.

Garbarino, J., Galambos, N. L., Plantz, M. C., & Kostelny, K. (1992). The territory of childhood. In J. Garbarino (Ed.), *Children and families in the social environment* (2nd ed.). New York: Aldine de Gruyter.

Garland, J., Jones, H., & Kolodny, R. (1976). A model of stages of group development in social work groups. In S. Bernstein (Ed.), *Explorations in group work* (pp. 17–71). Boston: Charles River Books.

Garnets, L. D., & D'Augelli, A. R. (1994). Empowering lesbian and gay communities: A call for collaboration with community psychology. *American Journal of Community, 22,* 447–470.

Garreau, J. (1991). *Edge city: Life on the new frontier.* New York: Anchor Books.

Garvin, C., & Reed, B. (Eds.). (1983). Group work with women/Group work with men. Special issue of *Social work with Groups, 6,* 5–18.

Gates, H. L., Jr. (1994). *Colored people: A memoir.* New York: Alfred A. Knopf.

Geis, G. (1999). Is incarceration an appropriate sanction for the nonviolent white-collar offender? Yes. In C. B. Fields (Ed.), *Controversial issues in corrections* (pp. 152–158). Boston: Allyn & Bacon.

Geller, A. (2003, August 10). Rural South reels as plants move out, ship jobs abroad. *The State* [Columbia, SC], pp. F1, F4.

General Accounting Office. (1999, December 28). *Women in prison: Issues and challenges confronting the U.S. correctional system.* Washington, DC: Author.

Gerbner, G., Gross, L., Morgan, M., & Signorielli, N. (1982). Charting the mainstream: Television's contributions to political orientations. *Journal of Communication, 32* (2), 100–127.

Gerbner, G., Gross, L., Morgan, M., & Signorielli, N. (1994). Growing up with television: The cultivation perspective. In J. Bryant & D. Zillmann (Eds.), *Media effects: Advances in theory and research* (pp. 17–41). Hillsdale, NJ: Lawrence Erlbaum.

Gerbner, G., Kilbourne, J. (Producers), & Jhally, S. (Director). (1994). *Media and the Culture of Violence: The Killing Screens* [videotape]. (Available from Media Education Foundation, 26 Center Street, Northampton, MA, 01060.)

Germain, C., & Gitterman, A. (1995). Ecological perspective. In R. L. Edwards (Ed.), *Encyclopedia of Social Work*, pp. 816–824.

Germain, C. B. (1991). *Human behavior in the social environment: An ecological view.* New York: Columbia University Press.

Gibelman, M. (2003). *Navigating human service organizations: Essential information for thriving and surviving in agencies.* Chicago: Lyceum.

Gifford, R. (1987). *Environmental psychology: Principles and practice.* Boston: Allyn & Bacon.

Gifford, R., & Gallagher, T. (1985). Sociability: Personality, social context, and physical setting. *Journal of Personality and Social Psychology, 48,* 1015–1023.

Gilbert, D. L. (1998). *The American class structure in an age of growing inequality* (5th ed.). Belmont, CA: Wadsworth.

Gillborn, D. (1992). Citizenship, "race," and the hidden curriculum. *International Studies in the Sociology of Education, 2,* 57–73.

Gilson, S. F., & DePoy, E. (2002). Theoretical approaches to disability content in social work education. *Journal of Social Work Education, 37,* 153–165.

Ginsberg, L. (1994). *Understanding social problems, policies, and programs.* Columbia, SC: University of South Carolina Press.

Ginsberg, L. (1995). Concepts of new management. In L. Ginsberg & P. R. Keys (Eds.), *New management in human services* (2nd ed.). Washington, DC: NASW Press.

Ginsberg, L. H. (1993). *Social work in rural communities* (2nd ed.) Alexandria, VA: Council on Social Work Education.

Ginsberg, L. H. (2001). *Careers in social work* (2nd ed.). Boston: Allyn & Bacon.

Girdner, E. J., & Smith, J. (2002). *Killing me softly: Toxic waste, corporate profit, and the struggle for environmental justice.* New York: Monthly Review Press.

Gitterman, A., & Shulman, L. (1994). *Mutual aid groups, vulnerable populations, and the life cycle* (2nd ed.). New York: Columbia University Press.

Goering, J., Kamely, A., & Richardson, T. (1997). Recent research on racial segregation and poverty concentration in public housing in the United States. *The Urban Affairs Review, 32,* 723–745.

Goffman, E. (1961). *Asylums: Essays on the social situation of mental patients and other inmates.* Chicago: Aldine.

Goffman, E. (1963). *Stigma: Notes on the management of spoiled identity.* Englewood Cliffs, NJ: Prentice Hall.

Goffman, E. (1974). *Frame analysis: An essay on the organization of experience.* Boston: Northeastern University Press.

Gold, S. J. (1999). Southeast Asians. In E. R. Barkan (Ed.), *A nation of peoples: America's multicultural heritage* (pp. 505–519). Westport, CT: Greenwood Press.

Golden, C. (1987). Diversity and variability in women's sexual identities. In the Boston Lesbian Psychologies Collective (Eds.), *Lesbian psychologies* (pp. 18–34). Urbana: University of Illinois Press.

Golding, P., & Murdock, G. (1992). Culture, communications, and political economy. In J. Curran and M. Gurevitch (Eds.), *Mass media and society* (pp. 15–32). London: Edward Arnold.

Goldstein, A. O., Sobel, R. A., & Newman, G. R. (1999). Tobacco and alcohol use in G-Rated children's animated films. *Journal of the American Medical Association, 281,* 1131–1136.

Goldstein, S. (1993). *Profile of American Jewry: Insights from the 1990 Jewish population study.* New York: North American Jewish Data Bank, Council of Jewish Federations.

Gomez, R. (2002, November 19). More women reach top jobs at top firms. *The State* [Columbia, SC], p. B7, B10.

Gonzales, P. B. (1993). Historical poverty, restructuring effects, and integrative ties: Mexican American neighborhoods in a peripheral sunbelt economy. In J. Moore and R. Pinderhughes (Eds.), *In the barrios: Latinos and the underclass debate* (pp. 149–171). New York: Russell Sage Foundation.

Gordon, D. M. (1973). Capitalism, class and crime in America. *Crime and Delinquency, 19,* 163–186.

Gottdeiner, M. (1997). *The theming of America: Dreams, visions, and commercial spaces.* Boulder, CO: Westview Press.

Gottleib, B. (1993). *The family in the Western world: From the black death to the industrial age.* New York: Oxford University Press.

Gould, E. (2003). *The university in a corporate culture.* New Haven, CT: Yale University Press.

Goulden, J. C. (1971). *The money givers.* New York: Random House.

Gramick, J. (1983). Homophobia: A new challenge. *Social Work, 28,* 137–141.

Greenberg, B. S. (1994). Content trends in media sex. In D. Zillmann, J. Bryant, & A. C. Houston (Eds.), *Media, children, and the family: Social scientific, psychodynamic, and clinical perspectives* (pp. 165–182). Hillsdale, NJ: Lawrence Erlbaum Associates.

Greenberg, D. F. (1988). *The construction of homosexuality.* Chicago: University of Chicago Press.

Greene, R. R. (1999). Ecological perspectives: An eclectic theoretical framework for social work practice. In R. R. Greene (Ed.), *Human behavior theory and social work practice* (2nd ed., pp. 259–300). New York: Aldine de Gruyter.

Grenier , G. J., & Perez, L. (1999). Cubans. In E. R. Barkan (Ed.), *A nation of peoples: A sourcebook on America's multicultural heritage* (pp. 138–155). Westport, CT: Greenwood Press.

Grusky, D. B. (1994). The contours of social stratification. In D. B. Grusky (Ed.), *Social stratification: Class, race, and gender in sociological perspective* (pp. 3–35). Boulder, CO: Westview Press.

Guerard, E. B. (2002). GAO: Tax credits help neediest students least. *Education Daily, 35,* (117). Retrieved November 25, 2003 from Expanded Academic database.

Guthrie, P., & Wahberg, D. (2002, July 15). Medical research widens gender gap. *The State* [Columbia, SC], p. A8.

Gutierrez, D. G. (1999). Mexicans. In E. R. Barkan (Ed.), *A nation of peoples: A sourcebook on America's multicultural heritage* (pp. 373–390). Westport, CT: Greenwood Press.

Hahn, H. (1991). Alternate views of empowerment: Social services and civil rights. (Editorial). *The Journal of Rehabilitation, 57,* (4), 17–20.

Halebar, J. (2002, September 9). Beauty shops offer breast cancer information. *The State* [Columbia, SC], p. B5.

Hall, M. (1995). *Poor people's social movement organizations: The goal is to win.* Westport, CT: Praeger.

Hamer, D., & Copeland, P. (1994). *The science of desire: The search for the gay gene and the biology of behavior.* New York: Simon & Schuster.

Hannan, M. T., & Carroll, G. R. (1992). *Dynamics of organizational populations: Density, legitimation, and competition.* New York: Oxford University Press.

Hannan, M. T., & Freeman, J. H. (1977). The population ecology model of organizations. *American Journal of Sociology, 82,* 929–964.

Harries, K. D. (1990). *Serious violence: Patterns of homicide and assault in America.* Springfield, IL: Charles C. Thomas.

Harris, D. A. (1999, June). *Driving while black: Racial profiling on our nation's highways.* [On-line]. Retrieved July 26, 2001 from http://archivedoc.aclu.org/profiling/report/

Hart, S., & Spivak, A. (1993) *The elephant in the bedroom: Automobile dependence and denial; impacts on the economy and environment.* Pasadena, CA: New Paradigm Books.

Hartman, T. (2002). *Unequal protection: The rise of corporate dominance and the theft of human rights.* New York: St. Martins Press.

Hate group growth continues. (2002, April). *SPLC Report.* Montgomery, AL: Southern Poverty Law Center.

Hawkins, D. (1996, February 12). Homeschool battles. *U.S. News & World Report,* pp. 57–58.

Hearn, G. (1979). General systems theory in social work. In F. J. Turner (Ed.), *Social work treatment* (pp. 333–359). New York. Free Press.

Heath, S. B. (1982). Questioning at home and at school: A comparative study, doing the ethnography of schooling. In G. Spindler (Ed.), *Educational Anthropology in Action.* New York: Holt, Rinehart, Winston.

Heilbroner, R. (1993). *21st century capitalism.* New York: W. W. Norton & Company.

Helgesen, S. (1990). *The female advantage: Women's ways of leadership.* New York: Doubleday.

Helling, A. (2002). Transportation, land use, and the impacts of sprawl on poor children and families. In G. D. Squires (Ed.), *Urban sprawl: Causes, consequences & policy responses* (pp. 119–139). Washington, DC: The Urban Institute.

Helminiak, D. A. (1994). *What the Bible really says about homosexuality.* San Francisco: Alamo Square Press.

Henry, S., & Schwartz, J. (1999, April 24). Hooked online: A computer savvy generation knows which cyberhoods to avoid. *Washington Post,* p. A1.

Henslin, J. M. (2001). *Sociology: A down-to-earth approach.* Boston: Allyn & Bacon.

Herman, D. (2001). The rape culture. In J. J. Macionis & N. V. Benokraitis (Eds.), *Seeing ourselves: Classic, contemporary, and cross-cultural readings in sociology* (5th ed.). Upper Saddle River, NJ: Prentice Hall.

Herring, R. D. (1999). *Counseling with Native American Indians and Alaska natives: Strategies for helping professionals.* Thousand Oaks, CA: Sage.

Herzberg, F. (1986). One more time: How do you motivate employees? In M. T. Matteson & J. M. Ivancevich (Eds.), *Management classics* (3rd ed.). Plano, TX: Business Publications, Inc. (pp. 282–297). (Originally published in the *Harvard Business Review,* January–February 1968).

Hickson, D. J. (1987). Decision-making at the top of organizations. *Annual Review of Sociology, 131,* 165–192.

Hill, J., & Cheadle, R. (1996). *The Bible tells me so: Uses and abuses of holy scripture.* New York: Anchor/Doubleday.

Hill, R. B. (1999). *The strengths of African American families: Twenty-five years later.* Lanham, MD: University Press of America.

Hillery, G. (1955). Definitions of community: Areas of agreement. *Rural Sociology, 20,* 111–123.

Hine, T. (2002). *I want that! How we all became shoppers. [a cultural history].* New York: HarperCollins.

Hirschkop, P. J. (1971). The rights of prisoners. In N. Dorsen (Ed.), *The rights of Americans: What they are—what they should be* (pp. 451–468). New York: Pantheon.

Ho, M. K. (1987). Family therapy with Asian/Americans. In M. K. Ho (Ed.), *Family therapy with ethnic minorities* (pp. 24–38). Beverly Hills, CA: Sage.

Hodge, B. J., Anthony, W. P., & Gailes, L. M. (1996). *Organization theory: A strategic approach* (5th ed.). Upper Saddle River, NJ: Prentice Hall.

Hodson, R., & Sullivan, T. A. (1990). *The social organization of work.* Belmont, CA: Wadsworth.

Hoff, M. D., & Rogge, M. E. (1996). Everything that rises must converge: Developing a social work response to environmental injustice. *Journal of Progressive Human Services, 7,* 41–57.

Holland, T. P. (1995). Organizations: Context for social service delivery. In R. L. Edwards et al., (Eds.), *Ency-*

clopedia of social work (19th ed., Vol. 2, pp. 1787–1794).Washington, DC: NASW Press.

Holland, T. P., & Petchers, M. K. (1987). Organizations: Context for social service delivery. In A. Minahan et al., (Eds.), *Encyclopedia of social work* (18th ed., Vol. 2, pp. 204–215). Silver Spring, MD: National Association of Social Workers.

Holtzclaw, J. (1993, Winter). America's autos on welfare: A summary of studies. *Transportopia Bulletin,* p. 11.

Homans, G. C. (1986). The Western Electric researches. In M. T. Matteson & J. M. Ivancevich (Eds.), *Management classics* (3rd ed.) (pp. 35–43). Plano, TX: Business Publications, Inc. (Originally published in *Fatigue of Workers* by George C. Homans, Reinhold, 1941, pp. 56–65.)

Home, A. M. (1991). Mobilizing women's strengths for social change: The group connection. *Social Work with Groups, 14,* 153–173.

Hooyman, N., & Kiyak, H. A. (2002). *Social gerontology: A multidisciplinary perspective* (6th ed.). Boston: Allyn & Bacon.

Household Economic Studies. (1995). *Household net worth and asset ownership.* Retrieved July, 3, 2002 from http:/www.census.gov/prod/2001pubs/p70–71.pdf

Howard, C. (1997). *The hidden welfare state: Tax expenditures and social policy in the United States.* Princeton: Princeton University Press.

Huffington, A. (2003). *Pigs at the trough: How corporate greed and political corruption are undermining America.* New York: Crown.

Hugh, D. S., Hickson, D. J., & Hinings, C. R. (1985). *Writers on organizations.* Beverly Hills, CA: Sage.

Huling, T. (2002). Building a prison economy in rural America. In M. Mauer & M. Chesney-Lind (Eds.), *Invisible punishment: The collateral consequences of mass imprisonment* (pp. 197–213). New York: The New Press.

Hunter, J. D. (1991). *Culture wars: The struggle to define American.* New York: Basic Books.

Huston, A. C., Donnerstein, E., Fairchild, H., Feshbach, N. D., Katz, P. A., Murray, J. P., Rubinstein, E. A., Wilcox, B. L., & Suckerman, D. (1992). *Big world, small screen: The role of television in American society.* Lincoln, NE: University of Nebraska Press.

Iannello, K. (1992). *Decisions without hierarchy: Feminist interventions in organization theory and practice.* New York: Rutledge.

Income and racial disparities in the undercount in the 2000 presidential elections. (2001, July 9). Retrieved November 8, 2001 from http://www.house.gov/reform/min/pdfs/pdf_inves/pdf_elec_nat_study.pdf

Irons, E. D., & Moore, G. W. (1985). *Black managers: The case of the banking industry.* New York: Praeger.

Ironson, G. (1992). Work, job stress, and health. In S. Zedeck (Ed.), *Work, families, and organizations* (pp. 33–69). San Francisco: Jossey-Bass.

Ishikawa, K. (1984). Quality control in Japan. In N. Sasaki & D. Hutchins (Eds.), *The Japanese approach to product quality* (pp. 1–5). Oxford: Pergamon.

Izumi, L. T., Schiller, M., & Hayward, S. (1996). *Corrections, criminal justice, and the mentally ill: Some observations about costs in California.* San Francisco: Pacific Research Institute.

Jackson, J. (2003, July 27). Old South holds back new South's potential. *The State* [Columbia, SC], p. D3.

Jackson, K. (1985). *Crabgrass frontier: The suburbanization of the United States.* New York: Oxford University Press.

Jackson, N. B. (1996). Arab Americans: Middle East conflict hits home. In P. M. Lester (Ed.), *Images that injure: Pictorial stereotypes in the media* (pp. 63–66). Westport, CT: Praeger.

Jacobson, M. F., & Mazur, L. A. (1995). *Marketing madness: A survival guide for consumer society.* Boulder, CO: Westview Press.

Janis, I. (1972). *Victims of groupthink.* Boston: Houghton Mifflin.

Janis, I. L (1982) . *Groupthink: Psychological studies of foreign policy decisions and fiascoes* (2nd ed.). Boston: Houghton Mifflin.

Jansson, B. S. (1993). *The reluctant welfare state: A history of American social welfare policies.* Pacific Grove, CA: Brooks/Cole.

Jansson, B. S. (1999). *Becoming an effective policy advocate: From policy practice to social justice.* Pacific Grove, CA: Brooks/Cole.

Jargowsky, P. A. (1997). *Poverty and place: Ghettos, barrios and the American city.* New York: Russell Sage Foundation.

Jargowsky, P. A. (2002). Sprawl, concentration of poverty, and urban inequality. In G. D. Squires (Ed.), *Urban sprawl: Causes, consequences & policy responses* (pp. 39–72). Washington, DC: The Urban Institute.

Jargowsky, P. A. (2003, May). *Stunning progress, hidden problems: The dramatic decline of concentrated poverty in the 1990s.* Retrieved May 28, 2003 from http://www.brookings.edu/es/urban/publications/jargowskypoverty.htm

Jasper, J. M. (1997). *The art of moral protest: Cultural, biography and creativity in social movements.* Chicago: University of Chicago Press.

Johnson, D. W., & Johnson, F. P. (2000). *Joining together: Group theory and group skills* (7th ed.). Boston: Allyn & Bacon.

Johnson, K. M. (1999). The rural rebound. *Reports on America, 1,* (3), 1–21.

Johnston, R. L. (1996). *Religion in society* (5th ed.). Englewood Cliffs, NJ: Prentice Hall.

Jones, E. C., & Rhoades, R. E. (2001). Comparative perspectives on international migration: Illegals or "guest workers" in the American south? In A. D. Murphy, C. Blanchard, & J. A. Hill (Eds.), *Latino workers in the contemporary south* (pp. 23–35). Athens, GA: University of Georgia Press.

Jones, L., & Newman, L. (2000). Our America: Life and

death on the south side of Chicago. In D. N. Sattler, G. P. Kramer, V. Shabatay, & D. A. Bernstein (Eds.), *Lifespan development in context: Voices and perspectives* (pp. 116–121). Boston: Houghton Mifflin.

Jones, M. J. (1994). Speaking the unspoken: Parents of sexually victimized children. In A. Gitterman & L. Shulman (Eds.), *Mutual aid groups, vulnerable populations, and the life cycle* (pp. 239–255). New York: Columbia University Press.

Kanter, R. M. (1993). *Men and women of the corporation.* New York: Basic Books (originally published in 1977).

Kantrowitz, B., & Wingert, P. (1998, October 5). Learning at home: Does it pass the test? *Newsweek,* pp. 64–70.

Kantrowitz, B., & Wingert, P. (2003, January 27). What's at stake. *Newsweek,* pp. 30–37.

Karau, S. J., & Williams, K. D. (1993). Social loafing: A meta-analytic review and theoretical integration. *Journal of Personality and Social Psychology, 65,* 681–706.

Karger, H. J., & Stoesz, D. (2002). *American social welfare policy: A pluralist approach.* Boston: Allyn & Bacon.

Kehoe, A. B. (1999). American Indians. In E. R. Barkan (Ed.), *A nation of peoples: A sourcebook on American's multicultural heritage* (pp. 48–74). Westport, CT: Greenwood Press.

Keil, J. E., Sutherland, S. E., Knapp, R. G., & Tyroler, H. A. (1992). Does equal socioeconomic status in black and white men mean equal risk of mortality? *American Journal of Public Health, 82,* 1133–1136.

Kendall, D. (2001). *Sociology in our times.* Belmont, CA: Wadsworth.

Kendall, D., & Feagin, J. R. (1983). Blatant and subtle patterns of discrimination: Minority women in medical schools. *Journal of Intergroup Relations, 9,* 21–27.

Kershaw, S. (2003, July 2). Wal-Mart policy seeks to protect gay workers. *The State* [Columbia, SC], p. A3.

Kerwin, A. M. (1992, June 13). Behind the waltzing. *Editor and Publisher,* p. 18.

Kilborn, P. T. (1997, August 1). Illness is turning into financial catastrophe for more of the uninsured. *New York Times,* A10.

Kilbourne, J. (1999). *Deadly persuasion: Why women and girls must fight the addictive power of advertising.* New York: The Free Press.

Kim, K. C. (1999). Koreans. In E. R. Barkan (Ed.), *A nation of peoples: America's multicultural heritage* (pp. 354–371). Westport, CT: Greenwood Press.

Kincheloe, J., Steinberg, S., Rodriguez, N., & Chennault, R. (Eds.). (1998). *White reign: Deploying whiteness in America.* New York: St. Martin Press.

Kinsey, A. (1948). *Sexual behavior in the human male.* Philadelphia: Saunders.

Kinsey, A. (1953). *Sexual behavior in the human female.* Philadelphia: Saunders.

Kinsley, M. (2003, January 27). How affirmative action helped George W. *Time Magazine,* p. 70.

Kirst-Ashman, K. (2000). *Human behavior, communities, organizations and groups in the macro social environment: An empowerment approach.* Belmont, CA: Brooks/Cole.

Klandermans, B. (1997). *The social psychology of protest.* Cambridge, MA: Blackwell.

Kohn, M. L. (1977). *Class and conformity: A study in values* (2nd ed.). Homewood, IL: Dorsey Press.

Korb, L. J. (1996, September 18). Holding the bag in the gulf. *New York Times,* p. A21.

Korten, D. C. (1995). *When corporations rule the world.* West Hartford, CT: Kumarian Press.

Kozol, J. (1991). *Savage Inequalities: Children in America's schools.* New York: Crown.

Kozol, J. (1995). *Amazing grace: The lives of children and the conscience of a nation.* New York: Crown.

Krauss, C. (2001). Women of color on the frontline. In M. L. Andersen & P. H. Collins (Eds.), *Race, class, and gender: An anthology* (4th ed.) (pp. 562–573). Belmont, CA: Wadsworth.

Kroll, L. (2003, September 17). Megachurches, megabusinesses. *Forbes.com.* [on-line] Retrieved October 22, 2003 from http://www.forbes.com/2003/09/17/cz_lk_0917megachurch.html

Kurland, R., & Salmon, R. (1998). *Teaching a methods course in social work with groups.* Alexandria, VA: The Council on Social Work Education.

La Brack, B. (1999). South Asians. In E. R. Barkan (Ed.), *A nation of peoples: America's multicultural heritage* (pp. 482–503). Westport, CT: Greenwood Press.

Lacayo, R. (1998, October 26). The new gay struggle. *Time,* pp. 32–36.

LaDuke, W. (1993). A society based on conquest cannot be sustained: Native peoples and the environmental crisis. In R. Hofrichter (Ed.), *Toxic struggles: The theory and practice on environmental justice* (pp. 98–106). Philadelphia: New Society Publishers.

LaFayette, J. (1998, August 10). News study: Violence still dominates. *Electronic Media,* pp. 22, 24.

LaFromboise, T. D., & Graff Low, K. (1998). American Indian children and adolescents. In J. T. Gibbs & L. N. Huang (Eds.), *Children of color: Psychological interventions with culturally diverse youths* (pp. 112–142). San Francisco: Jossey-Bass.

Lang, K., & Lang, G. E. (1961). *Collective dynamics.* New York: Crowell.

Langer, E. J., & Rodin, J. (1976). The effects of choice and enhanced personal responsibility for the aged: A field experiment in an institutional setting. *Journal of Personality and Social Psychology, 34,* 191–198.

Larson, J. (1996, February). Temps are here to stay. *American Demographics,* pp. 27–31.

Latané, B., Williams, K., & Harkins, S. (1979). Many

hands make light the work: The causes and consequences of social loafing. *Journal of Social Psychology, 5,* 822–836.

Laumann, E. O., Gagnon, J. H., Michael, R. T., & Michaels, S. (1994). *The social organization of sexuality: Sexual practices in the United States.* Chicago: University of Chicago Press.

Lawton, M. P. (1982). Competence, environmental press, and the adaptation of old people. In M. P. Lawton, P. G. Windley, & T. O. Byerts (Eds.), *Aging and the environment: Theoretical approaches* (pp. 33–59). New York: Springer.

Lawton, M. P., & Nahemow, L. (1973). Ecology of the aging process. In C. Eisdorfer & M. P. Lawton (Eds.), *The psychology of adult development and aging* (pp. 619–674). Washington, DC: American Psychological Association.

Lazar, B. A. (1994a). Under the influence: An analysis of children's television regulation. *Social Work, 39,* 67–74.

Lazar, B. A. (1994b). Why social work should care: Television violence and children. *Child and Adolescent Social Work Journal, 11,* 3–19.

Lazare, D. (2001). *America's undeclared war: What's killing our cities and how we can stop it.* New York: Harcourt.

Lazzari, M., Ford, H., & Haughey, K. J. (1996). Making a difference: Women of action in the community. *Social Work, 41,* 197–205.

Lee, D. (1986). Government policy and the distortions in family housing. In J. Peden & F. Glahe (Eds.), *The American family and the state* (pp. 305–335). San Francisco: Pacific Research Institute for Public Policy.

Lee, J. (2001). *The empowerment approach to social work practice: Building the beloved community.* New York: Columbia University Press.

Lee, S. M. (1998, June). Asian Americans: Diverse and growing. *Population Bulletin, 53,* 1–39.

Leighninger, R. D. (1978). Systems theory. *Journal of Sociology and Social Work, 5,* 446–480.

Leland, J. (2000, March 20). Shades of gay. *Newsweek,* pp. 46–49.

Lester, P. M. (Ed.). (1996). *Images that injure: Pictorial stereotypes in the media.* Westport, CT: Praeger.

Levitt, P. (1995). A todos les llamo primo (I call everyone cousin): The social basis for Latino small businesses. In M. Halter (Ed.), *New migrants in the marketplace: Boston's ethnic entrepreneurs* (pp. 120–140). Boston: University of Massachusetts.

Lewin, K. (1951). *Field theory in social science.* New York: Harper.

Lewis, M. (1996, July 21). God is in the packaging. *New York Times Magazine,* pp. 14–16.

Lewis, O. (1966, October). The culture of poverty. *Scientific American, 215,* 19–25.

Lewis, R. G. (1995). American Indians. In R. L. Edwards et al., (Eds.), *Encyclopedia of social work* (19th ed., Vol. 1, pp. 216–225). Washington, DC: NASW Press.

Liebow, E. (1967). *Tally's corner.* Boston: Little, Brown.

Lincoln, C. E., & Mamiya, L. H. (1990). *The Black church in the African American experience.* Durham, NC: Duke University Press.

Linder, M., & Nygaard, I. (1998). *Void where prohibited: Rest breaks and the right to urinate on company time.* Ithaca, NY: Cornell University Press.

Linton, S. (1998). *Claiming disability: Knowledge and identity.* New York: New York University Press.

Lippa, R. A., (2002). *Gender, nature, and nurture.* Mahwah, NJ: Lawrence Erlbaum.

Lips, H. M. (1993). *Sex and gender: An introduction.* Mountain View, CA: Mayfield.

Lipset, S. M. (1996). *American exceptionalism: A double-edged sword.* New York: W. W. Norton.

Lipset, S. M., & Raab, E. (1995). *Jews and the new American scene.* Cambridge, MA: Harvard Univeristy Press.

Lipsitz, G. (2002). The possessive investment in whiteness. In P. S. Rothenberg (Ed.), *White privilege: Essential readings on the other side of racism.* New York: Worth.

Lipsky, M. (1965). *Protest and city politics.* Chicago: Rand McNally.

Long-term care paradise, A. (1999, September). *Executive Solutions for Healthcare Management,* pp. 13–16. (Available from Capitol Publishing Group, a division of Aspen Publishers Inc, 1101 King Street, Suite 444, Alexandria, VA 22314.)

Lorber, J. (1994). *Paradoxes of gender.* New Haven, CT: Yale University Press.

Lott, J. R. (2000). *More guns, less crime: Understanding crime and gun-control laws* (2nd ed.). Chicago: University of Chicago Press.

Lowry, D. T., & Shidler, J. A. (1993). Prime time TV portrayals of sex, (safe sex) and AIDS: A longitudinal analysis. *Journalism Quarterly, 70,* 628–637.

Luey, H. S., Glass, L., & Elliott, H. (1995). Hard-of-hearing or deaf: Issue of ears, language, culture, and identity. *Social Work, 40,* 177–182.

Lukes, C. A., & Land, H. (1990). Biculturality and homosexuality. *Social Work, 35,* 155–161.

Maciel, D. R., & Herrera-Sobek, M. (1998). Introduction. In D. R. Maciel & M. Herrera-Sobek (Eds.), *Culture across borders: Mexican immigration and popular culture* (pp. 3–26). Tuscon: University of Arizona Press.

Macionis, J. J. (2001). *Sociology* (8th ed.). Upper Saddle River, NJ: Prentice Hall.

Mackelprang, R. W., & Salsgiver, R. O. (1999). *Disability: A diversity model approach in human service practice.* Pacific Grove, CA: Brooks/Cole.

Mackenzie, G. C. (1996). *The irony of reform: Roots of American political disenchantment*. Boulder, CO: Westview Press.

Madden, E. (2003, June 28). Ruling makes gays, at last, equal citizens. *The State* [Columbia, SC], p. A13.

Maguire, K., & Pastore, A. L. (Eds.). (2001). *Sourcebook of Criminal Justice Statistics 2000*. Washington, DC: U.S. Department of Justice, Bureau of Justice Statistics.

Majaj, L. S. (1999). Arab-America ethnicity: Locations, coalitions, and cultural negotiations. In M. S. Suleiman (Ed.), *Arabs in America: Building a new future* (pp. 320–336). Philadelphia: Temple University Press.

Makas, E. (1993). Changing channels: The portrayal of people with disabilities on television. In G. L. Berry & J. K. Asamen (Eds.), *Children & television: Images in a changing sociocultural world*. Newbury Park, CA: Sage.

Mander, J. (1991). *In the absence of the sacred*. San Francisco: Sierra Club Books.

Manning, R. D. (2000). *Credit card nation: The consequences of America's addiction to credit*. New York: Basic Books.

March, J., & Simon, H. (1958). *Organizations*. New York: Wiley.

Marks, G., & McAdam, D. (1994). *Collective behavior and social movements: Process and structure*. Englewood Cliffs, NJ: Prentice Hall.

Marriott, M. (1998, July 2). The blossoming of Internet chat. *The New York Times on the Web*, pp. 1–6.

Martin, P. Y., & O'Connor, G. G. (1989). *The social environment: Open systems applications*. New York: Longman.

Maslow, A. H. (1954). *Motivation and personality*. New York: Harper & Row.

Mason, J. (1982). *History of housing in the U.S.* Houston: Gulf.

Massey, D. S., & Denton, N. A. (1993). *American apartheid: Segregation and the making of the underclass*. Cambridge, MA: Harvard University Press.

Masterson, K., & Graves, R. (2001, September 22). Congress approves airline bailout. *Houston Chronicle*. Retrieved May 27, 2002 from www.chron.com/cs/CDA/story.hts/special/terror/impact/1057955

Masterson, P. (1993, January 11). Many editors report advertiser pressure. *Advertising Age*, p. 22.

Mauss, A. L. (1975) *Social problems of social movements*. Philadelphia: Lippincott.

Mayhew, M. (2003, December 14). Levi's zipping up last U.S. plant next month. *The State* [Columbia, SC], p. F3.

Mayo, E. (1933). *The human problems of industrial civilization*. New York: Macmillan.

McAdam, D., McCarthy, J. D., & Zald, M. N. (1996) Introduction: Opportunities, mobilizing structures, and framing processes—toward a synthetic, comparative perspective on social movement. In D. McAdam, J. D. McCarthy, & M. N. Zald (Eds.), *Comparative perspectives on social movements: Political opportunities, mobilizing structures, and cultural framings* (pp. 1–20). New York: Cambridge University Press.

McCarus, E. (Ed.). (1994). *The development of Arab-American identity*. Ann Arbor: University of Michigan Press.

McChesney, R. W. (2000). *Rich media, poor democracy: Communication politics in dubious times*. New York: The New Press.

McClain, L. (1986). More of a home to me now. In C. Page (Ed.), *A foot in each world: Essays and articles by Leanita McClain* (pp. 140–143). Evanston, IL: Northwestern University Press. (Originally published in the *Chicago Tribune*, May 24, 1981.)

McCormick, J. (1998, August 20). A gathering of men: African-Americans come to barbershops for haircuts, camaraderie. *The State* [Columbia, SC], pp. D1, D6.

McCracken, J. (2004, February 15). New jobs are out there, but the pay is lower. *The State* [Columbia, SC], pp. F1, F3.

McDavid, J., & Harari, H. (1968). *Social psychology: Individuals, groups, societies*. New York: Harper & Row.

McGeary, J. (1997, February 24). Echoes of the Holocaust. *Time*, pp. 36–40.

McGregor, D. (1960). *The human side of enterprise*. New York: McGraw-Hill.

McGuire, M. B. (1997). *Religion: The social context* (4th ed.) Belmont, CA: Wadsworth.

McIntosh, P. (1992). White privilege and male privilege: A personal account of coming to see correspondences through work in Women's Studies. In M. Anderson & P. H. Collins (Eds.), *Race, class, and gender: An anthology* (pp. 70–81). Belmont, CA: Wadsworth.

McLeod, P. L., Lobel, S. A., & Cox, T. H. (1996). Ethnic diversity and creativity in small groups. *Small Group Research, 25,* 248–264.

McLoughlin, (1978). *Revivals, awakenings, and reform*. Chicago: University of Chicago Press.

McNeely, R. L. (1992). Job satisfaction in the public social services: Perspectives on structure, situational factors, gender, and ethnicity. In Y. Hasenfeld (Ed.), *Human services as complex organizations* (pp. 224–255). Newbury Park, CA: Sage.

Menon, G. M. (2000). The 79 cent campaign: The use of on-line mailing lists for electronic advocacy. *Journal of Community Practice, 8,* 73–81.

Merton, R. K. (1949). *Social theory and social structure*. Glencoe, IL: Free Press.

Messner, M., Duncan, M. C., & Jensen, K. (1993). Separating the men from the girls: The gendered language of televised sports. *Gender & Society, 7,* 121–137.

Michels, R. (1949). *Political parties*. Glencoe, IL: Free Press. (Originally published in 1911.)

Middleman, R. R. (1992). Group work and the Heimlich maneuver: Unchoking social work education. In D. F.

Fike & B. Rittner (Eds.), *Working from strengths: The Essence of group work* (pp. 16–35). Miami, FL: Center for Group Work Studies.

Milham, S., Bullock, R., Hosie, K., & Haak, M. (1986). *Lost in care: The problems of maintaining links between children in care and their families.* Brookfield, VT: Gower.

Miller, J. (1991). *Last one over the wall.* Columbus, OH: Ohio State University.

Miller, J. (1996). *Search and destroy: African American males in the criminal justice system.* New York: Cambridge University Press.

Miller, L. S. (1995). *An American imperative: Accelerating minority educational advancement.* New Haven, CT: Yale University Press.

Mills, C. W. (1956). *The power elite.* New York: Oxford University Press.

Mills, R. J., & Bhandari, S. (2003, September). *Health insurance coverage in the United States: 2002.* [Online]. Retrieved May 28, 2004 from http://www.census.gov/prod/2003pubs/p60-223.pdf

Mills, T. (1967). *The sociology of small groups.* Englewood Cliffs, NJ: Prentice Hall.

Min, P. G. (1990). Ethnicity: Concepts, theories and trends. In P. G. Min & R. Kim (Eds.), *Struggle for ethnic identity: Narratives by Asian American professionals* (pp. 16–46). Walnut Creek, CA: Altamira.

Min, P. G., (1995a). An overview of Asian Americans. In P. G. Min (Ed.), *Asian Americans: Contemporary trends and issues* (pp. 10–37). Thousand Oaks, CA: Sage.

Min, P. G., (1995b). Major issues relating to Asian American Experiences. In P. G. Min (Ed.), *Asian Americans: Contemporary trends and issues* (pp. 38–57). Thousand Oaks, CA: Sage.

Miranda, S. M. (1994). Avoidance of groupthink. *Small Group Research, 25,* 105–136.

Mirowsky, J., & Ross, C. E. (1989). *Social causes of psychological distress.* New York: Aldine de Gruyter.

Mischel, W. (1977). The interaction of person and situation. In D. Magnussen & N. S. Endler (Eds.), *Personality at the crossroads* (pp. 333–352). Hillsdale, NJ: Erlbaum.

Mogelonsky, M. (1995, August). Asian-Indian Americans. *American Demographics, 17,* 32–39.

Mokuau, N., & Tauili'ili, P. (1992). Families with native Hawaiian and Pacific Island roots. In E. W. Lynch & M. J. Hanson (Eds.), *Developing cross-cultural competence* (pp. 301–318). Baltimore: Paul H. Brookes.

Moore, E. E., & Starkes, A. J. (1992). The group-in-institution as the unit of attention: Recapturing and refining a social work tradition. *Social Work with Groups, 15,* 171–192.

Moore, J., & Pinderhughes, R. (Eds.). (1993). *In the barrios: Latinos and the underclass debate.* New York: Russell Sage Foundation.

Moore, J., & Vigil, J. D. (1993). Barrios in transition. In J.

Moore & R. Pinderhughes (Eds.), *In the barrios: Latinos and the underclass debate* (pp. 27–49). New York: Russell Sage Foundation.

Morgan, G. (1986). *Images of organization.* Beverly Hills, CA: Sage.

Morgen, S. (1994). Personalizing personnel decisions in feminist organizational theory and practice. *Human Relations, 47,* 665–684.

Morris, A. (1993). Black southern student sit-in movement: An analysis of internal organization. In R. L Curtis & B. Aguirre (Eds.), Collective behavior and social movements (pp. 361–380). Boston: Allyn & Bacon.

Morris, A. D. (1984). *The origins of the Civil Rights Movement: Black community organizing for change.* New York: Free Press.

Morris, R. (1986). *Rethinking social welfare: Why care for the stranger?* New York: Longman.

Morris, R. (2003, October 7). For USC, the show must go on. *The State* [Columbia, SC], pp. C1, C4.

Mumola, C. J. (2000, August). *Incarcerated parents and their children.* U.S. Department of Justice, Office of Justice Programs. Retrieved March 17, 2003 from http://www.ojp.usdojgov/bjs/

Murray, H. A. (1938). *Exploration in personality.* New York: Oxford University Press.

Muscati, S. A. (2002). Arab/Muslim 'otherness': The role of racial constructions in the Gulf War and the continuing crisis in Iraq. *Journal of Muslim Minority Affairs, 22,* 131–148.

Myers, D. G. (1999). *Social psychology* (6th ed.). Boston: McGraw-Hill.

Myrdal, G. (1944). *An American dilemma: The Negro problem and modern democracy.* New York: Harper.

National Association of Social Workers [NASW]. (2000). Environmental policy. In *Social work speaks: National Association of Social Workers Policy Statements 2000–2003* (pp. 101–108). Washington, DC: Author.

National Center for Health Statistics. (1999). *Health, United States, 1998 with socioeconomic status and chartbook.* Available from the National Center for Health Statistics Website: http://www.cdc.gov/nchswww/data/hus98ncb.pdf

National Center for Health Statistics. (2001). *Health topic: Infants and children.* (Centers for Disease Control and Prevention). [On-line]. Available: http://www.cdc.gov/health/nfantsmenu.htm

National Center for Policy Analysis. (1995). *Bringing down costs through privatization.* Dallas, TX: Author.

National Center for Public Policy and Higher Education. (n.d.). Five national trends (Chapter one). In *Losing ground: A national status report on the affordability of American higher education.* Retrieved November 25, 2003 from http://www.highereducation.org/reports/losing_ground/ar2shtml

National Opinion Research Center [NORC]. (1999).

General social surveys, 1972–1998: Cumulative codebook: Chicago National Opinion Research Center.

Naughton, K. (2003, December 1). Three for the road: For today's family, two cars just aren't enough. *Newsweek,* p. 49.

Nelson, J. A. (1996). The invisible cultural group: Images of disability. In P. M. Lester (Ed.), *Images that injure: Pictorial stereotypes in the media* (pp. 119–125). Westport, CT: Praeger.

Newman, B. M., & Newman, P. R. (1999). *Development through life* (7th edition). Belmont, CA: Wadsworth.

Nguyen, A. (2000, July 31). The souls of white folk. *The American Prospect,* pp. 46–49.

Nirje, B. (1976). The normalization principle. In R. B. Kugel & A. Sheerer (Eds.), *Changing patterns in residential services for the mentally retarded* (pp. 179–195). Washington, DC: President's Committee on Mental Retardation.

Nishi, S. M. (1995). Japanese Americans. In P. G. Min (Ed.), *Asian Americans: Contemporary trends and issues* (pp. 95–133). Thousand Oaks, CA: Sage.

Norlin, J. M., Chess, W. A., Dale, O., & Smith, R. (2003). *Human behavior and the social environment: Social systems theory.* Boston: Allyn & Bacon.

Oakes, J. (1985). *Keeping track: How high schools structure inequality.* New Haven, CT: Yale University Press.

Oberschall, A. (1973). *Social conflict and social movements.* Englewood Cliffs, NJ: Prentice Hall.

Odendahl, T. (1990). *Charity begins at home.* New York: Basic Books.

Office of National Drug Control Policy. (1998). *The national drug control strategy, 1998.* Washington, DC: Author.

Oldenburg, R. (Ed.). (2001). *Celebrating the third place: Inspiring stories about the "great good places" at the heart of our communities.* New York: Harlowe & Company.

[One hundred] 100 questions and answers about Arab Americans: A journalist's guide. *Detroit Free Press.* Retrieved September 29, 2003 from http://www.freep.com/jobspage/arabs/arab1

Orum, A. M., & Orum, A. W. (1968). The class and status bases of Negro student protest. *Social Sciences Quarterly, 49,* 521–533.

Ostrander, S. A. (1980). Upper class women: The feminine side of privilege. *Qualitative Sociology, 3,* 23–44.

Ouichi, W. (1981). *Theory Z: How American business can meet the Japanese challenge.* Reading, MA: Addison-Wesley.

Pacyga, D. A. (1999). Poles. In E. R. Barkan (Ed.), *A nation of peoples: A sourcebook on America's multicultural heritage* (pp. 428–445). Westport, CT: Greenwood Press.

Padden, C. L., & Humphries, T. (1988). *Deaf in America: Voices from a culture.* Cambridge, MA: Harvard University Press.

Padilla, F. M. (1993). The quest for community: Puerto Ricans in Chicago. In J. Moore & R. Pinderhughes (Eds.), *In the barrios: Latinos and the underclass debate* (pp. 129–148). New York: Russell Sage Foundation.

Palen, J. J. (1995). *The suburbs.* New York: McGraw-Hill.

Palmer, L. D. (2003, September/October). Original intent? How corporations became "people." *Spirituality & Health,* p. 53.

Parenti, M. (1995). *Democracy for the few* (6th ed.). New York: St. Martin's Press.

Parfit, M. (1994, June). Powwows. *National Geographic,* pp. 85–113.

Parsons, T., & Bales, R. F. (Eds.). (1955). Family, socialization and interaction process. New York: Free Press.

Pascua, M. P. (1991, October). Ozette. *National Geographic,* pp. 38–53.

Passell, P. (1996, May 10). Race, mortgages and statistics. *New York Times,* pp. D1, D4.

Patai, D. (1991). Minority status and the stigma of "surplus visibility." *Chronicle of Higher Education, 38* (10), A 52.

Patterson, T. E. (2002). *The vanishing voter: Public involvement in an age of uncertainty.* New York: Alfred A. Knopf.

Payne, M. (1997). *Modern social work theory* (2nd ed.). Chicago: Lyceum.

Penn, M. (1998, Winter). Taming the suburban wasteland. *In Wisconsin, 99* (6), 28–35.

Perkinson, J. K. (1991). *Getting better: Television and moral progress.* New Brunswick, NJ: Transaction Publishers.

Perrow, C. (1961). The analysis of goals in complex organizations. *American Sociological Review, 26,* 856–866.

Perrow, C. (1991). A society of organizations. *Theory and Society, 20,* 725–762.

Perse, E. M. (2001). *Media effects and society.* Mahwah, NJ: Erlbaum.

Petersilia, J. (1983). *Racial disparities in the criminal justice system.* Santa Monica, CA: Rand.

Peterson, R. D. (1991). *Political economy and American capitalism.* Boston: Kluwer Academic Publishers.

Peyser, M., & Lorch, D. (2000, March 20). High school controversial. *Newsweek,* pp. 55–56.

Pfeffer, J. (1997). *New directions for organization theory.* New York: Oxford University Press.

Pfeffer, L. (1970). The right to religious liberty. In N. Dorsen (Ed.), *The rights of Americans* (pp. 326–347). New York: Pantheon Books.

Piotrkowski, C. S., & Hughes, D. (1993). Dual-earner families in context. In F. Walsh (Ed.), *Normal family processes* (2nd ed.) (pp. 185–207). New York: Guilford Press.

Piven, F., & Cloward, R. (1977). *Poor people's movements: Why they succeed, how they fail.* New York: Pantheon.

Piven, F. F., & Cloward, R. A. (1993). *Regulating the poor: The functions of public welfare* (updated edition). New York: Vintage Books.

Piven, F. F., & Cloward, R. A. (1997). Low income people and the political process. In F. F. Piven & R. A. Cloward, *The breaking of the American social compact* (pp. 271–295). New York: The New Press. (Essay originally published in 1963.)

Pollard, W. L. (1995). Civil rights. In R. L. Edwards et al. (Eds.), *Encyclopedia of social work,* (19th ed., Vol. 1, pp. 494–502). Washington, DC: NASW Press.

Polsky, H. W. (1962). *Cottage six: The social system of delinquent boys in residential treatment.* New York: Russell Sage Foundation.

Pope, E. (2003, November). Second-class care. *AARP Bulletin,* pp. 6, 7–8.

Popple, P. R., & Leighninger, L. (2001). *The policy-based profession: An introduction to social welfare policy analysis for social workers* (2nd ed.) Boston: Allyn & Bacon.

Postman, N., & Powers, S. (1992). *How to watch TV news.* New York: Penguin.

Powell, J. (2002). Sprawl, fragmentation, and the persistence of racial inequality: Limiting civil rights by fragmenting space. In G. D. Squires (Ed.), *Urban sprawl: Causes, consequences & policy responses* (pp. 73–118). Washington, DC: The Urban Institute.

Powell, T. J. (1995). Self-help groups. In R. L Edwards et al., (Eds.) *Encyclopedia of social work* (19th ed., Vol. 3, pp. 2116–2122).Washington, DC: NASW Press.

Pratto, F. (1996). Sexual politics: The gender gap in the bedroom, the cupboard, and the cabinet. In D. M. Buss & N. M. Malamuth (Eds.), *Sex, power, conflict: Evolutionary and feminist perspectives* (pp. 179–230). New York: Oxford University Press.

Prigmore, C. S., & Atherton, C. R. (1986). *Social welfare policy: Analysis and formulation.* Lexington, MA: Heath.

Pugh, D. S., Hickson, D. J., & Hinings, C. R. (Eds). (1985). *Writers on organizations.* Beverley Hills, CA: Sage.

Putnam, R. D. (2000). *Bowling alone: The collapse and revival of American community.* New York: Simon & Schuster.

Quadagno, J. S. (1994). *The color of welfare: How racism undermined the war on poverty.* New York: Oxford University Press.

Queralt, M. (1996). *The social environment and human behavior: A diversity perspective.* Boston: Allyn & Bacon.

Quinn, J. B. (2003, June 23). Tough course in tuition aid. *Newseek,* p. 51.

Radzilowski, T. C., & Radzilowski, J. (1999). East Europeans. In E. R. Barkan (Ed.), *A nation of peoples: A sourcebook on America's multicultural heritage* (pp. 174–199). Westport, CT: Greenwood Press.

Raines, J. P., & Leathers, C. G. (2003). *The economic institution of higher education: Economic theories of uni-*

versity behaviour. Northampton, MA: Edward Elgar.

Rainwater, L. (1970). *Behind ghetto walls: Black families in a federal slum.* Chicago: Aldine.

Ransom, S. (1998). The Eden Alternative: Creating human habitats in Texas nursing homes. *Texas Journal on Aging, 1* (1), 8–13.

Raspberry, W. (1999, September 26). Duty bound to pray for the heathen. *The State* [Columbia, SC], p. A6.

Ravitch, D., & Viteritti, J. (1996, Winter). A new vision for city schools. *The public interest,* pp. 3–16.

Rees, F. (1997). *Teamwork from start to finish.* San Francisco: Jossey-Bass.

Reid, K. (1997). *Social work practice with groups: A clinical perspective* (2nd ed.). Pacific Grove, CA: Brooks/ Cole.

Reid, S. T. (1987). *Criminal justice.* St. Paul, MN: West.

Reiman, J. (1998). *The rich get richer and the poor get prison: Ideology, class, and criminal justice* (5th ed.). Boston: Allyn & Bacon.

Reskin, B., & Padavic, I. (1994). *Women and men at work.* Thousand Oaks, CA: Pine Forge Press.

Retsinas, N. P. (2002, June/July). The housing divide. *Habitat world,* pp. 8–9.

Rey, L. D. (1997). Religion as invisible culture: Knowing about and knowing with. *Journal of Family Social Work, 2,* 159–177.

Reynolds, J. R., & Ross C. E. (1998). Social stratification and health: Education's benefit beyond economic status and social origins. *Social Problems, 45,* 221–245.

Richmond, R. (1998). TV sitcoms: The great divide—few shows bridge black, white audiences. *Variety, 370,* (9), 1.

Rist, R. C. (1970). Student social class and teacher expectations: The self-fulfilling prophecy in ghetto education. *Harvard Educational Review, 40,* 411–451.

Ritzer, G. (1996). *The McDonaldization of society* (rev. ed.). Thousand Oaks, CA: Pine Forge Press.

Ritzer, G. (1999). *Enchanting a disenchanted world: Revolutionizing the means of consumption.* Thousand Oaks, CA: Pine Forge Press.

Ritzer, G. (2001). *Explorations in the sociology of consumption: Fast food, credit cards and casinos.* Thousand Oaks, CA: Sage.

Robberston, T. (2003, January 6). Gay community invests in, revitalizes Detroit suburb. *Chicago Tribune,* p. 7F.

Robbins, S. P., Chatterjee, P., & Canda, E. R. (1998). *Contemporary human behavior theory: A critical perspective for social work.* Boston: Allyn & Bacon.

Roberts, K. A. (1995). *Religion in sociological perspective.* Belmont, CA: Wadsworth.

Rodin, J., & Langer, E. J. (1977). Long-term effects of a control-relevant intervention with the institutionalized aged. *Journal of Personality and Social Psychology, 35,* 897–902.

Rogge, M. (1993). Social work, disenfranchised communities, and the natural environment. *Journal of Social Work Education, 29,* 111–120.

Rogge, M. E., & Darkwa, O. K. (1996). Poverty and the

environment: An international perspective for social work. *International Social Work, 39,* 395–405.

Rose, J. D. (1982). *Outbreaks.* New York: Free Press.

Rosen, S. (2003, April 14). Teach youth well to avoid money woes. *The State* [Columbia, SC], pp. D1, D3.

Rosenbaum, D. E. (1997, February 2). Corporate welfare's new enemy. *New York Times,* pp. E1, E6.

Rosenblatt, R. (2001, December 17). God is not on my side. Or yours. *Time,* p. 92.

Rosener, J. B. (1990). The ways women lead. *Harvard Business Review, 68,* 119–125.

Rosenhan, D. L. (1973). On being sane in insane places. *Science, 179,* 250–258.

Ross, S. D. (1996). The emotional, irascible Irish. In P. M. Lester (Ed.), *Images that injure: Pictorial stereotypes in the media* (pp. 55–58). Westport, CT: Praeger.

Rothman, D. J. (1971). *The discovery of the asylum.* Boston: Little, Brown.

Rothschild, J., & Davies, C. (1994). Organizations through the lens of gender. *Human Relations, 47,* 583–590).

Rothschild, J., & Russell, R. (1986). Alternatives to bureaucracy: Democratic participation in the economy. *Annual Review of Sociology, 12,* 307–328.

Rothschild, J., & Whitt, J. A. (1986). *The cooperative workplace: Potentials and dilemmas of organizational democracy and participation.* New York: Cambridge University Press.

Rubin, L. B. (1976). *Worlds of pain: Life in the working-class family.* New York: Basic Books.

Ryan, W. (1976). *Blaming the victim.* New York: Vintage.

Sadker, M., & Sadker, D. (1994). *Failing at fairness: How America's schools cheat girls.* New York: Scribner.

Safdie, M. (1997). *The city after the automobile: An architect's vision.* New York: New Republic.

Safir, W. (2003, January 21). Old trustbusters now trust-trusters. *The State* [Columbia, SC], p. A7.

Sahyoun, N. R., Pratt, L. A., Lentzner, H., Dey, A., & Robinson, K. N. (2001). The changing profile of nursing home residents: 1985–1997. *Aging Trends;* No. 4. Hyattsville, MD: National Center for Health Statistics.

Salamon, L. M. (1993). The marketization of welfare: Changing nonprofit and for-profit roles in the American welfare state. *Social Service Review, 67,* 16–39.

Salant, J. D. (2002, December 25). Nearly half of new lawmakers millionaires. *The State* [Columbia, SC], p. A14.

Salazar, A. J. (1996). An analysis of the development and evolution of roles in the small group. *Small group research, 27,* 474–503.

Saleebey, D. (2002). *The strengths perspective in social work practice.* Boston: Allyn & Bacon.

Saltzman, A., & Proch, K. (1990). The rights of institutionalized adults. In A. Salzman & K. Proch, *Law in social work practice* (pp. 359–373). Chicago: Nelson-Hall.

Samhan, H. H. (1999). Not quite white: Race classification and the Arab-American experience. In M. S. Sulei-

man (Ed.), *Arabs in America: Building a new future* (pp. 209–226). Philadelphia: Temple University Press.

Sanger, D. E. (1996, January 1). A U.S. agency, once powerful, is dead at 108. *New York Times,* pp. 1, 9.

Schaefer, R. T. (2000). *Racial and ethnic groups* (8th ed). Upper Saddle River, NJ: Prentice Hall.

Schaefer, R. T. (2003). *Racial and ethnic groups* (9th ed). Upper Saddle River, NJ: Prentice Hall.

Schein, E. H. (1985/1991). *Organizational culture and leadership.* San Francisco: Jossey-Bass.

Schmid, R. E. (2002, March 21). Minorities slighted in health care, study says. *The State,* [Columbia, SC], pp. A1, A11.

Schneider, W. (1992, July). The suburban century begins. *The Atlantic Monthly,* pp. 33–44.

Schor, J. B. (1998). *The overspent American: Upscaling, downshifting, and the new consumer.* New York: Basic Books.

Schorr, L. B. (1989). *Within our reach: Breaking the cycle of disadvantage.* New York: Anchor.

Schriver, J. M. (2001). *Human behavior and the social environment: Shifting paradigms in essential knowledge for social work practice* (3rd ed.). Boston: Allyn & Bacon.

Schultz, W. (1958). *FIRO: A three-dimensional theory of interpersonal behavior.* New York: Rinehart.

Schulz, R., & Hanusa, B. H. (1979). Environmental influences on the effectiveness of control- and competence-enhancing interventions. In L. C. Permuter & R. A. Monty (Eds.), *Choice and perceived control* (pp. 315–337). Hillsdale, NJ: Erlbaum.

Schutz, A. (1967). *The phenomenology of the social world* (G. Walsh & F. Lennert, Trans.). Evanston, IL: Northwestern University Press.

Schwartz, D. (1996). Women as mothers. In P. M. Lester (Ed.) *Images that injure: Pictorial stereotypes in the media* (pp. 75–80). Westport, CT: Praeger.

Schwarz, J., & Volgy, T. (1992). *The forgotten Americans.* New York: Norton.

Scott, W. R. (1981). *Organizations: Rational, natural, and open systems.* Englewood Cliffs, NJ: Prentice-Hall.

Screen Actors Guild. (2001). *Casting data report.* Retrieved November 5, 2001 from www.sag.org/diversity/castingdata.html

Seabrook, J. (2002, September 2). The slow lane: Can anyone solve the problem of traffic? *The New Yorker,* pp. 120–129.

Seabury, B. A. (1971). Arrangement of physical space in social work settings. *Social Work, 16,* 43–49.

Secrest, D. K. (1999). "Three strikes and you're out" legislation: A cheap and effective crime control initiative? No. In C. B. Fields (Ed.), *Controversial issues in corrections* (pp. 129–135). Boston: Allyn & Bacon.

Segal, S. P. (1995). Deinstitutionalization. In Richard L. Edwards et al. (Eds.), *Encyclopedia of social work* (19th ed., Vol. 1, pp. 704–712). Washington, DC: NASW Press.

Selzer, M. (1972). *"Kike"—Anti-Semitism in America.* New York: Meridian.

Sennett, R., & Cobb, J. (1973). *The hidden injuries of class.* New York: Vintage Books.

Sensi-Isolani, P. A. (1999). Italians. In E. R. Barkan (Ed.), *A nation of peoples: A sourcebook on America's multicultural heritage* (pp. 294–310). Westport, CT: Greenwood Press.

Sentencing Project, The. (2002). *Mentally ill offenders in the criminal justice system: An analysis and prescription.* [On-line]. Retrieved February 14, 2003 from http://www.sentencingproject.org

Severson, M. M. (1994). Adapting social work values to the corrections environment. *Social Work, 39,* 451–456.

Shapiro, E. S. (1999). Jews. In E. R. Barkan (Ed.), *A nation of peoples: America's multicultural heritage* (pp. 330–353). Westport, CT: Greenwood Press.

Shapiro, J. P. (1993). *No pity: People with disabilities forging a new civil rights movement.* New York: Times Books.

Shaw, M. (1976). *Group dynamics: The psychology of small group behavior.* New York: McGraw-Hill.

Sherif, M., & Sherif, C. (1956). *An outline of social psychology.* New York: Harper & Row.

Sheth, M. (1995). Asian Indian Americans. In P. G. Min (Ed.), *Asian Americans: Contemporary trends and issues* (pp. 169–198). Thousand Oaks, CA: Sage.

Shichor, D. (1999). Has the privatization concept been successful? No. In C. B. Fields (Ed.), *Controversial issues in corrections* (pp. 113–120). Boston: Allyn & Bacon.

Siebert, S., & Gruenfeld, L. (1992). Masculinity, femininity, and behavior in groups. *Small Group Research, 23,* 95–112.

Signorielli, N. (1993). Television, the portrayal of women, and children's attitudes. In G. L. Berry & J. K. Asamen (Eds.), *Children and television: Images in a changing sociocultural world* (pp. 229–242). Newbury Park, CA: Sage.

Signorielli, N., & Lears, M. (1992). Television and children's conception of nutrition: Unhealthy messages. *Health Communication, 4,* 245–257.

Simon, B. L., & Akabas, S. H. (1993). Women workers in high-risk public service: Tokens under stress. In P. A. Kurzman and S. H. Akabas (Eds.), *Work and well-being: The occupational social work advantage* (pp. 297–315). Washington, DC: NASW Press.

Simon, D. R. (2002). *Elite deviance* (7th ed). Boston: Allyn & Bacon.

Simon, D. R., & Eitzen, D. S. (1993). *Elite deviance* (4th ed.). Boston: Allyn & Bacon.

Simross, L. (1992, April 5). When sharing the wealth, let the donor beware. *Los Angeles Times,* p. A6.

Sklar, H. (1997). Single mothers are unfairly blamed for poverty. In B. Leone (Ed.), *Single-parent families.* San Diego, CA: Greenhaven Press.

Slevin, P. (2000, April 24). Life after prison. *Washington Post,* p. A1.

Smeeding, T. M. (2004, February). *Public policy and economic inequality: The United States in comparative perspective.* Luxembourg Income Study, Working Paper Series, Working Paper No. 367. [On-line]. Available: www.lisproject/org/publications/LISwps/367.pdf

Smelser, N. J. (1962). *Theory of collective behavior.* New York: The Free Press.

Smith, E. (1992, Summer). The color of news. *Muckraker,* p. 3.

Smith, S. C. (1986). *Macmillan dictionary of anthropology.* New York: Macmillan.

Smith, T. W. (2002). Religious diversity in America: The emergence of Muslims, Buddhists, Hindus, and others. *Journal for the Scientific Study of Religion, 41,* 577–585.

Sneyd, R. (2002, June 12). Vermont to monitor drug companies' freebies to doctors. *The State* [Columbia, SC], p. A14.

Snipp, C. M. (1999). The first Americans. In N. R. Yetman (Ed.), *Majority and minority: The dynamics of race and ethnicity in American life* (6th ed.) (pp. 131–143). Boston: Allyn & Bacon.

Snow, D. A., Rochford, E. B., Worden, S. K., & Benford, R. D. (1986). Frame alignment processes, micromobilization, and movement participation. *American Sociological Review, 51,* 464–481.

Solomon, B. B. (1976). *Black empowerment: Social work in oppressed communities.* New York: Columbia University Press.

Solomon, B. B. (1987). Empowerment: Social work in oppressed communities. *Journal of Social Work Practice, 2,* 79–91.

South Carolina Coalition Against Domestic Violence and Sexual Assault. *Statistics* (2002). Retrieved July 3, 2002 from http://wwww.sccadvasa.org

Southern, D. (1987). *Gunnar Myrdal and Black-White relations.* Baton Rouge: Louisiana State University Press.

Southern Poverty Law Center. (1995, Spring). The ages of intolerance, *Teaching tolerance,* p. 27. Montgomery, AL: Author.

Spector, M., & Kitsuse, J. (1977). *Constructing social problems.* Menlo Park, CA: Cummings.

Spitzer, S. (1980). Toward a Marxian theory of deviance. In D. H. Kelly (Ed.), *Criminal behavior: Readings in criminology* (pp. 175–191). New York: St. Martin's Press.

Squires, G. D. (2001). Urban sprawl and the uneven development of metropolitan American. In G. D. Squires (Ed.), *Urban sprawl: Causes, consequences & policy responses* (pp. 1–22). Washington, DC: The Urban Institute.

Stack, C. (1997). *All our kin.* New York: Basic Books.

Staples, B. (1998, October 4). The push to broaden God's market share. *New York Times,* p. 14.

Statistical Abstract. Washington, DC: U. S. Bureau of the Census, published annually.

Stockard, J. (2000). *Sociology: Discovering society* (2nd ed.). Belmont, CA: Wadsworth/Thomson Learning.

Stolle, D., & Rochon, T. R. (2001). Are all associations alike? Member diversity, associational type, and the creation of social capital. In B. Edwards, M. W. Foley, & M. Diani (Eds.), *Beyond Tocqueville: Civil society and the social capital debate in comparative perspective* (pp. 143–156). Hanover, NH: University Press of New England.

Stone, M. (1978). *When God was a woman.* New York: Harcourt, Brace and Javonich.

Stringfellow, F. X. (Autumn 1990/Spring 1991). Society's rejection of the incarcerated. *Journal of Prisoners on Prisons, 3,* (1–2).

Strom, K., & Gingerich, W. (1993). Educating students for the new market realities. *Journal of Social Work Education, 29,* 78–87.

Stuart, G. E. (1991, October). Etowah. *National Geographic,* pp. 54–67.

Sudarkasa, N. (1997). African American families and family values. In H. P. McAdoo (Ed.), *Black families* (3rd ed., pp. 9–40). Thousand Oaks, CA: Sage.

Suleiman, M. S. (1999). Introduction: The Arab immigrant experience. In M. S. Suleiman (Ed.), *Arabs in America: Building a new future* (pp. 1–21). Philadelphia: Temple University Press.

Sutherland, E. H. (1940). White collar criminality. *American Sociological Review, 5,* 1–12.

Svestka, S. S. (1996). Headstart and early Headstart programs: What we have learned over the last 30 years about preschool, families, and communities. *International Journal of Early Childhood, 28,* 59–62.

Swartz, J. (1975). Silent killers at work. *Crime and Social Justice, 10,* 15–20.

Szymanski, E. M., & Trueba, H. T. (1994). Castification of people with disabilities: Potential disempowering aspects of classification in disabilities services. *The Journal of Rehabilitation, 60,* (3), 12–21.

Talbot, M. (2000, September 10). The maximum security adolescent. *The New York Times Magazine,* p. 42.

Takaki, R. (1993). *A different mirror: A history of multicultural America.* Boston: Little, Brown.

Tamura, E. H. (1999). Japanese. In E. R. Barken (Ed.), *A nation of peoples: A sourcebook on America's multicultural heritage* (pp. 311–329). Westport, CT: Greenwood Press.

TANF annual report to Congress (2002). Retrieved February 24, 2004 from www.acf.hhs.gov/programs/ofa/annualreport5

Tannen, D. (1994). *Talking from 9 to 5: How women and men's conversational styles affect who gets heard, who gets credit, and what gets done at work.* New York: Morrow.

Tarrow, S. (1994). *Power in movement: Social movements, collective action and politics.* New York: Cambridge University Press.

Taylor, F. W. (1911). *Scientific management.* New York: Harper.

Television Information Office. (1985). *A broadcasting primer with notes on the new technologies.* New York: Author.

Telhami, S. (2002, Winter). Arab and Muslin America: A snapshot. *Brookings Review, 20,* 14–15.

Thio, A. (1998). *Sociology* (5th ed.). New York: Longman.

Thio, A. (2000). *Sociology: A brief introduction* (4th ed.) Boston: Allyn & Bacon.

Thomas, P. (1992, October 9). Boston Fed finds racial discrimination in mortgage lending is still widespread. *Wall Street Journal,* A3.

Thomas, R. R. (1990, March–April). From affirmative action to affirming diversity. *Harvard Business Review,* 107–117.

Thomas, W. H. (1994). *The Eden Alternative: Nature, hope, and nursing homes.* Sherburne, NY: The Eden Alternative Foundation.

Tilly, C. (1978). *From mobilization to revolution.* Reading, MA: Harvard University Press.

Tobias, S. (1989, September). Tracked to fail. *Psychology Today,* pp. 54–58.

Toch, T. (1993, November 8). Violence in schools. *U.S. News and World Report,* pp. 31–36.

Tonnies, F. (1963). *Community and society.* New York: Harper & Row. (Originally published in 1887.)

Torres, S. (1999). Has the privatization concept been successful? Yes. In C. B. Fields (Ed.), *Controversial issues in corrections* (pp. 105–112). Boston: Allyn & Bacon.

Torrey, E. F. (1995). Jails and prisons: America's new mental hospitals. *American Journal of Mental Health, 85,* 1611–1612.

Toseland, R. W., & Rivas, R. F. (2001). *An introduction to group work practice.* Boston: Allyn & Bacon.

Trieschman, A., Whittaker, J. K., & Brentro, L. K. (1969). *The Other 23 Hours: Child care work in a therapeutic milieu.* Chicago: Aldine.

Tropman, J. E. (1989). *American values and social welfare: Cultural contradictions in the welfare state.* Englewood Cliffs, NJ: Prentice Hall.

Turow, J. (1992). A mass communication perspective on entertainment. In J. Curran and M. Gurevitch (Eds.), *Mass media and society* (pp. 160–177). London: Edward Arnold.

Uchitelle, L. (2003, October 5). U.S. companies 'offshoring' jobs. *The State* [Columbia, SC], p. A14.

Underwood, D. (1993). *When MBAs rule the newsroom.* New York: Columbia University Press.

Unger, R., & Crawford, M. (1996). *Women and gender: A feminist psychology* (2nd ed.). New York: McGraw Hill.

United Nations. (1994). *Human development report 1994.* New York: United Nations.

U.S. Bureau of the Census. (2000). *Statistical abstracts of the United States: 2000.* Washington, DC: Author.

U.S. Bureau of the Census. (2001). *Current population*

survey: 2001. [On-line]. Available: http://www.census.gov/hhes/www/poverty00.html

U.S. Bureau of the Census. (2002). *Population survey: 2002.* (Table F-2). [On-line]. Available: www.census.gov/hhes/www/income.html

U.S. Bureau of the Census. (2003, September). *Poverty in the United States: 2002.* Table 1. [On-line]. Retrieved November 8, 2003 from http://www.census.gov/hhes/www/poverty02.html

U.S. Bureau of Justice Statistics. (1999). *Criminal victimization 1998: Changes 1997–1998 with trends 1993–1998.* Washington, DC: Author.

U.S. Bureau of Labor Statistics. (1998, August 19). *Worker displacement, 1995–1997.* Washington, DC: Author.

U.S. Commission on Civil Rights. (1992). *Civil rights issues facing Asian Americans, 1990.* Washington, DC: U.S. Government Printing Office.

U.S. Committee for Refugees. (1996). *World refugee survey 1996.* Washington, DC: Immigration and Refugee Services of America.

U.S. Conference of Mayors. (2000). *A status report on hunger and homelessness in America's cities.* [On-line]. Retrieved December 11, 2001 from http://www.usmayors.org/uscm/news/press_releases/documents/hunger_release.htm

U.S. Department of Agriculture. (2000). *Prevalence of food security, food insecurity, and hunger for households and persons.* (Table 1). [On-line]. Available: www.ers.usda.gov/publications/fanrr21/fanrr21b.pdf

U.S. Department of Labor, Bureau of Labor Statistics. (2000, January). *Employment and earnings.* Vol. 47.

U.S. Federal Bureau of Investigation. (1999). *Crime in the United States 1998.* Washington, DC: Author.

U.S. National Center for Education Statistics. (1999). *Dropout rates in the United States: 1997.* Washington DC: The Center.

United Way of America. (1996). *Measuring program outcomes: A practical approach.* Alexandria, VA: Author. (Available from United Way of America, Effective Practices and Measuirng Impact, 701 North Fairfax Street, Alexandria, VA 22314-2045. To order call Sales Service/America (800) 772-0008.)

Valdez, A. (1993). Persistent poverty, crime, and drugs: U.S.-Mexican border region. In J. Moore & R. Pinderhughes (Eds.), *In the barrios: Latinos and the underclass debate* (pp. 173–220). New York: Russell Sage Foundation.

Van Den Bergh, N. (1995). Feminist social work practice. In N. Van Den Bergh (Ed.), *Feminist practice in the 21st century* (pp. XI–XXXIX). Washington, DC: NASW Press.

Van Wormer, K. (2001). *Counseling female offenders and victims: A strengths-restorative approach.* New York: Springer.

VanderVen, K. (1995). "Point and level systems": Another way to fail children and youth. *Child & Youth Care Forum, 24,* 345–367.

Vanneman, R., & Cannon, L. W. (1987). *The American perception of class.* Philadelphia: Temple University Press.

Verba, S., Schlozman, K. L., & Brady, H. (1995). *Voice and equality: Civic voluntarism in American politics.* Cambridge, MA: Harvard University Press.

Vergara, C. J. (1995). *The new American ghetto.* New Brunswick, NJ: Rutgers University Press.

Vieth, W. (2003, October 26). Erosion of factory jobs could haunt Bush in '04. *The State* [Columbia, SC], p. A15.

Violence Policy Center. (2000). *Unsafe in any hands: Why America needs to ban handguns.* Retrieved February 24, 2004 from http://www.vpc.org/studies/unsafe.htm

Von Bertalanffy, L. (1968). *General systems theory: Foundations, development, applications.* New York: George Braziller.

Wahl, H. (1991). Dependence in the elderly from an interactional point of view: Verbal and observational data. *Adult Residential Care Journal, 5,* 113–129.

Walbridge, L. S. (1999). Middle easterners and north Africans. In E. R. Barkan (Ed.), *A nation of peoples: A sourcebook on America's multicultural heritage* (pp. 391–410). Westport, CT: Greenwood Press.

Waldman, A. (2003, May 12). Some customer service jobs migrating to India. *The State* [Columbia, SC], p. A6.

Walker, J. E. K. (1999). African Americans. In E. R. Barkan (Ed.), *A nation of peoples: America's multicultural heritage* (pp. 19–47). Westport, CT: Greenwood Press.

Walzer, M. (1983). *Spheres of justice.* New York: Basic Books.

Ward, D. A., & Stone, L. H. (1996). *Sociology.* Minneapolis/St. Paul: West Publishing.

Warkentin, L. (2002, June/July). The security of a place called 'home.' *Habitat World,* p. 14.

Warren, M. R., Thompson, J. P., & Saegert, S. (2001). The role of social capital in combating poverty. In S. Saegert, J. P. Thompson, & M. R. Warren (Eds.), *Social capital and poor communities* (pp. 1–28). New York: Russell Sage Foundation.

Warren, R. L. (1978). *The community in American* (3rd ed.). Chicago: Rand McNally.

Wax, T. M. (1995). Deaf community. In R. L. Edwards, *Encyclopedia of social work* (Vol. 1, pp. 679–684). Washington, DC: NASW Press.

Weber, M. (1922/1978). *Economy and society.* Berkeley: University of California Press.

Weinhouse, D., & Weinhouse, M. (1994). *Little children, big needs: Parents discuss raising children with exceptional needs.* Niwot, CO: University Press of Colorado.

Weinrich, J. D. (1987). *Sexual landscapes: Why we are what we are, why we love whom we love.* New York: Charles Scribner's Sons.

Weinstein, L. B. (1998). The Eden Alternative: A new

paradigm for nursing homes. In *Activities, Adaptation and Aging, 22,* (4), pp. 1–8.

Weinstein, R. M. (1994). Goffman's asylums and the total institution model of mental hospitals. *Psychiatry, 57,* 348–367.

Wener, R., Frazier, W., & Farbstein, J. (1985). Three generations of evaluation and design of correctional facilities. *Environment and Behavior, 17,* 71–95.

Whalen, J., & Flacks, R. (1989). *Beyond the barricades: The sixties generation grows up.* Philadelphia: Temple University Press.

Wheelan, S. A. (1994). *Group processes: A developmental perspective.* Boston: Allyn & Bacon.

White, M. J. (1988). *The segregation in residential assimilation of immigrants.* Washington, DC: The Urban Institute.

White, R., & Lippitt, R. (1953). Leader behavior and member reaction in three "social climates." In D. Cartwright & A. Zander (Eds.), *Group dynamics* (pp. 586–611). Evanston, IL: Row, Peterson.

Whittington, M. (2001, October 22). Capitalism, meritocracy, wrong for our children, wrong for our world. *The State* [Columbia, SC], p. A9.

Whyte, G. (1991). Decision failures: Why they occur and how to prevent them. *Academy of Management Executives, 5,* (3), 23–31.

Wilhemus, M. (1998). Mediation in kinship care: Another step in the provision of culturally relevant child welfare services. *Social Work, 43,* 117–126.

Williams, A. (2003, January 27). But not at this cost. *Newsweek,* p. 33.

Williams, C. (1995). *Still a man's world: Men who do women's work.* Berkeley: University of California Press.

Williams, R. (1957). *American society: A sociological interpretation* (2nd ed.). New York: Alfred Knopf.

Wilson, K. L., & Orum, A. M. (1976). Mobilizing people for collective political action. *The Journal of Political and Military Sociology, 4,* 187–202.

Wilson, T. C. (1996). Compliments will get you nowhere: Benign stereotypes, prejudice and anti-Semitism. *Sociological Quarterly, 37,* pp. 465–479.

Wilson, W. J. (1978). *The declining significance of race: Blacks and changing American institutions.* Chicago: University of Chicago Press.

Wilson, W. J. (1987). *The truly disadvantaged: The inner city, the underclass, and public policy.* Chicago: University of Chicago Press.

Wilson, W. J. (1996). *When work disappears: The world of the new urban poor.* New York: Alfred A. Knopf.

Windhop, R. H. (1991). *Dictionary of concepts in cultural anthropology.* New York: Greenwood.

Wirt, G. L. (1999). Causes of institutionalism: Patient and staff perspectives. *Issues in Mental Health Nursing, 20,* 259–274.

Wolcott, R. M., & Milligan, R. (1992). Findings and recommendations of EPA's Environmental Equity Workgroup. *EPA Journal, 18,* 21–22.

Wolfe, A. (1998, June 14). Religion, with a grain of salt. *New York Times,* p. 15.

Wolfensberger, W. (1972). *The principle of normalization in human services.* Toronto: National Institute on Mental Retardation.

Wolfson, H. (2000, December 3). Tiny Indian tribe agrees to turn reservation into nuclear waste dump. *The State* [Columbia, SC], p. A4.

Woodbury, M. (1996). Jewish images that injure. In P. M. Lester (Ed.), *Images that injure: Pictorial stereotypes in the media* (pp. 47–54). Westport, CT: Praeger.

Wright, J. P., Cullen, F. T., & Blankenship, M. B. (1995). The social construction of corporate violence: Media coverage of the Imperial Food Products fire. *Crime & Delinquency, 41,* (1), 23–24.

Wright, J. W. (Ed.). (2002). *The New York Times 2002 Almanac.* New York: Penguin Reference Books.

Wright, R. (1995, August 28). The evolution of despair. *Time,* pp. 50–54, 56–57.

Wuthnow, R. (2002). United States: Bridging the privileged and the marginalized? In R. D. Putnam (Ed.), *Democracies in flux: The evolution of social capital in contemporary society* (pp. 59–102). New York: Oxford University Press.

Wysocki, B. Jr. (1991, January 15). Influx of Asians brings prosperity to Flushing, a place for newcomers. *The Wall Street Journal,* A1, A8.

Yalom, I. D. (1995). *The theory and practice of group psychotherapy* (4th ed.). New York: Basic Books.

Yung, J. (1999). Chinese. In E. R. Barkan (Ed.), *A nation of peoples: America's multicultural heritage* (pp. 119–137). Westport, CT: Greenwood.

Zachary, G. P. (1995, August 15). Mortgage deduction comes under fire. *Wall Street Journal,* A2.

Zald, M. N. (1970). *Power in organizations.* Nashville, TN: Vanderbilt University Press.

Zald, M. N., & McCarthy, J. D. (1987). *Social movements in an organizational society.* New Brunswick, NJ: Transaction Publishers.

Zarembka, A. (1990). *The urban housing crisis: Social, economic, and legal issues and proposals.* Westport, CT: Greenwood.

Zarit, S. H., Dolan, M. M., & Leitsch, S. A. (1999). Interventions in nursing homes and other alternative living settings. In I. H. Nordhus, G. R. VandenBos, S. Berg, & P. Fromhold (Eds.), *Clinical Geropsychology* (pp. 329–343). Washington, DC: American Psychological Association.

Zorn, E. (1995, May 4). American justice sees black and white over death penalty. *Chicago Tribune,* Section 2, p. 1.

Index